CHAREST

His Life and Politics

André Pratte
Translated by Fred Reed

Original title: L'énigme Charest
Copyright © 1998 Les Éditions du Boréal
English translation copyright © 1998 by Fred Reed

Published in 1998 by Stoddart Publishing Co. Limited
34 Lesmill Road, Toronto, Canada M3B 2T6
180 Varick Street, 9th Floor, New York, New York 10014

Distributed in Canada by:
General Distribution Services Ltd.
325 Humber College Blvd., Toronto, Ontario M9W 7C3
Tel. (416) 213-1919   Fax (416) 213-1917
Email customer.service@ccmailgw.genpub.com

Distributed in the United States by:
General Distribution Services Inc.
85 River Rock Drive, Suite 202, Buffalo, New York 14207
Toll-free tel. 1-800-805-1083   Toll-free fax 1-800-481-6207
Email gdsinc@genpub.com

02 01 00 99 98 1 2 3 4 5

Canadian Cataloguing in Publication Data

Pratte, André, 1957–
Charest: his life and politics

Translation of: L'énigme Charest.
Includes index.

ISBN 0-7737-3133-4

1. Charest, Jean, 1958–   . 2. Progressive Conservative Party of Canada.
3. Canada – Politics and government – 1993–   .*
4. Québec (Province) – Politics and government – 1994–   .*
5. Political leadership – Canada – Biography.* 6. Political leadership – Québec
(Province) – Biography.* I. Reed, Fred A., 1939–   .
II. Title.

FC636.C42P7212 1998   971.064'8'092   C98-931465-0
F1034.3.C42P7213 1998

*The translator wishes to thank Charles Phillips. Without his steadfast assistance
and dedicated collaboration, this translation would not have been possible.*

Jacket design: Bill Douglas @ The Bang
Text design: Tannice Goddard

Printed and bound in Canada

*We gratefully acknowledge the Canada Council for the Arts and
the Ontario Arts Council for their support of our publishing program.*

*This book was made possible in part through the
Canada Council's Translation Grants Program.*

For Vincent and François —
never forget that I love you

Contents

—⚭—

Acknowledgements

—m—

This book could never have been written without the generous collaboration of many individuals. Among them, I would like to express special thanks to Jean Charest, who granted me four exhaustive interviews. Despite his concern as to the final result, Mr. Charest responded to all of my questions with extraordinary courtesy and never once asked to approve what I had written. Michèle Dionne proved equally obliging, making available to me several photographs of her husband and his family. Mr. Charest's aide, Suzanne Poulin, bore gracefully the innumerable questions and special requests with which I inundated her over the months.

I would like to thank my employer, *La Presse*, and particularly president and publisher Roger D. Landry, as well as assistant publisher Claude Masson, who granted me several weeks' leave from my regular tasks to allow me to complete this political biography.

Thierry Giasson, a doctoral student in political science at the University of Montréal, proved a research assistant of extraordinary resourcefulness and efficiency.

Professor Denis Monière put at my disposal the television archives of the University of Montréal's political science department.

Renaud Gilbert, executive director of the Réseau de l'information (RDI), greatly facilitated access to certain archival documents, as did Denis Ferland, of Radio-Canada.

Huguette Pinard-Lachance arranged access to the fascinating archives of the Séminaire de Sherbrooke.

I owe much to my colleagues at *La Presse*, who generously agreed to read the manuscript and to share their knowledge with me. I'd particularly like to thank Chantal Hébert.

As for this English edition, I thank Fred Reed for a splendid translation, and all the people at Stoddart for making *Charest* a better book.

Thanks, above all, to Anne Marie who, as well as tolerating my prickly personality, listened with good grace as, for so many months, I spoke more of Jean Charest than of love.

"A Touch of Hamlet"

—◌◌—

It happened one evening at Hovey Manor, the swish North Hatley hostelry where Jean Charest likes to wine and dine. For the first time, I encountered what a significant number of Tory MPs, party organizers and rank-and-filers had warned me about: the opposite of the "Charest Effect" about which so much ink has been spilled in recent years. Call it the "Charest Enigma." A party worker perhaps put it best: "When Brian Mulroney called, he could be a hundred miles away but you still had the feeling he was standing right there beside you. Jean can be right in front of you, but he might as well be behind a sheet of Plexiglas. He doesn't hear a thing."

Jean Charest, his assistant Suzanne Poulin and I were sitting at the table. After a lengthy interview, the work was finished — it was time to relax, have a good meal and enjoy a bottle of fine wine. At times, Charest would be exactly as he comes across on television: charming, persuasive, amusing. He would talk about his favourite recipes: "First you marinate the duck breasts in teriyaki sauce, then you slap them on the grill . . ." Then a moment later his face would go blank, his blue eyes vacant. What was he thinking about? Had he tuned us out?

Maybe the conversation wasn't scintillating enough to hold his attention. But I wasn't the first to notice the effect. François Pilote, who was reorganizing the PCs in Québec for Charest, had told me earlier: "I'd have a two-hour meeting with Jean. And at the end of it he'd get up and say: 'Thanks a lot, François . . .' And that was that."

Jean Charest is a man possessed of enormous charisma. When you hear him speak or shake his hand after a meeting, it's easy to fall under his spell. But try to get the least bit close to him and you run up against a brick wall. For journalists, this paradox can lead to frustration. Michel Vastel, a distinguished columnist, told me he'd tried several times to do a profile of the Sherbrooke MP for the Québec monthly *L'Actualité*: "But each time, the piece was shorter than we'd anticipated because he didn't give me anything."

So much for journalists! But more surprising, and perhaps more disturbing, is that even Charest's people run up against the same brick wall. The Tories may have adored their leader, but they have sometimes wondered whether he was listening to them, whether he really cared about them, and that has ruffled more than a few feathers. Some feel they've detected a hint of condescension. Appearances to the contrary, Jean Charest is a headstrong, remote leader.

But there's another side to the enigma. "Jean Charest is the most gifted politician I've ever seen," confides former prime minister Brian Mulroney. "More gifted than Bourassa or Lévesque were at his age. But he has a touch of Hamlet about him." A touch of Hamlet? Jodi White, who organized Charest's 1993 leadership drive as well as the 1997 PC election campaign, also refers to the Danish prince when she describes her leader's tendency to hem and haw, and to agonize over questions a thousand times before taking action. Like Hamlet, Charest can be impossible to pin down. Is he as brilliant as he seems — or is he simply blessed with the gift of gab and an elephant's memory? Is he really interested in the common folk, or are they just so many stepping stones on the road to power? Does he have a mind of his own, or does he merely pick up any new idea that seems profitable? One Conservative likens Charest's brain to a black box: "You can see the decision come out, but you haven't the faintest idea how it got there."

I wanted to find the real Jean Charest. In the pages that follow, I hope you will come to know him along with me. The Charest I discovered is neither a monster nor a myth. He is obviously more complex than his political image. Hurt as a child, he has become a sensitive adult protected by a thick shell. He is a loyal friend. He can make people roll on the floor with laughter. A man of integrity and generosity, he is also, lest we forget, a hard-driving, demanding politician. A man who can sometimes be exacting, distant and ungrateful.

This book is not an authorized biography. Jean Charest has not given it his stamp of approval. Although he was kind enough to collaborate with me, Charest did not read a line before the book went to press.

Jean Charest is neither a close friend nor a casual acquaintance. Aside from the supper we shared at Hovey Manor, I have met him only in the course of my professional activities. Early on, we soon began to use the familiar "*tu*," but this may have been because we belong to the same generation, or simply because his personality invites *tu* rather than *vous*. Besides, it's hard not to appreciate the man, hard not to fall under his spell. When you study a person's character for a year, when you get to know his friends and family, his likes and dislikes and his dreams, you inevitably end up wishing him well. Some may find that I've been indulgent. Others may consider me overly harsh. Let me simply say that I have written nothing lightly, neither the compliments nor the criticism. On the contrary, I found myself torn between affection for Charest as a person and for his loved ones, and my instinctive distrust of politicians in general. Above all, I have respected the demands of accuracy. I have thought long and hard before drawing conclusions; my research has been as complete as I could make it.

In the end, I may like the man and admire the politician, but my obligation as a journalist is to report what I have seen, read and heard. Except to a few close friends, Jean Charest remains an enigma — to those who have travelled by his side, and to me.

The Hurt

—∿—

It's hard to spot the house as you drive up Portland Boulevard, the main street of Sherbrooke's Vieux-Nord district. The red-brick dwelling built over a hundred years ago in this quiet, well-to-do enclave is almost hidden behind the trees, well back from the street. It is here that Claude Charest is living out his retirement years. "Red" Charest — in Sherbrooke people call him "Red," or "Mr. Charest," but never Claude — bought the property in 1957. "There was hardly any traffic along Portland in those days," he tells visitors. "And there were fields in the back." In this house, Mr. Charest set up house and home with Rita Leonard, the fetching Irish lass he'd wed the year before. In this house, the couple raised their children: Louise, Robert, Jean, Carole and Christine — five newborns in six years. In this house, Rita spent her last days, as cancer destroyed her beauty and her life.

Since her death in 1978, not a room has been redecorated, not a piece of furniture or a book moved. When they left home, the children emptied their rooms, and that is how they've remained ever since. "I've kept the house just as it was when my wife was alive," Red explains hoarsely. "When the children come, it's their home, it hasn't changed."

If Mr. Charest were to invite you into his house, you would find it exactly as it was when Jean Charest was growing up. The walls of the little bedroom Jean shared with his older brother Robert are still covered with red-and-black patterned wallpaper that teens in the 1970s thought was "real cool." Laboriously easing his massive body down the stairs, Red would take you to the basement his children turned into a den. The decor is so frozen in time that you could easily imagine kids busting in noisily and flopping onto the couch to chatter about the day's skiing.

Then Mr. Charest would invite you into the dining room. Sitting down, he would leaf through photo albums as though he were leafing through his life. Finally, if he was in a particularly good mood — Red's moods are as changeable as Eastern Townships weather — he would take you into the living room and show you a film of his wedding. You could see for yourself just how lovely Rita was. You would understand why, for this oak-solid man, life came to a halt on October 16, 1978.

TORMENT

It was a cold, rainy autumn morning in 1978. Alone in his room, Jean could not concentrate. How was he supposed to focus on the Civil Code when, in the next room, his mother was dying, when her emaciated body, her withered bones, her puffy face made him want to scream? Charest's eyes glistened as he thought about the torment his beloved mom had been suffering since the doctors had spoken the fateful word: leukemia.

A few months before Christmas 1977, Rita Leonard, an energetic woman who had reared five children without so much as uttering the words "I'm tired," suddenly felt the strength flow out of her.

Getting dressed in the morning soon became a Herculean task. When her condition worsened, she entered Sherbrooke University Hospital for tests.

As she left the examining room, a bleak-faced doctor asked her youngest daughter, Christine, to call her father: "Your mother is very ill."

"Very ill?"

"We're going to give the usual treatment a try, Mrs. Charest," said the doctor, turning to his patient. "But it would be best not to get your hopes up. You probably have no more than six months to live . . ."

On the mantelpiece stands a photograph of Claude and Rita Charest, taken on Christmas Day, 1977. They're seated side by side on the sofa, laughter in their eyes. Looking at them, you can see a deep love, a love that has stood the test of time. But on that rainy fall evening, tears would take the place of laughter. The couple would spend the evening in each other's arms, weeping until they could weep no more. The Charests were fighters. They would fight to the bitter end. "Your mother won't die," Red told his children. But in those days, leukemia was always the winner. For nine months Mrs. Charest's suffering would endure; the rest of her life was to be a succession of short trips from her home to the hospital and back.

Someone had to look after Rita. The family decided that Carole, the second-youngest daughter, would leave college and stay at her mother's side during the day. At night, Red would look after her, holding her hand. When their mother was in hospital, the children stood watch by her bedside. One night in June is etched in the minds of Jean and his sister Christine. Rita lay burning with a fever so high that they had to change the sheets half a dozen times. "It's finished," Christine thought. Jean called the priest to administer the last rites. But, at dawn, a miracle had happened. "Let's go home!" said Rita with a broad smile, restored to life by a blood transfusion. The family would spend a last, unforgettable summer at

Île Charest, the little family property on Lake Memphrémagog. But death had only taken a few weeks' holiday.

Autumn came, and with it the grim reaper. Rita was determined to survive until her twenty-fifth wedding anniversary on September 28, 1978. The family celebrated the event at a local inn, far from prying eyes. "Mom" refused to let herself be seen in such a state of decay. Loretta Leonard could hardly recognize her sister. "In nine months," she says, "it was as if Rita had aged fifty years."

It was the memory of these painful months that haunted Jean on that cold autumn morning in 1978. As his eyes stared blankly at the pages of his textbook — what bloody good are laws when life is so unfair! — he was suddenly overwhelmed by a burden he would never be able to shed, the burden of guilt. Guilt for the moment when his mother called out to him in agony — "John!" — and he had not gone to her, for even to look at her was more than he could bear. Guilt for the moment when he heard Rita moaning softly and found himself, startled, wishing for her death.

THE END

In early October 1978, Rita's condition deteriorated. She had to be hospitalized again. On October 15, at around 11 p.m., Rita asked to see Red. Everyone sensed that it would be their last time alone together. "What should I do? Should I stay with her?" Red asked when he'd finally left the room. Christine and Robert persuaded their father to go home and rest. A half hour later, Rita was gone. "I think she knew she was going to die," says her daughter Christine, still shattered by the memory twenty years later. "I couldn't get over it — she was dying and there wasn't a thing we could do!" The family stayed in the room for over half an hour. But Rita's soul, the soul of the family, had departed.

The father gathered his children around him: "I want to see all of you at the house!" On Portland Boulevard, the old oak tree seemed more solid than ever. "It's all over. Your mother is dead. We must be brave. We can't give up now. Life goes on — that's how your mother would have wanted it."

John-John

―――

"Louise! Robbie! John! Carole! Christine! Get up before your father gets home!" Weekday mornings always started the same way in the Charest household. While Red was out jogging, Rita would call from her bed to wake up the children. Visitors were always struck by the order and discipline that ruled the old brick house on Portland.

At noon, Red would come home for lunch, sort through his mail and sit down to eat. Evenings, he'd arrive just in time for supper, served at five-thirty on the dot. "It seemed like a pretty strict life," recalls Martine Fortier, a friend of the children. "Monday was wash-day and shepherd's pie. Tuesday was spaghetti, and Wednesday . . . It was really impressive — all the meals were planned ahead of time."

"My father was a bit of a drill sergeant," recalls Jean Charest. The regimental atmosphere extended even to family outings. Sunday mornings, they attended mass at St. Patrick's Church, a meeting-place for Sherbrooke's Irish Catholics since 1887. After the service, the family would go for a spin in the car. In the summer they'd have a picnic. In the winter they would go skiing. While the children schussed down the slopes, Red and Rita chatted back at the chalet.

The kids were assigned the household chores, and there was no avoiding them. Every evening they did the dishes while their parents went for a walk. "Even at the chalet we worked hard," says Louise, the eldest of the Charest brood. "We washed the windows, cleaned the boats and mowed the lawn. Looking after the island kept us busy. There was a time for work and a time for play."

With his powerful build, gruff voice and terrifying mood swings, Red ruled with an iron hand. When the children got overexcited, came home with a disastrous report card or kept questionable company, Red laid down the law, and the kids toed the line. Meal-time in the early years saw the men seated at the table while the women served.

As in many families, the mother was the lightning rod, and she coached the children on the best time to announce bad news: "Today's not the day." When one of them came home with a rabbit, Rita devised a ruse to persuade her husband to let the children keep it. "If you tell him you found it, he won't have anything to do with it. But if *he* finds it . . ." That same day, at lunch time, Carole hid the rabbit under Red's car. When he spotted the animal, he shouted triumphantly, "Hey! Look what I found!" Rita knew her man. They called the animal "Bugsy" and brought it to Île Charest. Red fed it conscientiously. When wintertime came, he travelled miles looking for a farmer to adopt it.

After his wife's death, Mr. Charest ran the house. Routine became his life raft. Supper was still served at five-thirty sharp. The children were young adults by then, but if they arrived late they would find their meals in the fridge. Red handled all the cooking. "My mother always said, 'If you can boil water, you can cook!'" he chuckles. People who have tasted Mr. Charest's ham or meatballs know he's a better businessman than a cook. But he puts his heart into it, and his heart is as big as his shoulders are broad.

RED

Claude "Red" Charest was born in Sherbrooke on February 7, 1923. His father, Ludovic, had inherited the family construction business. After working for a time in the United States, Ludovic went bankrupt, a victim of the Great Depression of 1929. Mary Boucher, his mother, bailed him out by hiring him to do maintenance work on the buildings she'd inherited from her late husband, Joe Charest. Times were tough. "It was pride more than anything else that kept us away from the soup kitchen," says Red. "We had enough to eat, but nothing fancy, just the strict minimum."

Ludovic Charest had politics in his blood. He was a member of the Maurice Duplessis organization when Duplessis was elected leader of the provincial Conservative Party, in Sherbrooke, in October 1933. As a token of his gratitude, Duplessis rewarded Ludovic with some lumber contracts in northern Québec. Thanks to the man they called "le Chef," Claude's father was back in business.

Ludovic and his wife, Rose-Amande Dion, had only two children, both boys. Claude, the elder, got his nickname when he was small. "I had red hair," he says. "I didn't mind them calling me 'Red.' But 'Carrot-top' made my blood boil! I wouldn't stand for it." A bit of a hothead as a child, Red quit school after grade seven to play hockey. He must have been good, because when he turned twelve he was recruited by a team from nearby Bromptonville. The team agreed to pay his taxi fare so he could play, even though he was younger than his teammates.

When war broke out, Claude was recruited by a team sponsored by the Canada Car munitions factory in Montréal, which allowed him to avoid conscription. Then he was drafted by a semi-pro team from Baltimore, the Clippers. The players earned $150 a week, but the team didn't pay them a cent in the off-season or during training camp. Even so, in 1944, $150 a week was a good salary. "But there wasn't much left after you went out with the boys!"

The Sherbrooke defenceman's professional career lasted only a year. The team physician noticed that Red was still suffering from the after-effects of a serious childhood injury in which one of his uncles, a hunter, had accidentally shot him in the stomach. If he took a hard hit on the rink, he might never get up again, the doctor warned the team's owners. Hockey back then was even more rough-and-tumble than it is today. At the beginning of Charest's only season with Baltimore, the team's British-born coach had urged his players to play "clean hockey." "It didn't work," recalls Mr. Charest. "People weren't coming out to see us play. So they fired the coach. The new guy said: 'They want blood? Give 'em blood!' It wasn't long before we packed the arena."

With the season at an end and his career finished, Claude Charest returned to Sherbrooke. When he learned that the provincial police were looking for recruits, he borrowed his grandmother's car and headed straight for Montréal, where the entrance exams were taking place. By the time he reached Orford Lake, about thirty kilometres west of Sherbrooke, Granny's old clunker had started to overheat. Red stopped at a small hotel, hoping he could get a little alcohol to cool off the radiator. The owner was irate: "Only time anyone ever comes in here, for Christ's sake, is to get something for free! I'm going to sell this place!"

"How much do you want for your hotel?" the young Red shot back, already fast on his feet when it came to business.

"Twenty-five hundred, cash," said the owner. "We can work out the rest."

Red cajoled his grandmother into lending him the money. And so it was that the former hockey player became an innkeeper over-night. He expanded the Manoir Orford, installed a barbecue and cleared ski slopes. Hard work and post-war prosperity did the rest. "Veterans were coming back from the war. They had money in their pockets and they were looking for a good time." Wrestling stars Yvon Robert and Larry Moquin were also regular customers. After the Sherbrooke wrestling card, they'd drop by for a couple of drinks — a bottle of wine cost three dollars back then — and spend the night.

Lorenzo Boisvert, a former customer, still remembers Claude Charest's warm hospitality. Mr. Boisvert and his bride were on their honeymoon in 1953 and stayed at the Manoir. "On weekdays we were the only customers. We'd have dinner in the kitchen with Mr. Charest. Every evening he'd serve us steak sandwiches. Then he'd invite us over to the bar and treat us to every drink imaginable!"

THE LITTLE HOUSE ON THE PRAIRIE

Claude Charest was shopping one day in Magog when he noticed a gorgeous blonde chatting with a young man on the street. He managed to worm his way into the conversation and, great romantic that he was, invited Rita Leonard to a hockey game in Sherbrooke that very evening. It was the beginning of a love story that "on paper," as the sportswriters say, seemed to have little potential. "We couldn't see what she saw in him," some of the Leonards say to this day. Red was rough-hewn and uncouth; Rita was sweet and refined. People who knew her say she was "lovely on the outside, lovely on the inside — a saint."

Born on November 26, 1930, Rita was the fifth of six children. Her parents were of Irish descent and lived in Bury, a little village forty kilometres outside Sherbrooke. Founded in 1836 by British colonists, the village still exists, boasting a few hundred residents, four churches, a post office and a sawmill. The Leonards' former home still stands, only a few metres from the CPR tracks inaugurated by none other than Prime Minister John A. Macdonald. But the once neat white house with its wide verandah is now grey-stained and neglected. Like the village, it has aged badly.

Wood was Edward Leonard's business. He bought forested land, hired lumberjacks to work it and shipped off the logs to the nearby sawmills and paper mills. Business was so good that "Eddie" Leonard owned two cars. The children he raised with his wife, Margaret Green, share memories of pastoral childhood days in the rolling hills of the Townships. "We'd gather flowers in the fields and bring them to our mother to decorate the church," recalls Loretta, the couple's eldest child. Like most Catholics of the day, the Leonard family was deeply religious. In the evening, the family prayed together in the living room. In May, Margaret and the little ones would trek a kilometre to St. Raphael Church for daily prayers.

The Leonard children grew up surrounded by books. "Our parents bought us books instead of toys," Loretta Leonard says. Her brother Henry, who became a University of Sherbrooke professor, ordered his books by mail. And how this Irish family of sweet sensitive souls loved to sing! "The Irish are like that. It doesn't take much to make us cry, or to make us laugh," adds Loretta. The girl who would one day win Claude Charest's heart was no different. She was the only blonde in the family, and everybody remembers that her golden voice matched her hair.

Eddie Leonard didn't speak French, but he wanted his children to be bilingual. After French elementary school in Bury, Rita attended Collège Mont-Notre-Dame in Sherbrooke for high school and then for nurse's training. "The nuns," Loretta points out, "had lots of class." They passed it on to Rita. Red was hopelessly smitten.

Claude Charest and Rita Leonard were married at Saint Pat's on September 28, 1953. The wedding film shows a husky young man standing on the church steps, looking decidedly ill at ease. On his arm is a radiant young woman with a smile that could melt an iceberg. The reception at Red's hotel was attended by a mind-boggling array of friends and customers. "Half of Sherbrooke was there," Loretta recalls.

Within five years, Rita had persuaded her husband to sell the Manoir Orford and try his hand at another line. "She wasn't cut out for the hotel business," says Red. And it was becoming less prof-itable. The Mount Orford ski slopes had just been opened up, and the Manoir's trails, with their three rope-tows, couldn't compete. After a fire destroyed the hotel kitchen, Mr. Charest finally gave in to his wife's urging.

The couple moved to Sherbrooke, and settled down on Portland Boulevard, beside the house Rita's parents had just purchased. It was there that their third child, Jean, was born on June 24, 1958.

JOHN JAMES

"On his birth certificate his first name is John," thundered Bloc Québécois MP Suzanne Tremblay during the 1997 election campaign. "For us [Québeckers] it suits him to call himself Jean, but his real name is John." It was a stupid, racist remark to be sure, but one that inevitably focused attention on this particular tempest in a teapot.

The story is a familiar one. Charest and his staff have been telling it ever since the oddity was dredged up by an inquiring journalist during the 1993 Conservative leadership campaign. The same tale has been faithfully recounted by Jean Charest's first biographers: "His mother, who was of Irish extraction, wanted to call him James, but since he was born on June 24 [St-Jean Baptiste Day, Québec's national holiday], the Charest family chose Jean as a first name. However, Father Moisan, a priest of English-speaking descent from the Irish parish of Saint-Patrick in Sherbrooke, presided over the baptism. When the priest asked the parents what name they wanted to give their child they said 'Jean.' But Father Moisan entered John on the baptismal certificate [. . .]."[*]

The story may be a familiar one, but it's false. At least according to Red Charest: "My wife got along well with Father Moisan. They spoke English together, but they were both bilingual. She must have told him, 'Name him John James.' I didn't know anything about it. As far as I'm concerned, the priest didn't make a mistake. She must have said, 'Name him John.'"

This theory of an English-speaking priest misunderstanding the name "Jean" is highly improbable, since His Grace J. Rosario

* Henri Motte and Monique Gillot, *Jean Charest, l'homme des défis* (Montréal: Balsac-Le Griot, 1997).

Moisan spoke French fluently. In fact, says Father Pierre Doyon, St. Pat's current parish priest, "he was perfectly bilingual." The son of Franco-American parents, Moisan arrived in Québec when he was thirteen and did almost all his studies at the Séminaire Saint-Charles in Sherbrooke and the Séminaire de Montréal. According to Father Doyon, "it's impossible" that the priest would have mistaken "John" for "Jean." "It was John," acknowledges Loretta, who is also Jean's godmother.

No one seems to know where the story of the priest's slip-up originated. "That's the version I heard later. But maybe it didn't happen that way," Charest conceded when I laid out the evidence I had gathered. At any rate, John soon became Jean. For years, Rita called her youngest son John-John, but Red always used what he took to be his son's official name: "He was born on Saint-Jean Baptiste Day, so it was always perfectly clear to me that his name was Jean." As the five children attended French schools, and most of their friends were French-speaking, young people always called Charest "Jean," except for a handful who nicknamed him "Red" because of the shock of red hair he'd inherited from his father. The nickname didn't stick.

It wasn't until a few years later, during commencement exercises at the University of Sherbrooke Law Faculty, that Charest noticed the name on his baptismal certificate. The whole family, starting with Red, was stunned. The Québec Bar Association promptly insisted that the apprentice register his given name. So it was that Charest became a lawyer under the name of John James Charest, as his bar registration reads to this day. His earliest business cards carried the English name. Colleagues at the time remember half-jokingly calling him John James. "I felt obliged to practise under the name registered with the bar," explains the lawyer-turned-politician. "Then I realized that the name I usually went by was as legally valid as the name on my baptismal certificate. And everybody called me Jean, so . . ."

So Jean it would be. The English name did surface again briefly in 1984, when Charest stood for election for the first time. The rookie candidate would have put down his name as John James Charest if organizer Denis Beaudoin hadn't stepped in: "For God's sake, Jean, we need those Péquiste votes! I have PQ friends ready to work for us, so we'd better not put down John James Charest!" According to Beaudoin, Charest finally settled on "John James known as Jean Charest," enabling him to use Jean Charest on the ballot.

Why did Charest never lift a finger to change his legal name? Perhaps it was out of respect for his mother; perhaps because the Townshipper couldn't be bothered with such a minor detail. Whether he's called John James or Jean, how can anyone doubt the depth of his roots? "My father's family came to this country well over 300 years ago," he said heatedly during the 1997 federal election campaign. "My mother's name was Rita Leonard. Her family came to this country about 150 years ago. They were fleeing the potato famine in Ireland. Whether your ancestors are Irish or French-speaking, whether you are from Africa, from Europe, people from all over the world came to this country seeking freedom!"

"DIMWIT!"

Once he'd sold the Manoir Orford, Red Charest went into commercial real estate. He worked hard for thirty years and made enough money that his family could live in simple, secure comfort. He purchased four laundries and runs them to this day.

Rita's affection and cheerfulness made Red's irascible side bearable for the family. To point up the contrast between his parents' personalities, Jean describes their reaction when he broke his nose in a soccer game. "When my mother saw me, she was really worried: 'Oh, poor John! And you had such a beautiful nose!' But my father came into the bathroom and shouted, 'What have you done this time, you dimwit!'"

The children have fond memories of their mother singing arias, dancing and reading anything she could get her hands on, from newspapers to poetry. Despite a difficult life, she was always smiling. "It was very hard for her," Jean often says. A friend of the family whom I interviewed about Mr. Charest was adamant, saying, "I won't comment on that." Red Charest concedes he could be a "bit of a bastard" at times.

Rita found comfort in God. Carole remembers her mother reciting the rosary in the evening: "It was her way of coping with anxiety, of finding the strength to carry on." Carved above the words of devotion on Rita Charest's tombstone in Sherbrooke's Saint-Michel cemetery are a pair of hands joined in prayer.

It would be wrong, though, to draw too dark a portrait of Claude Charest. He was, and is, a very funny man, with a wry, deadpan sense of humour. The Charest clan has always enjoyed a good laugh. "Humour was the balm for all our little bruises," says Louise, the eldest. "We counted on it to make life more bearable." Today, the children point to the sensitivity that lies beneath their father's gruff exterior, a sensitivity they've discovered as the years have smoothed his rough edges. "Underneath it all, he's just a big baby!" laughs Carole.

Red's paternal discipline was born of a philosophy of life hammered out in the school of hard knocks. He would use anecdotes and precepts, dropping them like rocks in the middle of a conversation, to instruct his brood. "You've got to start young," he'd say. "Whatever you do, if you want to get ahead don't wait till you're forty . . . If a guy doesn't have a head on his shoulders at twenty-five, he won't be any smarter at forty." Or: "I never believed in dreaming. All the dreamers I've run into didn't have much in the way of guts. Dreaming may be okay when you're asleep — then you get up the next morning and the dream's gone." One day, when a dinner guest complained that too many immigrants were coming to Canada without a penny to their names, Red replied, "All I know is that my ancestors didn't come here because they had a castle back home." End of discussion.

Red was generous to the destitute around him. He hired people who'd fallen on hard times to work in his laundries. Every year on Christmas Day, he would cook them a meal and deliver it himself. Christmas was also an occasion to invite people who were alone to share the family dinner. Sometimes he would even adopt the visitors, inviting them to the house so often that they ended up becoming part of the family. The children still remember a "strange old" Mr. Cummings, whom they came to look upon almost as a grandfather.

Rita and Claude, as different as they were from one another, agreed on basic values. First came perseverance: "There are three important things in life," Red liked to say. "Work, work and work." When you start something, see it through to the end: "If you don't have the guts to do it, don't bother!" Red would say.

"To us," explains Louise, "it meant that if you do something, it has to come from the heart. You have to give 150 percent. If you're not ready to commit yourself, don't do it — don't waste your time."

If one of the children was going through a rough patch, if they'd run up against an obstacle, Rita would listen with tenderness and patience. Then she'd pat her child on the back and say, "When you fall, you have to get back on your horse!" Or, "Don't worry, we'll find a solution. There's a solution for everything."

Autonomy and responsibility were the other basic principles. All the children had chores and, from the time they were thirteen or fourteen, they had to pay a part of their expenses. Which meant they had to work. "That explains our serious side," says Louise. "It's all right to play and to play hard, but we had our responsibilities, and they came first."

Finally, both Claude and Rita laid a strong emphasis on school. Explains Jean: "My parents hammered into us the idea that to get a decent job, we had to go to university." Rita kept a sharp eye on the children's schoolwork, made sure they did their homework every night and met with their teachers regularly. If one of the children came home with bad marks, Red would hit the ceiling. But he never asked for the impossible. Acquiring the tools to succeed was far more important than finishing at the top of the class. Judgment, courage and initiative were qualities no university could teach. Their father was living proof of that.

"I Love You"

Every morning, John-John and his mother played a little game that showed how much they loved each other. As he left for school, the little boy would trot through the front door, hide for a moment, then run back inside shouting "I love you!"

"I love you too, John-John. Now, go to school!"

Again the little boy would run out of the house and hide behind the garage, then come racing back and leap into his mother's arms: "I love you!"

"It may seem a little silly to talk about it now . . ." says Jean Charest apologetically. But there's the hum of real emotion here, strong enough to pierce the thick shell.

John-John was the family clown, the most rambunctious of the five children. He was always running around imitating someone, teasing his sisters, building forts with Robert, with whom he was inseparable, or plotting some prank: "I don't know how many times I ran away from home!"

A new French-speaking elite had moved into the once exclusively English-speaking Vieux-Nord district. At the Charests', as in many homes in the neighbourhood, French and English were interchangeable. The Charest children usually spoke French with their father and English with their mother, but as both parents were bilingual, sometimes it was just the opposite. On one point, however, Mrs. Charest was uncompromising: the children had to speak one language or the other, they must never mix the two languages. They were not to say: "*Tu mettras mes* socks *dans le* dryer"!

The young Charest liked to play the mediator in disputes between French- and English-speaking gangs, relates childhood friend Jean Desharnais: "Jean was the referee. He liked to negotiate . . . But when a fight was unavoidable, he stood down. He didn't want to take sides." Charest himself recalls that relations between English- and French-speaking children were harmonious: "We played together, we mixed. I learned about white socks and penny-loafers when I was very young. It was a very Anglo style; French-speakers didn't dress like that." Some people, however, say Charest has forgotten what life was really like, that relations between the two communities in the Eastern Townships were not nearly as cordial as he suggests.

It all depends on the era, explains Jean-Pierre Kesteman, a University of Sherbrooke historian: "As a French-speaking elite grew and the role of the English diminished, there was less and less hostility. Since the 1960s, English-speakers have accounted for barely 10 percent of the population, and they no longer control the economy. They've had to face facts." Sherbrooke has many mixed families, like the Charests, which makes peaceful co-existence easier. "Even Johnny Bourque, the leader of the nationalists in the Union Nationale in the region, came from an English-French-speaking family," Professor Kesteman points out. "These were people with a vision in which both communities had a place." Official census figures bore out the reality: in 1961, 35 percent of Sherbrookers said they were bilingual.

There were relatively few children in the Charests' immediate area, a neighbourhood inhabited by judges, doctors and even Senator Paul Desruisseaux. For excitement, the children would sneak onto the senator's property to play — and risk getting kicked out. "It was a dull 'keep off the grass' type of neighbourhood," says Christine, the youngest of the Charest brood.

To Mrs. Charest's amazement, her little clown blossomed into a model pupil in elementary school. Charest's earliest teachers describe him as a relatively placid, though inquisitive, boy. Michel Dufour, his eighth-grade geography teacher, remembers Jean as one of his best students. Jacques Blais, his French teacher, recalls that the boy was quiet in class and well organized. "I remember when he'd go home for lunch, he'd have his hands stuck in his pockets and a grin on his face. He seemed mature for his age." Already. "He was a very quick little fellow. He understood everything," says Louise Meunier, his seventh-grade homeroom teacher at École Sainte-Anne.

To this day, Charest has vivid memories of grade seven. That was the year Mrs. Meunier assigned her class Germaine Guèvremont's masterpiece *Le Survenant*. This novel was his first contact with Québec literature: "I found my family in it, my roots." Perhaps Jean also saw his father in the character of Didace: "[. . .] with a love that was gruff and unspoken, but strong and undeniable."*

---

*   Germaine Guèvremont, *Le Survenant* (Montréal: Presses de l'Université de Montréal, 1989), p. 95.

The Kid

—ʍ—

.

What was Jean Charest like as a teenager? "Have a look at the ski camp poster!" Bernard Bonneau, former pastoral counsellor at École Montcalm, advised me. A couple of Charest's boyhood friends had mentioned the same notorious pin-up earlier. One of them even dug up a faded copy from a corner of his basement. There, perched on the hood of a school bus, sits teenage Jean Charest sporting a mop-top and sideburns, sticking out his tongue and giving the world the classic middle finger. "That's him all right," laughs Bonneau. "He was quite a kid!"

To be perfectly frank, Jean Charest's friends and teachers at Montcalm don't remember him for his intellectual prowess. Red Charest's second son made his mark as an incorrigible party animal. "Studying came well back, in second place," he prudently avows two decades later. "We didn't really study all that much at École Montcalm," says his best friend of the day, Bruno Hallé. "It was an accomplishment if we cracked the books for half an hour a month!"

The temper of the times hardly encouraged academic pursuits. In

the early 1970s, the young people who attended Québec's compre-
hensive high schools simultaneously discovered liberty, sexuality,
alcohol, drugs and political protest. Teachers and principals were
helpless to keep the lid on a bubbling cauldron. Some advocated a firm
approach, while others let themselves be swept away by the tide of
craziness. Montcalm was no exception; in fact, it ranked high on the
list of Québec's most troubled schools. "Those were wild and crazy
years," says Martine Fortier, a one-time girlfriend. "In the eleventh
grade, I must have skipped at least half my classes!"

An open letter published during the 1972–73 school year (when
Charest was a ninth-grade student) hints at the climate that prevailed at Montcalm. In it, the writer lashes out at principal Jean-Paul
Laurendeau's "travesty of justice": "Are they paying you to hold
the students back or to help them become adults? [. . .] Your police
tactics are right in line with the society we live in, and fit your role
perfectly." The letter was signed by a tenth-grade student named
Guy Gendron, today a political reporter at Radio-Canada. That
winter was a season of student strikes, and by the time it was over
the principal had been forced out.

Jean Charest was not particularly involved in the upheaval. Most
of his time was taken up with soccer, skiing and his first serious
romantic involvement, with a young woman called Brigitte Charland.
The two could often be seen lounging against a wall not far from the
students' entrance. As Bernard Bonneau tells it, Charest was an
"ordinary" student, a judgment confirmed by his report cards. After
three years of maintaining a satisfactory average, his grades
suddenly plummeted in his fourth and fifth years. It's not hard to
imagine Red Charest's reaction when he saw his son's final grade-
eleven report. Sure, Jean had scored 76 percent in French and
80 percent in oral English — Charest already had a way with words
— but how was he going to explain that 31 percent in introductory
economics? Or the 21 percent in religious studies? "He wasn't really
all there," says Bonneau.

When the wake-up call finally came, it was not in the classroom.

As a tenth-grader, the kid had been elected class representative on the student council. And on the eve of the next school year, Father Bonneau persuaded him to stand for council president. "I don't know why I pushed him," says Bonneau. "I could see him as president. Yet I can't say I noticed anything special about him."

Father Bonneau graciously leads the way backstage at the Montcalm auditorium; it was here that he forced the young Charest to make his first speech, before hundreds of students.

"He didn't want to go on stage!" recounts the priest. "I had to give him a shove! But to my surprise, he didn't even take the prepared text we'd drawn up out of his pocket. He just ad-libbed." The crowd greeted the future politician's speech with thunderous applause, and he won the election hands down.

"I was overwhelmed by the favourable response," Charest says today. "It gave me confidence. 'Hey, I can do that,' I said to myself." But his friend Bruno Hallé remembers how the young president "trembled like a leaf" every time he had to speak in public.

That year — 1974–75 — was a great deal less eventful than the "travesty of justice" term that had preceded it. Even so, the students walked out once or twice, for reasons nobody can quite recall. "He was a top-notch president," says Bernard Bonneau, "dynamic and outgoing. It wasn't long before he became fully independent, able to lead the council, make decisions and take responsibility for them."

There were times, too, when the new president showed an authoritarian streak. At one council meeting, his friend Hallé told him: "Jean, it looks to me like you're running council all by yourself. You make decisions without consulting anyone. You just do whatever you feel like."

"Have you got a problem with that?" Charest shot back, looking his friend straight in the eye.

When Hallé explained "his problem," Charest mumbled, in an attempt to mask his obvious embarrassment, "You're right. I'll do something about it."

Charest could be surprisingly serious when he wanted to be,

when the time came to amend the council's by-laws, for instance. Already he was interested in constitutions! But the young president devoted most of his energy to enjoying his youth. "We did things we're better off not talking about," admits Hallé. "Jean might not have been the wildest of the bunch, but he was no wallflower, either. He was just like all the other kids back then. He loved to party, to go out dancing or drinking, to get home late. We used to have parties at the student council, we played underground music full blast. We had a wild time." And Charest's popularity grew. "He could get people together. You felt like hanging out with him."

"He was a leader," recalls a close friend, Marie Fabi. "He was full of good ideas. He was mischievous, always full of tricks!" When she was bedridden with a nasty fracture, Jean showed up with a huge bouquet of daisies. "I was sure he'd robbed a florist's. He could hardly get his arms around the bouquet!" Another time, a few days after he had been Miss Fabi's dinner guest, Charest published his thanks in *La Tribune*, the Sherbrooke French-language daily. What young woman could resist such charm?

SURROUNDED BY PRIESTS

Jean Charest was finding it difficult to juggle studies, school politics and an active social life. In grade eleven, he skipped history class thirty-four times and economics forty-three times!

"He was always partying," says Martine Fortier. "He was loaded with charisma. Fun to be around. He wasn't the serious Jean Charest we know today, not at all."

Not by a long shot. And his parents were alarmed. What to do with a son who was perpetually up to his ears in mischief? they wondered. Rapidly, they made up their minds to enrol him in a private school. And not just any private school: the Séminaire Saint-Charles was the most prestigious private educational institution in the region. If the ultra-modern École Montcalm's futuristic architecture seemed designed for protest and the lax standards that breed it, the Séminaire's venerable corridors, lined with portraits of the scores of priests trained there since the nineteenth century, exuded religion, authority and tradition. "For old Sherbrooke families, the Séminaire was the place one had to attend. The CEGEP was, well, unthinkable," explains René Poitras, a childhood friend of the young Charests.

Eighty years earlier, the future prime minister of Canada, Louis Saint-Laurent, had studied at the Séminaire. In those days, students were forbidden to read newspapers. Boys had to wear a tie in class, call each other "Monsieur" and use the formal "*vous*" when addressing each other. While Saint-Laurent was at Saint-Charles, Wilfrid Laurier, who was then prime minister, visited the institution. "I have devoted my political career to a single concept," Laurier told the students. "Whether I succeed or fail, when I will have been laid in my tomb I will have won the right to have inscribed on my monument the words: 'Here rests a man who sought to make of the French-Canadian and English-Canadian families a single family, united and living in harmony under a single flag.'"* Words that Jean Charest might well utter today.

But the winds of youthful rebellion that had sprung up in the 1970s were too powerful for the venerable institution to resist. Though the administration had granted the students some concessions — for example, the compulsory uniform requirement had been abolished two or three years before Charest arrived — nevertheless, the 1975–76 school year, Red's son's first term at the Séminaire, was a particularly turbulent one. The students formed an association and began to protest, and by November, the young bourgeois of Sherbrooke had hit upon their issue: co-education. Since 1972, the Séminaire had been lending a helping hand to Collège Sacré-Coeur, a nearby girls' school that was short on classroom space. Sacré-Coeur students used the Séminaire's facilities for vari-

---

* Dale Thomson, *Louis St. Laurent: Canadian* (Toronto: Macmillan of Canada, 1967).

ous classes, particularly for science labs and physical education. The number of girls grew year by year, but they continued to take most of their courses apart from the boys, shuttling back and forth between the Collège and the Séminaire every day.

Come 1975, the young people, exasperated by a situation they saw as absurd, demanded that the Séminaire officially declare itself a co-educational institution and integrate the girls from Sacré-Coeur into the student body. All in the name of principle, of course. Led by their president, Jean Desharnais, and Charles Larochelle (now an influential Parti Québécois activist), the students went on a three-day strike, demanding a meeting with the rector. They even enlisted the support of popular Québec comedienne Clémence DesRochers. *La Tribune* devoted two articles to the issue. The first ran under a picture of a student holding a placard that read: "Co-eds or clerical collars." The next day, the newspaper published an editorial ridiculing the strikers: "No one expects Sherbrooke's private college students to be submissive. But, if we may say so, it's high time they showed enough maturity to realize the privileges they enjoy."

And where was Jean Charest? As usual when he talks about the past, Charest tends to exaggerate his role: "Since I was good at organizing strikes . . ." As if he had done everything all by himself. If the testimony of participants and the documents of the period are to be believed, he wasn't even one of the leaders of the movement. They were mostly second-year students. But not many students new to the Séminaire would have jumped in head first the way he did. The young man didn't seem intimidated by the institution's reputation, even though he was one of the few students to have transferred from a public school. "Most of us came from private schools. But Jean had gone to Montcalm, which had a very bad reputation," says former student Lucie Émond. "We heard they were doing drugs, that students cheated on the provincial exams." Drugs? Imagine that!

When the students met rector Georges Cloutier, Charest was one of the spokesmen. He proved to be both eloquent and moderate. He was asked to chair a students' assembly. And it wasn't long before he was elected to the "co-education committee" that was negotiating with the administration.

However, young Charest had more pressing concerns. His was a less noble cause: he wanted the Séminaire to organize a ski week in the Laurentians, like the ones he'd gone on at École Montcalm. All autumn long he badgered student affairs director Maurice Ruel. The good Father was less than enthusiastic about the idea. "The séminaire was quite a traditional institution," he explains. "So the idea of boys and girls going up north for a weekend, you get the picture . . ." Indeed. Ski weeks were "wild and crazy" times, as Martine Fortier might have put it. That would explain Charest's eagerness. He liked nothing better than a wild and crazy time. He was so persistent — "When he wanted something, nothing could stop him," says Father Ruel — that he ended up convincing the administration.

"To the Victor . . ."

There was something else on Jean Charest's mind — and in his heart. During his wild and woolly final year at Montcalm, he'd made the acquaintance of a young woman after making a wager with his pal Bruno Hallé. One evening, the two lads were comfortably but illegally ensconced at a table in a local watering hole — they were both under age — when Martine Fortier introduced them to her friend Michèle Dionne, an eye-catching Sherbrooke lass with flowing hair whose parents had sent her off to Montréal to study at Villa Maria, the cream of Québec's private girls' schools. Immediately after the encounter, the two skirt-chasers made a bet: who would be the first to date Michèle?

Jean proved too fast for his friend; the next weekend he announced he'd won. "It was love at first sight!" says Michèle. All was not sweetness and light, however. When she learned a little later that their romance had begun with a wager, she was fit to be tied. It would be quite a while before Jean would be allowed to forget the incident.

It soon became clear that there was more to the relationship than the usual adolescent crush. "While the rest of us went from one girl-friend to another," recalls their friend Bruno Fortier, "they were already getting serious." Who would have believed it? "They weren't the type of people you could see as a couple. She was a serious girl, and he was such a party animal. It didn't look to us like the perfect match," says Martine Fortier. A little like Red and Rita, perhaps?

Michèle Dionne is the youngest of surgeon Philippe Dionne and Lisette Plourde's three daughters. Philippe and Lisette are an affluent, slightly formal couple, people who patronize the arts. Michèle's parents were also stern disciplinarians. "They stood on ceremony," says Martine Fortier. "When you were at her house you didn't fool around, you behaved yourself."

Every summer the Dionne family spent a month in Provence. The parents led their daughters on the round of museums and concerts. "We were happy to go, they didn't have to force us," Lise Dionne, Michèle's senior by one year, assures us.

Dr. Dionne is a music lover, a passion he inherited from his father Luc, a farmer from Kamouraska. Every Saturday afternoon, Luc Dionne would tune in the Metropolitan Opera radio broadcast from New York; every Sunday he would buy a classical record. His son Philippe loved to play the violin. For many years he would play in the evening after the day's work was done, and then again on Sunday mornings. Dr. Dionne adores Beethoven, Mahler, Schubert and Chopin. But when asked to name his favourite composers, he replies, "I love all beautiful music." Marie Fabi, who went on to become a pianist, has fond recollections of her visits to the Dionne household, where she might step through the front door and into a Mahler symphony or a stimulating conversation with Michèle's father.

Dr. and Mrs. Dionne are also movie buffs. In the mid-1950s, the surgeon started a film club in Sherbrooke. "Before, we had to go to New York to see films like Truffaut's *The 400 Blows*," says Lisette

Dionne. Once a year, of course, the couple would treat themselves to the Montréal Film Festival. They'd spend a week in the theatres, from eight o'clock in the morning to midnight. But that was only once a year. With the film club, they could order great movies and show them to their friends in Sherbrooke. "I set up a projection room," says Dr. Dionne. "And after the film, we'd sit around and discuss it." The day before, the Dionne girls would have their own sneak preview.

In short, Michèle Dionne was a particularly refined and cultivated teenager. "She had so much class, she stood head and shoulders above the other girls," recalls Bruno Hallé. "She had a savoir-vivre that Jean found immensely appealing."

Slowly, Michèle overcame an almost debilitating shyness. According to Martine Fortier, "She was a rather cold girl. She wouldn't make friends with just anyone." A few years earlier, at the summer camp in the United States to which her parents had sent her, Michèle had refused to go into the cafeteria without her sister Lise. And when her ballet school put on a recital, Michèle stubbornly remained in the wings until the teacher relented and let the curtain fall. "The first word she learned was 'no,'" confides her father. "We couldn't force her to do a thing. If she felt she couldn't do it or if she didn't want to, she just said no!"

Against all odds, as the years went by, the couple became a perfect match. Michèle Dionne would keep her husband on an even keel and help him aquire a sense of organization, which he lacked. She brought out the perseverance and discipline his parents had instilled in him. These same values are visible in everything "Michou" says and does, right down to the way she brings up their children. "If they start something, they have to finish it," she says. "'If you want to go skiing, you'll have to study all week.' No studying, no skiing. There's a time to have fun and a time to be serious." Even on vacation.

Following the death of Jean's mother, he rediscovered with the Dionne family the warmth that had vanished from the house on Portland Boulevard. "The support Mrs. Charest had given him was no longer there," says his friend René Poitras. "Jean found a family atmosphere at the Dionnes'."

Michèle took charge of Jean's artistic education. Now he enjoys showing guests the paintings in their North Hatley home: "The region is well known for its folk art," he explains.

Jean gave Michèle's life a touch of fantasy, humour and the unpredictable. "When he dropped by to see Michèle," says Michèle's mother, "he didn't bring her one flower, he brought an armful!" Sherbrooke florists rubbed their hands in glee when they saw Jean pull up. And once, Lise Dionne was about to go for a drive in the evening and found Jean stretched out on the driveway, blocking the way. Who else could have pulled off a stunt like that at the Dionnes'? One thinks of a sentence in Alexandre Jardin's *Le Zubial* a novel that Michèle adores: "He was my clown, my Hamlet and my d'Artagnan, my Mickey Mouse and my favourite trapeze artist."*

But the romance did not always go so smoothly. In point of fact, the couple split up during Jean's first year at the Séminaire, at the same time his fellow students were entering his name in the "sexiest collegian of the year" contest. The intense extra-curricular activity had had an impact on Jean's marks. His report cards were mostly average, or slightly above average, but he flunked two courses, scoring an inglorious 28 percent in poetry. No Cyrano, Jean let flowers do his courting!

It was then that Father Ruel took the gifted young man aside. "If you want to get into university, you're going to have to work harder," he told Jean. The message hit home — and at the same time, Jean's ambition started to surface. In his final semester, Charest took nine courses and even managed to do extremely well in Russian history (88 percent). When graduation rolled around, Maurice Ruel quipped in the college newspaper: "He'll call his next speech 'How to earn a diploma in one semester (the fourth).' It's bound to be a fine piece of oratory. Don't miss it!" About Michèle

---

* Alexandre Jardin, *Le Zubial* (Paris: Gallimard, 1997).

Dionne, the priest wrote this intriguing remark: "The echo does nothing but multiply solitudes."

HAPPY BIRTHDAY, MARIE!

Was the young bon vivant finally settling down? Let's not jump to conclusions. True, he was spending more time cracking the books, but he still enjoyed playing the clown. He even concocted one of those patented stunts that he's been tight-lipped about until now, for fear of tarnishing his sacrosanct image.

One May evening in 1976, after he'd had supper at the local St. Hubert barbecue restaurant with his pal Bruno Hallé, he pulled two cans of red paint out of his bag.

"What's that for?" asked Bruno.

"You'll see. We're going to make a birthday card for Marie Fabi!"

Later that night, the two musketeers spelled out "HAPPY BIRTHDAY MARIE!" in giant red letters on the pavement of Lomas Street, in front of the restaurant. Just as they were putting the finishing touches to their masterpiece, Hallé spotted approaching headlights. The police! The merry pranksters took to their heels. Hallé got away, but the police nabbed the mastermind and shoved him in the back of the squad car:

"Who's the other guy?"

"What other guy? I didn't see any other guy."

"What's your father's name, kid?"

"Claude Charest."

"Not Red Charest?"

"Yeah."

The cop turned to his colleague and laughed: "Boy, is he in deep shit!"

Then he told the prime suspect, "Well, you're really going to get your butt whipped!"

When they got to the station, the cops called Jean's parents. "Your son's been arrested. You'd better come and get him!" But they didn't say what he'd been arrested for. Jean's mother was worried sick. And by the time he got to the station, Red was fuming. "I'll take care of him!"

The epic showdown between father and son was a turning point in their relationship. "The argument was very lively, very frank," says Jean. "We said some harsh words. He said what was on his mind, I said what was on mine, and we haven't said a word about it since."

What did Jean tell his father? Jean's friends think it probably went like this: "I'm sick of being bawled out! Stop calling me a dimwit and an imbecile!" Jean's outburst must have had an effect. "We let it all hang out," Red Charest recalls. "I finally realized it was more foolishness than anything else. You look in the mirror and you remember you made your own mistakes, too." Since then, Red and Jean's father-son relationship has been a man-to-man relationship. Or pretty close to it.

A few months later, Jean Charest was hauled up in youth court before Judge Albert Gobeil. The sentence from the future chief justice of the Québec court consisted of one piece of advice: "Next time, send a birthday card!"

THE UNION NATIONALE: CHAREST TO THE RESCUE

The Charests lived and breathed politics, a passion Red inherited from his father. But unlike Ludovic, Red avoided active involvement: "In the hotel business, you keep your trap shut in public," he says. "In those days, if you were against the government, you lost your licence." As a true-blue conservative, though, the proprietor of the Manoir Orford had nothing to worry about. To this day, Red's admiration for Maurice Duplessis and his Sherbrooke henchman Johnny Bourque still burns bright. "Duplessis's organization may have been corrupt," he admits on mention of the somewhat tarnished reputation of "Le Chef." "But Duplessis himself was not. People respect someone who knows how to speak his mind. Like

Lucien Bouchard. I'm no fan of Bouchard's, mind you, but there's a man who can really speak his mind! Duplessis, he was like that."

Federally, Red Charest didn't much care for John Diefenbaker but voted for him anyway. "It seemed like he was giving everything to the West, even though the farmers in our neck of the woods weren't exactly rolling in dough. Some of them lived near the hotel. They had maybe three or four hens, a sow, a couple of horses, a cow and that's about all." Still, back then, true-blue Tories voted blue.

Every evening the family sat around the table talking politics. Jean and his brother Robert inherited the family fixation. Later, Robert became an aide to the federal environment minister, a certain Lucien Bouchard. Jean's elder brother has also played an important role in his younger sibling's political campaigns, and has been at his side at every key moment in his career.

As a youngster Jean didn't read newspapers; he devoured them. Other students followed the papers too, but rare were the French-speakers who pored over Sherbrooke's English-language daily, the *Record*, the way Jean did, or walked around with a copy of *Time* magazine under his arm, or religiously watched *60 Minutes* on CBS. Jean was absorbing politics, talking politics all day long, but his interest was still mostly theoretical. He did take part in a demonstration against Premier Robert Bourassa's Bill 22, which made French the official language of Québec. The nationalists were attacking the legislation, which they claimed made it too easy for people to send their children to English schools. "I was just demonstrating for demonstration's sake," is Charest's assessment. "And I hesitated to get too involved because I didn't really understand the issues." Clearly, though, Charest had picked up the vibrations of the nationalist upsurge that was carrying young people before it. In November 1976, he voted for René Lévesque's Parti Québécois. And Red, like many French-speaking Québeckers, cast his ballot for the PQ too, even though he wasn't a sovereign-tist. "The first time [1976], it wasn't about independence," Red explains. "The Union Nationale wasn't around any more. The only way to get rid of the Liberals was to vote for Lévesque."

At the Séminaire Saint-Charles, Jean was surrounded by Péquistes. A students' association poll showed the PQ with 40 percent support, compared with only 24 percent for the Liberals. Although a mere 2 percent of the students supported the Union Nationale, Charest continued to show a keen interest in the moribund party for some time. In fact, he informed Bernard Bonneau, his former mentor, that he intended to "relaunch the Union Nationale." A tall order! Near the end of Jean's freshman year at Saint-Charles, a family acquaintance invited him to attend the Union Nationale's leadership convention in Québec City as a delegate. He and Bruno Hallé headed off to Québec. According to Bruno, Jean turned down the party's offer to pay for his hotel room and refused to use the credit card his father had lent him: "He wanted to be strictly independent."

The May 1976 convention was a curious affair. Delegates were not elected by the rank and file; they were chosen by the party brass. Most of the candidates were political unknowns. The interim leader, wily old veteran Maurice Bellemarre, was probably more popular than all of them put together. The outcome of the election hung on back-room deals by politicos known as the "colonels." Rodrigue Biron, a Lotbinière industrialist, scored a first-ballot victory. "The winner," wrote Le Devoir's Lise Bissonnette, "has practically no political experience."

The two young men had a fine time in Québec City, but Charest was not pleased. "I wasn't very impressed," he sighs. "Maurice Bellemarre was everywhere. I was disillusioned. I could see the party wasn't going anywhere. I couldn't identify with it." Even so, two years later, with a few drinks under his belt, he swore to his pal Michel Coutu: "Someday, I'll be head of the Union Nationale and premier of Québec." (Premier of Québec? Well, well . . .)

Coutu burst out laughing. "But, Jean, the party's all but dead."

"Well then, I'll go into federal politics. I'll become leader of the Progressive Conservative Party and prime minister of Canada. But one thing's for sure, I'll always be true-blue!"

So he still had a soft spot in his heart for the Union Nationale. Union Nationale or Progressive Conservative Party, it made little difference — what mattered was finding a vehicle for his budding aspirations. "I was probably kidding around when I said 'I want to become prime minister,' but I was lucid enough," says Charest defensively. Then he concedes, "It was a joke. But humour is just another way of saying things. There's always a pinch of truth. I could feel the urge. It seemed to me that I would be happiest if I could make a difference, help people."

Charest was only seventeen and already he had his eye on a political career. "After my student council days, I could see myself as an MP. I'd say to myself, 'Someday, I wouldn't mind getting into politics.'" When he suggested to Bruno Hallé that they get together every week to discuss politics, his friend protested, "But Jean, we see each other every day and that's all we talk about."

"Yes, but maybe our discussions should be more organized!"

"You've got to be kidding!"

The signs were multiplying like loaves and fishes. The kid was changing, turning deadly serious. Twenty years later, as Tory leader, Jean Charest would find himself in a restaurant, scolding his MPs for some high-spirited behaviour: "Throwing bread around in a restaurant, for God's sake!"

THE WISDOM OF SUN TZU II

Bruno Hallé has yet another revealing tale to tell. Jean didn't waste a minute, he says, while they were driving to the Union Nationale convention in Mrs. Charest's Vega. "Jean had visualized the whole weekend. He imagined how he would react to what would happen. He thought: 'So what's the score? Who's going to be there? What are they going to talk about? Where will I be seated?'"

The need to be prepared and the fear of being caught off guard have become permanent traits of the Jean Charest personality. On the coffee table of his North Hatley home, I came across *The Lost Art of War*, the book of maxims by the ancient Chinese strategist Sun Tzu II. Charest swears by the book's strategic injunctions, especially: "Do not act before you are prepared."* According to Hallé, "[Charest] has always been like that, since his student council days. Even when he's meeting friends he visualizes events before they happen so he can control the situation." For all but the most intimate occasions, Charest's assistant, Suzanne Poulin, has standing orders to find out who will be attending the event, how it is expected to unfold and whom he'll be sitting beside. This is the standard drill in practical politics, but the Charest clan take it a little further than most. Sherbrooke organizer Jacques Fortier was stung to learn that, when his wife invited Charest to Jacques's fortieth birthday party, she was subjected to a grilling by Poulin: "Who will be there? What time are we supposed to arrive? Let me get back to you. Jean may have something else on his schedule."

"Listen, Suzanne," said Fortier's wife a few calls later. "Jacques has been working for Jean Charest for ten years. I hope he'll find a way to be there!"

Chalk it up to insecurity. Or, perhaps more than anything else, to caution overlaid with pride. It's a need for control, a fear of embarrassment. The Sherbrooke MP was unfailingly co-operative with me as I was preparing this book, but he never stopped protecting himself. I had to insist on interviewing his younger sisters, Caroline and Christine, two delightfully straightforward and sincere women. "The family doesn't give any interviews," Suzanne Poulin explained. "They don't feel comfortable with the media." Translated into everyday language, that meant there was always the risk they might tell the truth without first passing it through the political-correctness filter. They might be as candid and outspoken as Red had been. Charest even asked relatives who were going to meet with me to record the

---

* Sun Tzu II, *The Lost Art of War* (New York: Harper Collins, 1997), p. 22.

interviews — though I was already taping them myself.

It took weeks of manoeuvring to persuade Charest to let me see his report cards. Suzanne Poulin's initial response was, "He'd prefer not to. He'd rather keep them for a book he's thinking about writing himself." Then she agreed, but with one proviso: "All right, but we'll send for the files ourselves from the school board." A little later she told me, "Sure I have them. But first I have to get Jean's final approval," followed by, "I haven't had time to talk to him about it." In the end, a purely political argument probably won the day: how would the saviour of his country look if I were to recount that he had refused to show me his report cards?

The incident revealed an image-conscious Jean Charest who, in the end, places a great value on frankness. Though he is a master of the art of political double-speak, there are limits beyond which he will not go. By nature as much as by expediency, Charest is straightforward and above board. Few politicians would have supplied a journalist with their school transcripts, especially if they showed little to boast about. There were real risks involved. The Suzanne Tremblays of this world are always lying in wait: "How can you take his economic program seriously? He failed his economics course in high school!"

It would be an error to read too much into Jean Charest's academic record. His marks show him as a typical young man of his day, drawn more to action than to study, a characterization that remains true today. Besides, academic success has never been a reliable measure of a person's ability.

This curious blend of openness and caution, candour and secretiveness, is one component of the Charest enigma. "So," Suzanne Poulin asked over supper with Charest, "After all your research, are you starting to understand our leader a little better?"

"No," I replied, unsure about the conclusions I would reach.

"It's just as well!" sighed Charest.

Red. Claude Charest was twenty-two when he joined the Baltimore Clippers. "I was no star," he says. *Claude Charest collection*.

The gorgeous blonde. Red Charest and Rita Leonard were married in 1953.
People who knew Jean Charest's mother say she was "beautiful on the outside,
beautiful on the inside." *Claude Charest collection*.

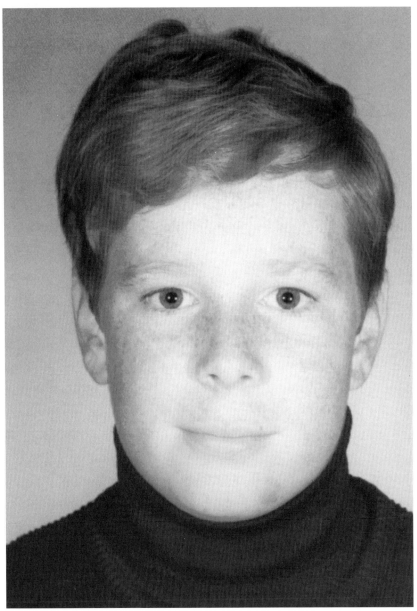

John-John. His mother baptized him John James and called him John-John. His father called him Jean. Everyone agrees that he was the family clown. *Jean Charest/Michèle Dionne collection.*

The family. The Charest family gathered around Rita several months before her death. Front: Red, Rita, Christine and Louise. Rear: Jean, Carole and Robert. *Jean Charest/Michèle Dionne collection.*

The future minister of Sport. An avid soccer player, the teenaged Jean Charest poses with his École Montcalm teammates (front row, far right). *Jean Charest/Michèle Dionne collection.*

The kid. "That's him," say friends from his teen years: Jean Charest mugs for the camera during the annual École Montcalm ski week. *André Pratte collection.*

The young and the restless.
Freshly graduated from the
University of Sherbrooke Law
School, Jean Charest begins his
brief career as a lawyer. *Jean
Charest/Michèle Dionne collection.*

A perfect couple. Michèle
Dionne and Jean Charest at the
École Montcalm senior prom,
1975. An unlikely pair slowly
became an ideal couple. *Jean
Charest/Michèle Dionne collection.*

A perfect family. Michèle Dionne, Jean Charest and their children, Alexandra, Antoine and Amélie, on a winter's day at the family home in North Hatley. *Jean Charest/Michèle Dionne collection.*

Three generations of Charests. Jean Charest and father Red are wild about politics. Any guesses about Antoine? *Claude Charest collection.*

"Have you done your homework?" Concerned parents on the campaign trail, keeping tabs on the children by telephone. *Photo: Bill McCarthy. Jean Charest/Michèle Dionne collection.*

PERRY MASON JR.

One evening when he was twelve, Jean Charest sat down at the family dinner table and announced, "I know what I want to do when I grow up. I'm going to be a lawyer." He'd just finished watching a *Perry Mason* episode on TV.

The idea stuck in his mind. When he graduated from law school at the University of Sherbrooke, he chose to work on criminal cases. "It was Perry Mason, the widow and the orphan," he explains. "I liked the idea of giving people a hand, helping them." Most of all, the silver-tongued Charest wanted to plead cases in court. "Criminal law per se never really attracted me. What I wanted to do was to try cases before a judge and jury. And the only place you get judge and jury trials is in criminal law." But university criminal law courses did not exactly inspire our aspiring Perry Mason. Surprisingly, he was more interested in philosophy. This came after he encountered Michel Krauss, a young professor from Ontario who had just moved to Québec. "It was a real eye-opener!" Charest says.

Krauss gave a few compulsory courses, but he was best known for the philosophy of law seminar that attracted a dozen or so of the law school's top students. High marks were few and far between. "I gave the lowest marks in the faculty," admits Krauss, now a professor at George Mason University, near Washington, D.C. Ever curious, Charest was drawn to the professor's unconventional approach, and signed up for the seminar for the fall semester in 1979. Every week, Krauss drove his students through weighty tomes written by professors from Oxford and Cambridge, which they would then discuss in class. "Jean didn't get the highest marks," recalls Krauss. "He knew full well when he took my course that he was at a relative disadvantage and that he was unlikely to improve his average. He was well aware he wasn't a philosopher, but he felt he needed exposure to the subject."

"He was an amiable enough chap, very eager to learn, but certainly no genius," concludes Professor Krauss. "He didn't give me very high marks," laughs Charest. "I was annoyed at him because I had worked so hard!"

LIFE

Michel Krauss soon became convinced that this particular student was destined for a career in politics. "He had presence, a kind of charisma. When he spoke, people listened." It came as no surprise to Krauss when the young Sherbrooker ran for federal office five years later. No surprise, but a bit of disappointment.

"I can't blame him for seizing the opportunity," says Krauss. "But I wonder if, deep down, he wouldn't have preferred to do something else for ten years or so before getting into politics. If I had wanted to have a political career, I think I would have wanted to hold other positions beforehand so that I'd have a chance to look more deeply into certain issues." Sherbrooke businessman and former Liberal adversary Dennis Wood puts it more bluntly: "Jean knows politics; he doesn't know life."

Charest learned on the job. There's little doubt that now, at forty years of age, he's built up a wealth of experience that is the envy of many. Still, from time to time, some surprising lapses occur. Perhaps he started too early and has climbed the ladder too fast. In one interview, Charest confused Premier Jean-Jacques Bertrand's Bill 63 with Robert Bourassa's Bill 22, and ended up calling it the "Bourassa government's Bill 69." And in 1994, he claimed federalism could be considered a form of sovereignty association, since, as he put it, "The concept of sovereignty association has never, to my knowledge, been defined in detail." A curious assertion, bearing in mind that René Lévesque wrote a book on the subject in 1968 and that in 1980 the Parti Québécois published a white paper to define the concept.

SEVERAL SPEECHES, ONE TEXT

In addition to philosophy, Charest loved the course in constitutional law taught by Pierre Patenaude, a jurist as brilliant as he was flamboyant. "It was an extraordinary course," says Michel Coutu, a friend at the time. "Jean saw a bit of himself in Patenaude. He tried to debate him in class." Charest's passion for debate earned him a bit of a reputation among his classmates. "Jean didn't ask questions in class. He made speeches!"

It's no easy matter to discern, from what we know of his ideas, the older man's influence on Jean Charest's thinking about the constitution. A federalist at the time (that would change after the repatriation of the Constitution in 1982), Patenaude was convinced that the country's political system needed a thorough overhaul. He did not conceal his views from his students: "It is essential to bring about a substantial reform in power sharing," he wrote. "Above all to enable Québec's language and culture to thrive, which is not now the case because of Ottawa's spending power. When there are two centres of decision-making with regard to culture, often taking contradictory positions, cultural planning becomes an illusion."

Urged on by Michel Krauss, Charest took an interest in the issue of religious freedom. He sat on a committee to examine whether the University of Sherbrooke should end its affiliation with the Catholic Church. And in the heat of the debate over the religious status of École Notre-Dame-des-Neiges, which the parents wished to become a non-confessional school against the wishes of the Montréal Catholic School Commission, Charest fired off a letter to *Le Devoir*, one of his few youthful writings.

He was responding to an opinion piece published in the Montréal daily by a school commissioner opposed to any change in the school's confessional status. In it, the traits that have since become typical of today's politician are clearly visible. First, a respect for the opinions of others. "Your argument in favour of the Catholic religion does not disturb me," he starts off. "I myself am a Catholic, so I appreciate the fervour and sincerity with which you profess your faith."*

Even then, tolerance and openness had become core values for the young Charest, anchoring his opposition to the imposition of Catholic education on Québec's growing immigrant population. "The grave social injustice which allows those who believe themselves to be possessed of the truth to impose their dogma on those who don't share this particular truth must be corrected," he wrote. In his mind, not only must non-Catholic children be exempted from religious instruction, there must be non-confessional institutions as well. Otherwise, continued Charest, he "would be forced to conclude that the integration of immigrants into the French-speaking community in Québec is little more than the pious wish of an ethnic group turned inward on itself, and not the desire of a nation seeking to build its future." Already his mistrust of a certain variety of nationalism has manifested itself; yet note the use of the word "nation" to describe the French-speaking people of Québec.

In the long run, Charest argued, all schools should cut their religious ties and the teaching of religion should be left to the churches, as in the United States: "[. . .] it is not certain that religious education will be the responsibility of the State in a pluralistic, French-speaking society."

"Now, as Québec must give its answer to the 'question,'" Charest concluded (he was writing four months prior to the May 1980 referendum), "I hope that Québeckers will not forget that their future is made up of a number of questions." The style may be a little heavy-handed, but Charest had already developed a sense of formula.

Friends from his law school days describe him as a determined, disciplined student who worked hard, at least in the courses that interested him. Mario Proulx remembers him quoting one of Red's maxims: "In life, there are three things that count: work, work and work." Twenty-year-old Jean Charest was already teaching that particular course.

---

* Jean Charest, "Une question à laquelle il faut aussi répondre," *Le Devoir*, January 17, 1980, p. 5.

His natural courtroom flair blossomed in his first mock trials. Says friend Marc Lapointe, "He wasn't self-conscious in the slightest. Everyone else was intimidated, but he immediately felt at ease." But for all his efforts, Charest got slightly below-average marks. True, he earned a sensational 91 percent in Constitutional Law I. But there were some disasters, too, like the 43 percent in Penal Law I.

In those days, conditions were not exactly propitious for study. It was during his second year in law school that Charest lost his beloved mother.

"I love you!"

"I love you too, John-John."

"It was a trying time for him, but he bore his grief with dignity," recalls Mario Proulx, who visited the family at the funeral home. "He kept his mourning to himself. His tears were silent."

There followed a painful period that the family is reluctant to talk about. "Those were hard times for us," Charest admits. "The family went through deep feelings of guilt. It took several months for us to get over it, to rebuild our relationships."

But, as Red had ordained, life must go on. When he graduated from the University of Sherbrooke, Jean Charest quoted Lebanese mystic Kahlil Gibran beside his photo in the school yearbook:

And you who would understand justice, how shall you unless
    you look upon all deeds in the fullness of light?
Only then shall you know that the erect and the fallen are but
    one man standing in twilight between the night of his
    pigmy-self and the day of his god-self,
And that the corner-stone of the temple is not higher than the
    lowest stone in its foundation.

Inspired by this spirit, twenty-two-year-old Jean Charest set forth to defend widows and orphans.

THE DISCOVERY OF CANADA

Apart from ski holidays and a few visits to Montréal and Québec City, the young Jean Charest had never left Sherbrooke. Now it was time to put to sea, to prove to himself and to his father that he was independent. And put to sea is what he did, literally, for two whole summers.

On a tip from a friend, Charest travelled to the port of Montréal to look for a job on one of the freighters that ply the St. Lawrence River and the Great Lakes. After cooling his heels for a few days in the Seafarers' Union hiring hall and plunking down union dues — $260 in cash — he got the break he was looking for. The *J. N. McWaters*, a 16,000-tonne laker with a cargo of grain bound for Québec City, needed an assistant mechanic.

"What was your last job?"

"Uh . . . driving a beer truck," said Charest, stretching the truth a bit (in fact, he'd only loaded the trucks).

"Okay, you've got the job: assistant mechanic."

Red Charest was furious. "You're telling me your mother and I raised you to become a sailor!" Yet another angry face-off ensued.

At two o'clock the following morning, at the St. Lambert locks, the would-be grease-monkey shipped out on a freighter for the first time in his life. The massive vessel was 220 metres long and 22 metres wide. The look of awe on Charest's face betrayed his total inexperience. The chief engineer could hardly believe his eyes: "The bastards, so that's what they handed me for a mechanic!"

The two summers he spent working the river were hard ones — "The only thing that comes close to life on ship board is life in prison!" says Charest — but the experience was fascinating and the pay was good. Jean Charest put his capacities to the test; he grew a beard, went hungry for ten days and hung out in topless bars, often the only places open when the boats docked.

And Charest discovered Canada, its geography, economy and people.

First, the geography. He saw the Great Lakes and the St. Lawrence River. Ah, the river! Charest speaks about it with emotion: "I'll never forget one Sunday afternoon on the river. We were sailing from Les Escoumins to Québec City. The church steeples in the sunshine, and in the evening, the lights of the Chateau Frontenac! Unforgettable!" Farther upstream lay the Thousand Islands. "When you see them for the first time . . . !" And the great American cities: Detroit, Cleveland, Chicago.

Then came the economy. The laker carried grain from West to East, and iron ore from the mines of northern Québec to the steel mills that line the American shores of the Great Lakes. "I still remember my first trip to Port-Cartier. Those were hard times — the mines were closing down."

Finally, there were the people — the native people of Thunder Bay, and the "Newfies." There was intolerance, too. Sailors, especially when under the influence of alcohol or drugs, weren't the most receptive of Canadians when it came to debating Québec's aspirations. "You could talk politics on the boats, but you had to be careful."

There was nothing there to spark a love affair between the greenhorn sailor and his country. Meanwhile, the May 1980 referendum was approaching. What would Charest the nationalist do, the self-same Charest who had voted for the PQ three and a half years earlier? Nothing. When his final semester in university ended, he fled by freighter. On the day of the vote he was not even in Québec. Saved by the bosun's pipe. How was it that a young man with politics in his blood did not do everything he could to cast his vote for the future of his country? Today, Charest claims he was in desperate straits. He needed money to take his bar exams in the fall and, above all, he needed money to get married. The summer before, he had asked for Michèle's hand. It had been a romantic proposal: Jean, from a telephone booth on the Welland Canal; Michèle, in a hotel room in Greece, where she had gone rather than spend the summer bored and lonely in Sherbrooke while her boyfriend plied the St. Lawrence.

Who knows? Had he remained ashore, perhaps Jean Charest would have been swept along on the Yes tide. Today, of course, the federalist leader claims, "I would have voted No. Like so many people, I considered myself a nationalist deep down. But the sovereigntists hadn't convinced me. Canada still meant something to me. I'd lived on the boats; I'd seen the country and its vastness. I had a different perspective."

PERRY MASON DOES LEGAL AID

Jean Charest passed his bar exams in the fall of 1980. He and his friend Mario Proulx then articled for six months under attorney Claude Leblond, handling legal aid cases. His hard work and enthusiasm made an immediate impression. On one occasion, when his supervisor asked him to prepare a case that had to be defended the following day, Charest worked until five o'clock in the morning. "He prepared extremely detailed comparative tables. I was fortunate to have had such a resourceful and industrious trainee," says Leblond.

Charest's self-assurance set him apart from the other budding lawyers who were making their courtroom debuts. "You could see the guy's confidence in court right away," Proulx recalls. "He never made the same mistake twice. He could keep his stress under control. He was a born litigant. He may have had a few hesitations, but it was clear that he had the will to perform."

"It was as if he'd been speaking in court all his life," says Judge Laurent Dubé, who presided over several cases involving clients of Charest's.

Criminal lawyer Michel Dussault, then an associate in a small Sherbrooke firm, first noticed the curly-headed novice in the courthouse waiting room, thronged by dozens of poor souls accused of every crime in the book. "He spoke to everybody and looked them straight in the eye. People were drawn to him. He hooked a lot of new clients that way," relates Dussault. Charest had just landed his first job. Henceforth, lawyer John James Charest would work for the Wellington Street legal firm of Beauchemin, Dussault.

The novice attorney was a little too zealous for certain tastes. One night, he brought home a client in trouble. The next morning, when Michèle Dionne went downstairs in her dressing gown to prepare breakfast, she found a stranger fast asleep on the living-room sofa. Alarmed, she ran upstairs. "Jean, there's someone sleeping in the living room!"

"Yeah, I know. He's a client," said Charest.

"A client! What did he do?"

"Robbed a bank . . ."

"Robbed a bank!? Get that guy out of here right this minute!"

Attorney Leblond felt it necessary to dampen his trainee's enthusiasm. "Jean, I've noticed how concerned you are about your clients. I'd just like to remind you that your clients are entitled to a lawyer. When you try to be a social worker, you deprive them of that lawyer."

To hear Jean Charest describe it, his law career was a long and tumultuous one. Once again, this is Charest embellishing his image. Some might even say that he lays it on thick. So rapid has been his rise to the top that he sometimes speaks with the all-knowing tone of a man of vast experience. When the young Sherbrooke MP first sat in the House of Commons, Liberal MP Jean-Claude Malépart would criticize this condescending tone and suggest that he "stop strutting just because he happens to be a lawyer." Jean Charest practised law for a total of three years. All in all, he pleaded eight cases before a jury. No one, neither his supervisor nor Michel Dussault, not even Charest himself, can recall a single remarkable court case. On the eve of his leap into politics, attorney Jean J. Charest was still a neophyte — but a neophyte with a promising career ahead of him, the kind of young lawyer that Sherbrooke law offices fight over.

A SURPRISING PARALLEL

There are striking similarities between Charest and another politician, born a quarter of a century earlier. Like Charest, he too had only a brief law career in small-town Québec under his belt when he was catapulted into the political arena in Ottawa. He too lacked depth, people said.

Like Charest, he had been raised by a strict father and protected by a very gentle mother. His mother died when he was nineteen, practically the same age as Jean Charest when Rita Leonard died. Like Charest, this politician of another generation married his childhood sweetheart, who, like Michèle Dionne, was a serious, ambitious young woman. She would make sure that her man got over his youthful folly and landed with both feet on the ground. Throughout his lengthy political career, she would be his rudder, his guardian angel.

The similarities are striking indeed. But what lessons can we draw from them? The man whose life in certain respects so closely resembles Jean Charest's is Jean Chrétien.*

LIFE ON THE WRONG SIDE OF THE TRACKS

The young Charest learned much during his three years at the bar. He has always been able to make the most of every experience, no matter how modest. The Sherbrooke courthouse taught Charest about what might be called "the lower depths": "I don't know whether you've ever waved goodbye to someone who's being put away for seven years," he says. To his astonishment, he discovered that many young people his age did not know how to read or write. For a bon vivant, the destitution soon became too hard to bear. "There was no way I was always going to be looking at the bad side of life."

---

* See Lawrence Martin, *Chrétien: The Will to Win* (Toronto: Lester Publishing, 1995).

Charest was ambitious, Michèle perhaps even more so. But criminal law offered few high-profile career opportunities. Jean considered doing a Master's degree in maritime law in England or the United States. At the same time, Monty, Coulombe, Sherbrooke's largest law firm, offered him a position practising labour law. Charest accepted, at first. Then, to Michou's profound dismay, he changed his mind. He was a young man in a hurry: "I didn't want to get into a firm where it would take twenty years to become a senior partner. I preferred working on my own."

It was the winter of 1983. Jean Charest was twenty-five years old. His professional life was at a crossroads. Should he go into criminal, labour or maritime law? One Sunday evening, at the traditional family dinner, Jean and his father were in the kitchen. "Jean," Red blurted out, "if you're thinking about getting into politics someday, check out what's going on in the Progressive Conservative Party."

What was going on in the Progressive Conservative Party was the rise of another hard-driving, ambitious man. A man by the name of Brian Mulroney.

The Tory Tide

—⚬—

In Sherbrooke, to be considered the father of Jean Charest's political career is something to brag about. In fact, there are several claimants to the paternal title.

Psychiatrist Pierre Gagné, head of the University of Sherbrooke's department of psychiatry, is one of the leading aspirants. A long-time back-room operator, Dr. Gagné was one of the few dozen Tories who held the fort for the Sherbrooke Conservatives during Pierre Trudeau's reign in Ottawa, from 1968 to 1984. "I'm a born Tory," he says. His paternal grandfather was called "Johnny" in honour of Sir John A. Macdonald; maternal grandfather Wilfrid Labbé served in the Duplessis cabinet.

So no one was surpirsed when the doctor turned up one evening in the fall of 1982 at a Progressive Conservative Party association meeting in Sherbrooke. The Tories were choosing delegates for the upcoming national convention, to be held in January 1983. The event, which was to take place in Winnipeg, would have a decisive impact on leader Joe Clark's political future. After a brief career as prime minister in 1979, Clark had lost a non-confidence vote in the House following the presentation of his first budget. He then proceeded to lose the early election that ensued and was relegated to the Opposition. Almost miraculously, Pierre Elliott Trudeau once again became prime minister of Canada. The evening of his triumphant return, Trudeau declared with his customary haughtiness: "Well, welcome to the Eighties!" Tory party workers were beside themselves. In Winnipeg, they would vent their frustrations by secret ballot, in a leadership review.

All across the country, pro- and anti-Clark forces were locked in a pitched battle for the hearts and minds of the delegates. Most of the Tory delegates who wanted to dump the former prime minister were in the pocket of Brian Mulroney, then president of the Iron Ore Company of Canada. Opposition to the Mulroney camp in Sherbrooke was almost non-existent. "There were thirty people in the room at the most, including spouses," says Dr. Gagné of the party association meeting. Since most of the local Tory notables wanted to get rid of Clark, they proceeded to elect a delegation hostile to the leader.

Gagné left the Le Baron Hotel disgusted with the disloyalty of the Sherbrooke Conservatives. Shunned by the local delegation, he did not attend the Winnipeg leadership review where Clark, with a feeble 67 percent endorsement, promptly called a leadership convention. "Until we have silenced all the serious critics in these ranks, we will not prove our capacity to form a government to the people of this country," thundered the man from Alberta. Once again, delegates would be chosen from each of Canada's 282 constituencies. The Clark-Mulroney duel would be particularly bitter in Québec. As most ridings lacked a Conservative Party association, the organization that sold the most memberships would carry the day.

In the weeks following the Winnipeg convention, Joe Clark asked Pierre Gagné to head the Sherbrooke organization. But Gagné, who was no great shakes as an organizer, admits to being "a bit desperate." So he began knocking on doors and buttonholing friends, including defence attorney Michel Dussault, who had called Gagné as an expert witness in a number of court cases. Joining the two men at Le Brasier, a King Street steak house, was Dussault's law partner, Michel Beauchemin. "Would you mind if I brought Jean Charest along?" Dussault had asked. The doctor, who had encountered the young man on several occasions at the courthouse, had no objection. Over lunch, Gagné laid out his strategy, but his friends were less than enthusiastic. "You know, Mr. Gagné," said Charest, "I'm leaning toward Mulroney myself." The young lawyer would need some convincing. In glowing terms, the psychiatrist described the possibility of delegate status at the Ottawa convention. A political convention? A weekend in Ottawa? Say no more. Charest jumped at the chance, promptly forking over fifteen dollars for his membership card, three times the going price.

FATHER NUMBER TWO

That, according to Pierre Gagné, is how Jean Charest's political career began. But there is a second version of the Sherbrooke Kid's first steps on the road to the nation's capital: Denis Beaudoin's. One of Joe Clark's top advisers in Québec, Beaudoin knew the Eastern Townships like the back of his hand. His father, Léonel Beaudoin, had been the Créditiste MP for Richmond. Denis had run there as the Tory candidate in 1979 and 1980. When the battle broke out between Clark and Mulroney, Beaudoin wasted little time setting up pro-Clark organizations in Sherbrooke and a number of other ridings. One of his contacts — Judge Léo Daigle swears he's the man — advised Beaudoin to call "Red Charest's boy." "One Friday evening," says Beaudoin, "I met him in his Wellington Street office and told him, 'Joe's authorized me to offer you a deal: help us in the leadership race. If we win, we'll help you become the Conservative candidate in the next election.'"

Why would a seasoned organizer seek out a political neophyte he didn't know to organize the Sherbrooke campaign? Because, says Beaudoin, the entire local organization was leaning toward Brian Mulroney: "I had to go outside the party apparatus. I had to find another outfit, an outfit that would catch those people unawares, and sell a fistful of membership cards."

Before reaching a decision, Jean Charest invited Beaudoin to the family's Sunday dinner on Portland Boulevard. Everyone put in his two cents' worth. The elder Charest put Beaudoin to the test: Did Clark have a chance? What did the polls say? For her part, Michèle wasn't eager to see her husband abandon his budding legal career. In the Dionnes' house, where names like Riopelle, Truffaut and Beethoven dominated the conversation, politics had never ranked high on the agenda. "The whole family got into the act," says Beaudoin. Finally, Jean accepted the Clark organizer's proposal.

That, according to Denis Beaudoin, is how Jean Charest's political career began. According to Judge Daigle, Beaudoin's version contains several inaccuracies; the truth probably falls somewhere in between Gagné's, Beaudoin's, and Daigle's versions. But Jean Charest is not about to settle the issue; after all, he might offend one of his friends: "All these things were happening at the same time . . . "

SUGAR-COATING

Beaudoin and Gagné do agree on one point. Both remember Charest as a lukewarm supporter of Joe Clark's bid for confirmation of his leadership. Beaudoin recalls Charest saying, "You know, between the two of them, I prefer Brian." Longtime friend Bruno Fortier also found Charest's sudden interest in Clark's future astonishing: "Before he hadn't shown any . . . Then all of a sudden, look who's Joe Clark's man in Sherbrooke: Jean Charest! Save Joe Clark in 1983? If Clark had been a rising star on the national scene, it might have made more sense!"

Charest doesn't recall being a Brian Mulroney fan. On the contrary: "Clark's position on the repatriation of the Constitution really impressed me back then," he maintains. Joe Clark, let it be remembered, had been critical of Québec's exclusion from the constitutional agreement of 1981, while Mulroney supported the machinations of the Trudeau government. Had the young lawyer joined the Clark camp because he endorsed the Albertan's vision of Canada? The reality was a good deal more prosaic. Jean Charest gives his entrance into politics an ideological sugar-coating that his friends cannot confirm. To hear them tell it, their friend's real motives could not have been more down to earth. Charest's position, says Fortier, was this: "I'm supporting Joe Clark because I want to be a delegate and go to the convention."

The new convert sold memberships with the enthusiasm he brings to everything he does. The upshot was that, when the Conservative association met to choose its delegates, not thirty but several hundred people jammed the room in the Auberge des Gouverneurs, and the full Clark slate was elected, including Jean Charest.

As Charest scaled the political heights, the legend grew that he was the architect of the pro-Clark victory in Sherbrooke. Charest has done nothing to dispel the impression: "So I backed Joe. He needed someone to organize, I accepted the job and I did it." There was more to it than that. Charest certainly sold a great many memberships, especially to dozens of young people who normally would not have wasted an evening on a bunch of old Tory fogies. He might even have outsold everyone else, though that honour has been contested. But in claiming to be the chief organizer, he is going a little too far. "Charest sold membership cards. He wasn't in charge of anything," says Léo Daigle. Dr. Gagné says the same thing.

In early June 1983, Jean Charest arrived in Ottawa to take part in the election of the next Tory leader. Those who attended the convention remember it as one of the most exciting events in the history of Canadian politics. The three thousand delegates packed into the Ottawa Civic Centre braved nine hours of voting and waiting in the stifling heat.

The young Sherbrooke lawyer had brought along his wife: "It was our first outing together since Amélie's birth." To each his idea of a romantic weekend . . . A few weeks earlier, a very pregnant Michèle had burst into tears when Jean announced his intention to plunge into the battle for delegates. She joined him on the Ottawa trip reluctantly, but ended up having a wonderful time. Today, the Charests love to describe how Michou, up until then the perfect apolitical spouse, would get up at four o'clock in the morning to slide leaflets under delegates' hotel room doors.

Still, Michèle did have real cause for concern. Her husband had found a mistress. Jean Charest had missed his rendezvous with destiny at the Union Nationale convention a few years earlier, but this time he'd fallen in love — with politics. "I had a few delegates under my wing; it felt like I was on the front lines, though I wasn't, neccessarily." He was just one out of three thousand, in point of fact. "When he came back from Ottawa, his feet barely touched the ground," recalls attorney Michel Dussault.

Pierre Gagné was also smitten — by Jean Charest, budding politician. The psychiatrist was greatly impressed with his recruit's energy, his way with people and his loyalty. Charest had stuck with Clark right to the end, while many others had abandoned him to join the victor's camp.

At 9:20 p.m., on Saturday, June 11, the result of the fourth and final ballot was announced: Joe Clark, 1,325 votes; Brian Mulroney, 1,584. While Mulroney and wife Mila were making their way across the packed convention floor to the stage, the Clark loyalists, who had been fighting for three years to save their irreproachably well-meaning champion, broke into sobs.

An embittered Gagné and his group returned to Sherbrooke, bent on revenge. They would elect *their* candidate in the next election. The undertaking was a bold one, considering that Brian Mulroney would be assuming full command of the party machine. And the project took on a near-comic aspect when the party's big brass picked its candidate: Claude Métras, an insurance adjuster known for his active involvement in the Sherbrooke community.

KAMIKAZE WANTED

The former Clark supporters were united in their desire to wreck the Mulroney camp's prospects in Sherbrooke. To do it, they would need a sacrificial candidate to go up against Métras for the riding nomination. Young Charest, Pierre Gagné told his friends, might make a good choice. There was a good deal of skepticism: "Who is this guy anyway?" "People wondered how he could get by Métras, let alone beat the Liberal MP," says the psychiatrist. But no one else was willing to play the kamikaze, and soon they'd fallen under Charest's spell. In the end, everybody agreed: Jean Charest was it. "No one had any illusions about Charest's chances of beating the Liberal, or Métras, for that matter," Gagné continues. "We were doing it to prepare for the next election." The rookie didn't take much persuading. He was keen to run. But they did have to sell Michou on the idea. "She was reluctant," Charest admits. Nobody knows how he did it, but somehow he managed to convince her.

In early January 1984, Pierre Gagné and Léo Daigle brought together a few dozen friends to launch Jean Charest's campaign for the Sherbrooke riding PC nomination. The meeting took place in the faculty lounge at the University of Sherbrooke law school. "That's where I made my first speech," laughs Jean Charest, "a little sales pitch. It was absolutely terrible! I must've looked like a kid with my long hair! Not that anybody there was paying much attention!" Bruno Fortier chuckles when he remembers the speech. Charest spoke cautiously, as he always did, going to great lengths not to paint himself into a corner. "He started out by saying, 'I'm very surprised to see you here,' even though his father had paid for the cocktail party!" Charest went on to say, "I am working to find Canadian solutions for Canadian problems, and one day perhaps I'll work for the Conservative Party."

Charest's handlers introduced him to Sherbrooke's upper crust. He charmed "Le club de la Relève," a group of up-and-coming entrepreneurs and professionals who were intent on taking over from the city's old guard. Its members included accountant Denis Berger, city councillor Jean Perreault, another councillor and businessman Jean-Yves (Jerry) Laflamme and the director general of the Eastern Townships' regional health and social services commission, Albert Painchaud. With the federal elections approaching, "La Relève" was looking for a standard-bearer.

After breakfast at the New Wellington Hotel, Painchaud asked Charest point blank: "Can you win?"

"If I've decided to get in," he said, "it's because I think I can go far!"

"When we saw how determined this guy was," says Berger, "we thought, 'He's one of our knights!'" "The city establishment was going to back someone from the old guard," says Painchaud. "So we put our money on someone entirely new."

Jean Charest might have been eyeing Ottawa, but his political career began with a very local struggle, a fight for the political and economic control of Sherbrooke. To understand Charest's political career, we must never lose sight of this fact. Or as Tip O'Neill, the sly old fox of American politics, used to say, "All politics is local."

On February 29, 1984, Pierre Elliott Trudeau resigned as prime minister and leader of the Liberal Party. It was the Grits' turn to face a leadership race. But there was no doubt about the eventual winner: John Turner would be squaring off against Brian Mulroney.

A CIRCUS

The Sherbrooke PC nomination meeting was scheduled for May 15, 1984. Once again, selling memberships was the name of the game, with the rival camps handing out cards by the hundreds. Not only did Mr. Métras enjoy an enviable reputation, he also had the backing of the Montréal party machine, which supplied him with funds and volunteers. Nevertheless, the Charest organization seemed unstoppable. "We called on our friends, our parents — everyone we could think of," says René Poitras, Jean's boyhood friend. "I brought out my elderly aunts and even my father, a hard-core Liberal! We brought out plenty of sovereigntist friends who normally didn't vote in federal elections. How did we convince them? They identified with Jean. Those were the days of Lévesque's '*beau risque*,' after all. And we had to kick out the Grits." Red took a month's holiday to sell membership cards to his friends, customers and suppliers. "I must've sold seven hundred," says Jean's father, an extremely persuasive salesman.

The Claude Métras camp was confident. Too confident. The evening of the vote, 2,100 people jammed into the Eugène-Lalonde Arena amidst brass bands, posters, streamers and cheerleaders. All these people had turned out to choose one Conservative candidate. Hard to believe that, a few months earlier, the party had seemed to be in its death throes!

Métras and Charest delivered workmanlike speeches. Charest portrayed himself as "the kind of leader who can bring men and women together, the kind of man who won't vanish into thin air when the going gets tough." But speeches aren't what count at such meetings. Everything boils down to the number of memberships a candidate sells, and especially the percentage of the candidate's cardholders who actually take the trouble to vote. Certain of victory, many of Claude Métras's supporters stayed home, while the young people recruited by the Charest machine answered the call. And they had good reason to do so: "We had sold cards to people who would go and vote because they'd been promised a beer bash [after the meeting]," says Léo Daigle. Charest won by 908 votes to 800.

Métras's top political strategist, Sherbrooke PC association president Guy Bureau, who had grown accustomed to more intimate party meetings, lashed out at the "circus atmosphere." "Revolting," he fumed. "At least 50 percent of the people here are one-night Conservatives. We certainly won't be able to beat the Liberals in the next election with voters like this." Charest retorted with aplomb, revealing his now-famous flair for the well-turned phrase: "We'll need plenty of 'one-night Conservatives' next election night."

RALLYING THE TROOPS

The next day, the loser showed up at the riding office at 8:30 a.m., as if nothing had happened. At 9:15, his secretary told him an unexpected visitor had arrived, someone named Jean Charest.

"Mr. Métras," said Sherbrooke's new Conservative candidate, "I would like us to work together to give the Liberals as tough a fight as the one we've just had."

"Jean, you can count on me. But you'd better give my organization a little time to catch its breath."

The two camps were to merge, but there would be some gnashing of teeth. The rivalries of that period would never quite vanish.

The twenty-five-year-old lawyer's victory over Métras, a local star and party favourite, made a few waves. At Tory headquarters in Montréal, Bernard Roy, the head of the Québec wing and a close associate of Brian Mulroney, expressed concern. He called George MacLaren, the publisher of the *Sherbrooke Record*. MacLaren was quick to reassure him: "I saw how the young man handles himself. In my opinion, he's an excellent candidate." One small wave reached PC national headquarters in Ottawa, where party bigwig Harry Near heard Jean Charest's name for the first time.

George MacLaren was sufficiently impressed with Charest to agree to handle the fundraising for his campaign. MacLaren counted both Mulroney and Roy as friends; all three had studied law at Laval University in Québec City. Well connected in the business community, he proved a valuable ally and an astute counsellor for the curly-headed Sherbrooker.

Two days after their victory, Dr. Gagné and his protégé drove to Montréal to pick up the documents that would confer the party's seal of approval. The reception, recalls Gagné, was decidedly chilly: "We sat down in the waiting room. A half hour later, the room had emptied and we were still waiting." Finally, Bernard Roy greeted them "courteously but coolly." Charest left the brief encounter with a feeling of concern: "Well, I don't think I'll be getting much support from the party for the campaign!"

"Don't worry, Jean," Gagné told his startled young friend. "You're not only going to beat [Liberal MP Irénée] Pelletier, but after that we're going to take on another project, to make you prime minister of Canada!" A jest, of course. "I was only half kidding," assures the psychiatrist. "Because if there was ever anyone who had the potential to become the prime minister of Canada — you know, a long, long shot — it was someone like Charest."

THE APPRENTICESHIP OF MICHÈLE DIONNE

Michèle Dionne doesn't say much about it today, but her early days in the world of politics were a time of trial. The day before the nomination meeting, the Charest camp had chosen to call all the riding's card-carrying Tories, including the Métras supporters, to encourage them to get out and vote. On Daigle's insistence, Michou was asked to lend a hand. He set her up in one corner of his office, dialled a number and handed her the receiver: "Did she ever get an earful! She started to cry, 'I won't make another call. I'm leaving,' she said, 'I never liked politics anyway!'" But the organizer cajoled Michèle into making a second call. It was one of her husband's fans. Then she reached a stream of Charest supporters. The evening didn't turn out so badly after all.

A few months later, the election campaign began. Michèle revolted against the traditional role she was asked to play. Painchaud describes it as follows: "You put the wife beside the candidate, then you

take her away when it's over, then you put her back again."
Painchaud goes on to say, "Michou was fed up hearing about politics and she wasn't easy to deal with . . ." In other words, she
couldn't be led by the nose. Painchaud attempted to put his foot
down: "Either you do the campaign our way and we forget about
feminism and whatever else is bothering you, or you don't."

Inconveniently, Michèle refused to be called "Mrs. Charest."

"My name isn't Mrs. Charest, it's Michèle Dionne!" she insisted.

"Listen," Painchaud fired back. "If you call yourself Michèle
Dionne, nobody's going to know who you are or where you're from."

Michèle refused to back down. During her husband's second election campaign, in 1988, the party brass agreed to let her have her
own campaign itinerary. And no one ever called her Mrs. Charest
again. Even today, however, Michèle still gets on stage and does a
few dance steps with Jean, to the delight of his supporters, then sits
down demurely while he delivers his speech, rejoining him when
he's finished. The scene bears a strange resemblance to Albert
Painchaud's prescription: "You put the wife beside the candidate,
then you take her away when it's over."

Concerned with giving Jean's career a positive image, Michèle
steers discussion away from those early dustups. Instead, she describes the 1984 campaign in glowing terms: "It was really fantastic.
We started at the bottom of he ladder. We didn't have anything.
Jean's father found us an office. His brother lent us a refrigerator;
my father gave me a filing cabinet. There was a Ping-Pong table
and some overstuffed orange furniture. We were setting out on a
real adventure!"

Asked if she had any hesitation or reservations, she replies: "No,
we went into it body and soul."

Body and soul, yes. Without hesitation or reservation? That's not
exactly the way the couple's entourage remembers it.

THE FIRST DEBATE

Irénée Pelletier had been the Liberal member for Sherbrooke for twelve years. He had won the 1980 election with a crushing 23,000-vote majority. Though he was not a cabinet minister and never would be, he had earned the respect of the riding's voters. Charest's opponent looked like an impregnable fortress.

When the newly anointed Liberal leader and prime minister, John Turner, called an election for September 4, 1984, the polls gave the Grits an overwhelming lead over Brian Mulroney's Conservatives. In Sherbrooke, the situation was no different. Initial polling by Denis Beaudoin revealed high levels of popularity for Pelletier. Dropped from the party machine by the new Conservative leader, Beaudoin set up a small business, Majoricom, which offered to organize Tory candidates' election campaigns for a few thousand dollars. Jean Charest was one of the five candidates who retained Beaudoin's services. "My polls showed that Charest was an unknown. Not one person in five had heard of him. His profile was zero!" recalled Beaudoin when I met him a few months before his death in April 1998.

But soon, across Canada, John Turner's ratings began to waver. The day he called the election he announced nineteen political appointments, Trudeau's delayed rewards to the party faithful. The patronage appointments would haunt Turner throughout the campaign, especially when the issue came up during the televised debate in English. "I had no option," said the Prime Minister. "You had an option, sir," responded Mulroney. "You could have said: 'I'm not going to do it. This is wrong for Canada!'" From that moment on, the Liberals' national campaign floundered, and Canadians' profound discontent with the party that had governed them for more than twenty years rose to the surface.

Certain that he would crush his opponent, Irénée Pelletier agreed to a televised debate. "I was convinced he would refuse," said Beaudoin. "If I'd been in his shoes, that's what I would have done.

He had everything to lose." Charest made his preparations, "just like I used to prepare my legal briefs." He pored over files and statistics. "He knew nothing about local issues," Léo Daigle had observed. And though such ignorance was nothing for a twenty-six-year-old lawyer to be ashamed of, it did point up his true motive for getting into politics. Charest may claim he ran for office in 1984 because "the Liberals didn't care about what was happening to the economy of the region" and because he saw a new day dawning on the federal horizon, "a new period of reconciliation." But in fact, all his close friends say that he got into politics for the sheer pleasure of the game. Charest was backed by people looking for revenge against the Mulroney camp and by others who wanted to replace Sherbrooke's old establishment with a new establishment. "Charest was the victim of his own ambition," says Léo Daigle. "He didn't control very much; he didn't know anything!"

Nevertheless, the young lawyer was well prepared when he showed up late at the CHLT studio. "I arrived at the last moment on purpose," he says. "I sat down in my seat and *pow!* the program began!" He did his best to look confident, but the rookie politician had a bad case of nerves. "It was very intimidating. There I was, sitting across from a man who had been there for twelve years, an intelligent man who had been a good MP." A good MP? Those were not Charest's words on the hustings in the summer of 1984.

Charest's preparation proved its worth. Pelletier focused on his opponent's inexperience; the young Tory probably didn't even know the riding's unemployment rate, he challenged. But Charest responded with the precise percentage, then ripped into the Liberal government's economic policy. When Pelletier insinuated that many of the Tory's supporters had voted Yes in the 1980 referendum, Charest sprang to their defence, pointing out that these Québeckers represented 40 percent of the province's population. "If Conservative Jean Charest was an Olympic boxer," the *Tribune* commented editorially the next day, "we would have to award him the decision for most blows landed." At the end of the debate, the station polled the viewers: 51 percent called Charest the winner, compared to 44 percent for Pelletier.

It was the first debate of Jean Charest's political career. Those who saw it will never forget it. They consider it the turning point in the Sherbrooke campaign. On the evening of September 4, 1984, Charest was elected, along with 210 other Conservatives from coast to coast. Pelletier's 23,000-vote majority had turned into a 7,000-vote deficit.

Nevertheless, a hoary political truism holds that local candidates are responsible for only 5 percent of the votes they end up with. The remaining 95 percent of their support is the result of national trends. This was undoubtedly true of Jean Charest in 1984. A glance at the Sherbrooke dailies confirms it: the campaigns by the leaders — Mulroney, Turner and Broadbent — dominated the front page; the rare articles on local candidates were buried deep in the inside pages. Charest is the first to admit that he owed his victory to the Tory tide that swept the country on September 4, 1984, and not to his own efforts, whether in the debate or during the rest of the campaign: "If the debate had never happened, or even if I had lost it, I would still have gotten elected." Nevertheless, the debate proved a pivotal point in his career. "Psychologically, it was very important for me, because from that moment on, I had confidence. I thought, 'I can handle myself in situations like these.'"

If it had not been for the Tory landslide, Jean Charest would not have become an MP in 1984. Perhaps he would have moved to the United States to get a Master's degree in maritime law, or perhaps he would have hung up his shingle in Sherbrooke. But one thing was certain: he would never have lost the political bug.

Pleasing Brian

—⁓—

Visions of his protégé as prime minister might well have been dancing in Dr. Gagné's head, but on September 5, 1984, Jean Charest was little more than a twenty-six-year-old tyro. His three-year law practice had made no lasting impression. His political speeches were short on originality. Of course, everyone realized he was good at selling memberships and "getting out the vote." "At the time, I thought of him as an organizer," recalls Pierre-Claude Nolin, who was doing that kind of work for Brian Mulroney. "When [Charest] came to Ottawa in 1984, he was just another MP."

Just another MP? Well, not exactly. It wasn't long after he arrived in Ottawa that Charest began to display an uncommonly keen eye for the political main chance. At his election night victory party, he announced that his constituency office would be open bright and early the next morning. The September 6 edition of *La Tribune* noted, "the new member for Sherbrooke opened his office at 780 King West yesterday morning, the day after the election."

Then, at the party's election nerve-centre in Ottawa, the Tory bigwigs, still intoxicated with their landslide victory, were packing their boxes. As Harry Near puts it: "Who shows up at headquarters two days after the election but this kid, Charest! And he basically says: 'Thanks!' It's one of those things you stick in the back of your head, and you know: 'This guy gets it!'"

Heeding the advice of George MacLaren and Denis Beaudoin, Charest wasted no time setting up shop in Ottawa, even though the House would not begin sitting for another two months. While the Québec Conservative MPs who had been swept into office by the Tory landslide were still coming down from the euphoria of victory, their Sherbrooke colleague was already prowling the corridors of power. "We weren't planning to settle in before mid-November," recalls François Gérin, elected in the neighbouring riding of Mégantic-Compton, "but there he was, in the middle of September, making contacts, especially with the English-speaking MPs."

For all its bilingual pretensions, Parliament was and is a fundamentally English-speaking institution. The freshman MP from Sherbrooke easily navigated these English waters, while most of his Québec colleagues were splashing about, dictionaries in hand, like drowning men. Richelieu MP Louis Plamondon recalls an invitation sent to members of the Québec caucus on the eve of the first session: "It was from Jean Charest, inviting us to a reception at his apartment. Already he wanted us to regard him as a leader."

Most caucus members felt the most powerful political figure in the Townships would be Mégantic-Compton MP François Gérin, not the ambitious — some might say pretentious — young Charest. At a meeting in Coaticook, Brian Mulroney had promised, "You'll be hearing from François Gérin in the riding, in the province and in the nation." Gérin had played the statement for all it was worth during the campaign. It's not hard to imagine his disappointment when he learned he'd been left out of the Mulroney cabinet, while Charest was named Assistant Deputy Speaker of the House of Commons. From that day on, a Charest-Gérin rivalry was obvious to every member of the Québec Conservative caucus.

Why did Brian Mulroney pick Jean Charest for a cabinet post when he didn't know the young man from Adam? "Something must have happened between September 4 and the time the cabinet was formed," says Pierre-Claude Nolin, who kept a watchful eye on the situation from his office at Dessau, a Laval-based engineering firm. In fact, something *had* happened — and it carried George MacLaren's imprint. The publisher of the *Sherbrooke Record* had taken Charest under his wing. In the days following the election victory, MacLaren sent a videotape of the televised debate between Charest and Pelletier to Peter White in the Prime Minister's Office. White was impressed. "He was fast on his feet," recalls the former Mulroney adviser. MacLaren had also sung Charest's praises within easy earshot of his friend Mulroney.

"Charest and you are like two peas in a pod! He's a French-speaking Irishman, he's perfectly bilingual, and he's loaded with charisma!"

Says the former prime minister: "When we came to power, I began to keep an eye on him. I handed him some responsibilities even before I got to know him because I trusted MacLaren's judgment."

As positions go, Assistant Deputy Speaker is better than nothing, but it's about as dull as they get. "A nice quiet job," says Marcel Danis, Mulroney's Deputy Speaker. In the House of Commons, the Speaker supervises debate at key moments, especially during Question Period. The Deputy Speaker then chooses the next best assignments, and his two assistants get the leavings, the pointless end-of-the-day debates that usually involve only the handful of MPs who are obliged to remain in attendance. Charest, says Danis, wasn't enthusiastic about the appointment. "He was disappointed. He wanted a cabinet post. He was ambitious."

"Were you pleased with the appointment?" I asked Charest.

He hesitated a moment. "I was pleased, sure. There was a fresh crop of MPs from Québec, so I thought, maybe . . . But you've got to be realistic. I was only twenty-six." As Danis says, the young man was ambitious.

Charest promptly resolved to make the most of the position he'd been handed. "For on-the-job training, it's hard to beat," says Danis. "If you think someone's got ministerial potential, there's no better place to gain an understanding of the way the House of Commons works." The Sherbrooke MP buckled down to the task at hand. He learned the rules of the House. But most of all, he kept his eyes open. The Newfoundland MPs quickly won his admiration: "The Newfies have an extraordinary oral tradition," he says, mentioning both Liberals and Conservatives: John Crosbie, George Baker and Brian Tobin.

Inevitably, he spent long hours listening to speeches. "It was slow going . . . really slow," he admits. To pass the time, Charest fell back on his sense of humour. One evening, assistant clerk Robert Marleau sent him a note. The procedure is normally used to provide the person handling the Speaker's duties with information on the rules. But Marleau's message read: "Look at the pretty girl in the Civil Service Gallery." The Assistant Deputy Speaker of the House of Commons looked up at the gallery, rolled the note into a ball and swallowed it!

CHAREST, THE CLOWN

Ottawa soon discovered that beneath the young man's serious exterior lay a playful side. People who have worked for Charest will tell you how he would regale them with jokes, facial contortions and imitations. "He cracked us up!" says former minister Monique Vézina, who sat next to him in the House of Commons for a time.

Camille Guilbeault, who handled the liaison chores between the PMO and the Québec Conservative caucus, tells an amusing story. Impeccably attired as usual, Ms. Guilbeault was walking along Wellington Street in front of the Parliament Buildings, when she heard a man hail her. Turning around, she saw a minister's limo; in it was the environment minister of Canada, the Honourable Jean Charest. He lowered the rear window and stuck his head out. On his nose were perched a pair of glasses with plastic eyes dangling on long springs!

Camille Guilbeault's collection includes a videocassette of a Jean Charest routine worthy of the country's top comedians. "It's a very rare video," she says before letting me see it. The first part features a satire of a newscast, cooked up in 1996 for the annual get-together of an informal group of politicians and journalists called the Gatineau Hills Gentlemen's Club. In it, Jean Charest imitates General Jean Boyle, former Canadian Forces commander-in-chief. The best part of this segment is the decor. Seated behind a desk, Charest is wearing an enormous military beret bearing the Progressive Conservative Party coat of arms, and hanging from the wall, as in every armed forces office, is a photograph of the head of state. But in the video, the face is Kim Campbell's!

The fictitious news bulletin over, Charest keeps on improvising while the camera rolls. Never distributed, the item has remained the special preserve of a lucky few. Charest starts off with a carica-ture of Jean Chrétien and his promise to abolish the GST: "Maybe you got me out of context, that's not what I said. I didn't say that. Okay, okay, so I said those words. So what, so I exaggerated a bit. Big deal. I told them I'd get rid of the GST. Abolish, scrap . . . Look it up in the dictionary. Harmonizing is close. It is. Scrap the harmonizer, harmonize the scrap . . . It's the same, you know . . ." Then Charest imitates a woman who might well be Sheila Copps: "Gee, you're so technical! You're so picky!" Next we see the false Chrétien frothing with fury: "What do you expect, for God's sake! Any player in the NHL makes more money than I do. Do you think I'm Einstein? You think it's easy? You think it's funny? How do you think I feel when my wife walks around the house with one of those damn statues and hits the staff over the head!"* Suddenly con-trite, he slumps over, crumples up the sheet of paper he's holding

---

* Charest is referring to an incident that had happened a few months earlier at the Prime Minister's official residence when an armed intruder entered the house. While the PM was sleep-ing, Mrs. Chrétien took an Inuit statue in her hands, ready to defend herself and her husband.

and, with the cameramen splitting their sides with laughter, sighs, "I tried . . ."

In the basement of his house in the posh Ottawa district of Rockcliffe, Charest's former deputy minister, John Edwards, keeps a similar souvenir: a tape of a speech given by Charest at a dinner in Edwards's honour. Charest, who had just been appointed minister of state for Youth, steps up to the podium, a vacant look on his face. He begins his speech sounding like a man who has had too much to drink, "La . . la . . . ladies and gentlemen . . . Very happy to be here at the Rotary Club . . . Ottawa . . . Wrong speech again . . . !" By now, he has the audience eating out of his hand. Next he makes fun of Barry Carin, one of his favourite public servants: "I was informed that Barry Carin had written his speech not knowing that ministers would be present. So we have a deal with him. Benoît [Bouchard] and I are going to the washroom while he talks . . . 'cause if we're going to get shit, might as well get the real thing!" Then Charest imitates a series of telephone conversations with his deputy minister, using his shoe as a receiver.

"My sense of humour is a safety valve," says Charest, who won't hesitate to make himself the butt of his own jokes. "In politics, you become a sort of caricature of yourself. When you understand that, it helps you survive, keeps things in perspective." Laughing at yourself is one thing, but being laughed at by someone else is another. "Maybe it's the same for everyone," he admits when someone makes the point. Maybe . . . His old college friend, Bruno Fortier, told me in an interview that he had categorically refused to help *Surprise sur prise*, the popular Québec TV show, play a practical joke on Charest. "I didn't think it was wise to put him in a situation like that."

"But he has appeared on comedy shows, hasn't he?"

"Yes, but only when he was in control!"

Former cabinet minister Pierre Blais, one of Charest's closest political friends, remembers a 1989 roast celebrating Charest's first five years in politics. "I laid it on a little thick. Jean wasn't used to being on the receiving end. He was a little . . . let's say his self-esteem was hurt . . . But it didn't take him long to get his revenge." And how! Blais laid into Charest with a will, making fun of his colleague's constant travel and proclivity for the spotlight. But Charest's stinging reply left the audience squirming in their seats. "Pierre is a good fellow, but a little limited . . . Let's face it: he's not the swiftest guy in the world." Bruno Hallé, who witnessed the scene, explains, "The whole family is like that. Never attack, never humiliate a Charest in public, because the response will be scathing."

FINE PAPERS, CRAFTY POLITICS

What began as a typical regional economic controversy over plans to modernize the Domtar paper mill in Windsor, in the Eastern Townships, soon became the backdrop for the premier appearance of "the Charest way" — perhaps best described as a subtle blend of hard work, back-room wheeling and dealing and wily media management. "He spreads his web like a spider," says Monique Vézina, his one-time cabinet colleague.

In February 1985, *La Presse* announced that the federal government had turned down Domtar's application for a $100-million grant. The company wanted to build the world's most modern fine-paper plant in Windsor, for an estimated total cost of $1.2 billion. The decision by the minister for regional economic expansion, Sinclair Stevens, touched off an uproar not only among the Township elite but all across Québec, which was then painfully emerging from a deep recession. A common front for the survival of the Domtar mill was quickly set up, followed by a salvo of public meetings and demonstrations. Elected representatives in Québec and Ottawa were bombarded by more than 450,000 letters. The media began to zero in on the affair, forcing Mulroney and Parti Québécois Premier René Lévesque to act.

The Domtar plant was located in Liberal MP Alain Tardif's riding. But Jean Lapierre, Tardif's flamboyant Grit colleague from the neighbouring electoral district, led the charge. Charest found himself between the rock of his government duties and the hard place of local interests. For a freshman MP to neglect one for the benefit of the other could prove fatal. With Mulroney casting about for a form of financial assistance that would not be a grant, and promising to discuss the problem with Premier Lévesque, Charest urged the members of the common front to be patient. "I often got calls from him late at night asking me to cool it a bit," recalls spokesperson Michel Bousquet.

"The Prime Minister has said that he'll look after the matter personally," Charest explained. "To me, that means the parties concerned will be getting what they want, and they should recognize the fact." It was an attitude that earned him a chorus of boos at a public meeting. "Charest is talking out of both sides of his mouth," charged Windsor Mayor Adrien Péloquin.

Instead of verbal pyrotechnics, Charest preferred to exert gentle but insistent pressure on his caucus colleagues. And when there was a favourable development, he was quick to get in touch with local media to take the credit.

When the common front leaders arrived in Ottawa, Jean Charest was unable to arrange for them to meet with the Prime Minister. But they saw the PM, nevertheless, thanks to the efforts of rival Jean Lapierre. "Lapierre took the floor," says Péloquin, who was observing the scene from the visitors' gallery in the House of Commons. "He said, 'I don't understand why the Prime Minister refuses to meet the group from Windsor that's come all this way for that purpose!' And he challenged Mulroney to meet with us!" The PM thought it the better part of valour to surrender: "It will give me a great deal of pleasure to see you right after Question Period."

"The security guards came up to the visitors' gallery to lead us to the PMO. We were walking on air," adds Péloquin.

After a few weeks of bargaining, the matter was finally resolved with federal financial assistance in the form of a guaranteed loan. It was an achievement that Jean Charest would take credit for in his 1988 campaign literature. Was he justified in doing so? Since the matter had been handled at the highest level, it's far from certain that rank-and-file MPs like Charest had much impact on the outcome. But in the minds of most of the people involved, Jean Lapierre was the true hero. "Lapierre was very skilful," Charest acknowledges. But it should be noted that, for a Liberal on the Opposition benches, things were easier. The rookie Conservative was in a much more delicate position.

Luc Lavoie, then parliamentary correspondent for the TVA network, describes a scrum given by the member for Sherbrooke after a caucus meeting on the Domtar affair: "With his hair à la Robert Charlebois, he looked even younger than his years, but he was extremely articulate and appeared to be very sure of himself." Charest did pretty well. He impressed his colleagues — and local decision-makers — with his grasp of the issues and his ability to manoeuvre between binding party discipline and the legitimate requirements of his constituents. "The success of MPs depends on their capacity to reconcile the two," concludes the Sherbrooker, twelve years later. Jean Charest has always performed this particular high-wire act to perfection.

The Mini-Minister

—ɯ—

It was the day before the cabinet shuffle of June 30, 1986. The telephone rang in Jean Charest's apartment in Gatineau, Québec. On the line was Fred Doucet, Brian Mulroney's chief of staff. "The Prime Minister wants to see you tomorrow," he said. Charest had been handed a full-fledged cabinet portfolio. "I was walking on cloud nine," says Charest. "I remember because I came back to earth on my way back to Sherbrooke, when I was hauled over by the police [for speeding]."

Even as a cabinet minister Charest continued to make the long commute between Ottawa and his home town, firmly behind the wheel. Jules Pleau, Charest's friend, who was then chief of staff to Treasury Board president Robert René de Cotret, warned him, "It's not safe to drive, with all the built-up fatigue."

"No way I'll use a chauffeur, I want to be able to chat with Michou without anyone listening in!"

"It was the rebelliousness of youth," Pleau believes. "And it lasted until he finally realized he really wasn't using good judgment."

Making matters worse was Charest's weakness for speed. René Poitras, a boyhood friend, recalls returning from a trip to Florida in a Volkswagen Bug when they were students at the Séminaire. Poitras handed Jean the wheel, told him not to exceed the 55-miles-per-hour speed limit, then promptly fell asleep in the back seat. A few minutes later, he was awakened by the flashing light of a patrol car.

"What's happening, Jean?"

"Uh, maybe I was going a little bit fast."

"How much too fast?"

"Uh, a fair bit . . ."

The fine amounted to more than $100 U.S., payable on the spot. The only alternative was a night at the police station. As Charest had not a penny in his pockets, Poitras had to empty his wallet. For the rest of the trip, the young men survived on a jar of peanut butter.

Bruno Hallé remembers a hair-raising drive along Montréal's mid-town Décarie Expressway when he and Charest were university students. Jean was driving a used Opel without a radiator cap, "hitting 160 kilometres per hour with the steam whooshing out like a geyser!"

Over the years, Charest has undoubtedly paid his share of speeding tickets. "Do you like speed?" I asked shortly after he had made the leap to provincial politics.

"I don't drive . . . I don't allow myself to drive."

Jean Charest is a man in a hurry who has learned the benefits of caution.

THE MINISTER FOR YOUTH

On June 30, 1986, with his father and several members of his family in attendance, Jean J. Charest was sworn in as Minister of State for Youth. At twenty-eight, he had become the youngest MP in Canadian history to be appointed to the cabinet. Brian Mulroney had liked what he'd seen in George MacLaren's protégé. "Charest was a comer," says the former prime minister. "It was obvious to me he had a bright future. He showed a great deal of maturity for his age. And he had his priorities in the right place." Once, Mulroney recalls, the young man from Sherbrooke arrived late for a breakfast that the PM gave every Wednesday morning for a few select MPs: "For an MP, an invitation to 24 Sussex, knowing that the Prime Minister wanted to take a close look at what he was doing . . ." Such a command performance, Mulroney implies, was not to be taken lightly. "So, I noticed Charest had arrived late. Without telling him, I looked into it. I found out the reason: it was because he drove his children to school every morning." Nothing could have melted the Baie Comeau Irishman's heart any faster.

Arriving late for early-morning meetings in Ottawa became part of the Charest legend, proof of his devotion to his family. He told senior minister Marcel Masse, who had grown irritated with Charest's tardiness, that all he had to do was schedule his meetings later in the day. More than once, Charest would draw attention to himself by appearing at meetings or public events with little Amélie in his arms. It's not certain, however, that the children are the sole cause of Jean Charest's lack of punctuality. Friends have pointed out that, in his youth, he was far from an early riser. Denis Beaudoin recalls how, during Jean's first election campaign, he literally had to drag Charest out of bed: "I had a key to the house. I would arrive around 5:45 and put on the coffee. Then I'd walk right into the bedroom. Michou would be furious . . ." Charest quite simply has his own notion of time, says longtime aide Suzanne Poulin. "He's never stressed out by time. It's as if he has his whole life ahead of him. You'll never catch him looking at his watch to end an appointment."

Jean Charest was now a cabinet minister. But he was a minister of state, a kind of second-class minister. Without the "real" minister's stamp of approval, a minister of state is helpless. In Charest's case, the senior minister was the member for Roberval, Benoît

Bouchard, a former CEGEP principal whose stock was on the rise. In the last cabinet shuffle, Bouchard had inherited a heavyweight portfolio, Employment and Immigration, an assignment that further inflated an already robust ego. "The senior minister's civil servants don't exactly open their arms wide for the minister of state," Bouchard told me. "They don't look upon him as a key player unless the senior minister is very explicit about it." Bouchard swears up and down that he always supported his young colleague, but it would appear that the two men didn't always see eye to eye. The senior minister probably didn't appreciate Charest's ambitious projects. Charest looks back on this period in his career with a sigh, describing it as "one long apprenticeship, my God!" "The relationship between a senior minister and a junior minister," he goes on to say, "is like putting two children in a sandbox and telling one of them: 'You're in charge of the toys and you can decide which ones you want to lend your friend.' As a minister of state, you're totally at the mercy of the senior minister."

In any event, the Prime Minister hadn't appointed the young MP to the position to launch a slew of new programs. "The minister of state job was really a political invention," says Benoît Bouchard. "It was something the Prime Minister created to show the country's youth the government cared." Charest seems to agree: when Brian Mulroney gave him the good news that he'd been appointed to the cabinet, the PM advised him to travel as much as possible. The rookie minister didn't need much persuasion. He discovered what was to become one of his favourite political pastimes: crisscrossing the country, meeting as many people as he could. Not a bad way to get oneself known and to form alliances that would come in handy further down the road.

But Charest was not going to be satisfied with being a mere figurehead. He wanted to get things done. In August 1986, Charest and his bureaucrats spent a day on a cabinet retreat. The deputy minister, John Edwards, happened to be an acquaintance of George MacLaren's. The young minister couldn't have been more fortunate.

Edwards was — and remains, even in retirement — a man with a finely honed sense of organization. In the course of an interview, he makes constant use of his diaries and notebooks, quoting dates, speeches and policies with painstaking accuracy. At the retreat, which took place "at the country club on the ninth of the month," Edwards sat down with the minister of state and painted his situation in sombre colours. A year earlier, the government had introduced its Canadian Jobs Strategy, a $2-billion program that included some measures specifically for youth. Given the grand scale of the strategy, the government was not prepared to inject any further funds to stimulate youth employment. Either Charest would make the rounds of the ridings, doling out summer employment cheques as his predecessors had done, or he would have to find a niche, an area that the federal government had overlooked. "Our top policy people had identified a problem area of national significance that was not being well addressed, and that was the high rate of high school dropouts," recalls John Edwards. The minister of state jumped on the issue like a dog on a bone. In the months that followed, Charest and his staff would set up the $300-million, five-year "Stay in School" program.

Secondary education is exclusively within the jurisdiction of the provinces, and Jean Charest knew it. But he believed the situation was serious enough to warrant federal intervention, in conjunction with the provincial governments. He explained his point of view in the Commons: "The paternalism and the sectarianism that the issue has touched off arise in part from the fact that, even though everyone admits it is our most significant problem, up until now no one has taken the trouble to define it, or to ask other Canadians what they think." The "Stay in School" program was coolly received in Québec. "It really got our dander up," says Thomas Boudreau, then provincial deputy minister of Education. The federal program was being launched just as the Québec government was putting the finishing touches on its own anti-dropout strategy. Boudreau and his minister, Claude Ryan, made "vigorous" appeals to Charest in an attempt to persuade Ottawa to transfer the funds directly to the Québec government, which would then inject the money into its own program. "Obviously, from the standpoint of visibility, our proposal wasn't very attractive," admits Boudreau. "A young minister wants his name associated with a program."

Soon after, Thomas Boudreau and Claude Ryan met Jean Charest to discuss the issue. The deputy minister came away impressed. "He was very charming. He had gone to the same school as my daughter. He said, 'Oh! So you're Hélène's father.' I don't know whether he really remembered her. At any rate, he wasn't conceited at all. And he was not the kind of man to run after controversy."

Charming Charest might have been, but he was also determined. The federal government turned down Québec's request. "That meant that the federal government could get its foot in the door," the former deputy minister points out. "It got the two governments involved in education. The Parti Québécois would never have agreed to it, but Mr. Ryan did."

"Stay in School" was Jean Charest's first major initiative. He still speaks of it with pride. A consultant's report in 1994 concluded that "the importance of the program has been unanimously recognized" by educators and school administrators across the country.

NO MEANS NO

The minister was on a roll. Now he envisioned a sweeping "strategy for youth" that would see young citizens lose their eligibility for social assistance or unemployment insurance benefits unless they enrolled in a skills-training program. The strategy would also establish one-stop access to federal and provincial youth services. "He was highly ambitious, very astute, always looking for opportunities to make a difference," recalls Edwards, who no doubt had put up with many less talented ministers of state over the years. "There was a strong idealistic streak in him. And at the same time he had a political side. He wanted not only to do something worthwhile but also to get credit for it. He always had one eye on the media."

Charest's new youth strategy went down to defeat in cabinet. Politically, it was too costly and too risky. Like "Stay in School," it encroached on provincial jurisdiction in the areas of education and social assistance. The project's fate was decided at a cabinet committee meeting on social development, presided over by Jake Epp. Following the strict rules of government procedure, Privy Council civil servants prepared a Record of Decision (RD), an official document recording the committee's final ruling. All that remained was ministerial approval. When the committee reconvened, Charest made a last-ditch attempt to reverse the verdict. The discussions had gotten bogged down, and so he produced an RD of his own, which his chief of staff had thoughtfully drafted on Privy Council letterhead. The trouble was, the document was a fake. Charest's newly appointed deputy minister, Nick Mulder, was aghast. "What the hell is going on? You're not supposed to do this!" he hissed in Charest's ear. "That's considered a real no-no," Mulder maintains to this day. "The Record of Decision is prepared by the officials from the Privy Council Office based on what they think the discussions were at a particular committee, and it's signed by the chairman of that committee. So for a minister to come in with his own write-up, his own version of what went on . . . You can't run a cabinet if every minister decides on his own what he thought the decisions were!" But, at the time, Charest could hardly be bothered with rules and protocol. When he was appointed Assistant Deputy Speaker, he refused to wear the robe. No robe, no chauffeur . . . Why worry about cabinet procedure?

His youth strategy might have sunk, but it produced positive ripples on the way down. Agreements would be signed between Ottawa and two of the Atlantic provinces, New Brunswick and Newfoundland, creating one-stop access for youth programs. And the rookie minister had found out how vital it was to sell his colleagues on a project before bringing it before cabinet. He had also learned to recognize how "no" is expressed in political parlance. "I realized they had told me 'no' several times without ever pronouncing the word. They had been sending me plenty of signals. It must have been embarrassing for my colleagues," Charest admits. Embarrassing for him, actually. When the Finance minister dismissed the project with the wave of his hand, Charest had persisted, even raising his voice. Norman Spector, a senior civil servant at the time, remembers the scene vividly: "Here you have the most junior minister in the government getting into a shouting match with the Finance minister! Michael Wilson, who was always cool as a cucumber, just shook him off. That's what you call career-shortening behaviour. But Charest learned." He certainly did. "I was surprised to see how much clout the Finance minister had," Charest says. "There really wasn't any discussion. When the minister made up his mind, there was practically no appeal."

"I also remember," the former MP goes on to say, "the enormous influence of the Prime Minister. One word, one nod from Mulroney could totally change the fate of any initiative."

THE WHIPPING BOY

Charest studied the Prime Minister's every move. "He drank in his words," colleagues recall. The same colleagues soon noted that "Brian" had taken the Sherbrooke MP under his wing. "The Prime Minister paid special attention to him," recalls Chicoutimi MP André Harvey. "The way he talked to him, the way he kept him at his side. We could see that he thought Jean was a man with potential, and that one day he'd be able to carry the party on his shoulders."

Recollections embellished by subsequent events are not invariably trustworthy, but more than a few people recall the PM's attitude, the sense of favouritism that must have provoked a fair bit of envy. A case in point was Mégantic-Compton MP François Gérin, who confided his feelings to his "friends" from across the floor, Jean Lapierre and Alain Tardif. Others must have been envious too, even though they didn't express it openly. "The world of politics is very guarded, even prudish," former Conservative MP Gabriel Desjardins points out. Not to say hypocritical.

Generally speaking, however, colleagues appreciated the Honourable Member for Sherbrooke. They considered him dedicated and level-headed. At Québec caucus meetings, on Tuesday evenings, he would sit in the back row and listen. He rarely spoke, but when he did, his way of going to the heart of the issues made him stand out. "He had a broader viewpoint than we did," says Guy Saint-Julien, former Tory MP for Abitibi. "He spoke from a *national* perspective. We would just talk about our ridings."

Some considered him too much of a loner, even a snob. At noon, a dozen or so Québec MPs would sit down for lunch together at the "Québec table" in the parliamentary restaurant. Regulars don't recall ever seeing Jean Charest there. Nor do the MPs who dined together on Tuesday evenings after the Québec caucus meeting, often accompanied by a minister — Benoît Bouchard, Marcel Masse or Pierre Blais — remember seeing him. Charest? Never. "Sure, he had his family . . ." concede people who took part in those evenings. By necessity, but also by inclination, Jean Charest has never been an enthusiastic mixer.

It did not take long for the Minister of State for Youth to emerge as one of the Liberals' prime targets. "His problem was that he had a short fuse," says Jean Lapierre, then Liberal member for Shefford. "Every time we put the pressure on, *bang!*" But let's not forget what Charest's pal Bruno Hallé said: "Never humiliate a Charest in public . . ." So the Liberals cranked the pressure up another notch. "Mini-minister," they called him, or "Minister of State for Small Stuff." Jean-Claude Malépart, the colourful inner-city Montréal MP, ridiculed him with fierce delight, accusing Charest of wasting time "driving around in his limousine talking to his chauffeur." "The Minister of State and the other ministers from Québec say they're happy — I guess that's what 'French Power' means!" Malépart would say. "They have their little jobs, their limos. Every once in a while they get to cut a ribbon and they're happy. And he has his hair curled, and that's 'French Power!'" When he heard it, the young bantam rooster would fly off the handle. More than anything else he wanted to be taken seriously. Waxing indignant, he would deplore the tone of the debate and call for a ruling from the Speaker. There was nothing to be done. "We kept pecking away at him," says Lapierre.

"I was a junior minister. I wanted to have my place in the sun, to accomplish something," Charest later explained. "Maybe there was some ego involved, too."

In those days, the atmosphere in the Commons could best be described as wild and woolly. There were few Liberals in the House, but Copps, Tobin, Dingwall, Nunziata and Boudria behaved so aggressively that they were dubbed the "Rat Pack." Charest and a handful of other young ministers, like Bernard Valcourt, were more than ready for a good dust-up. "Mulroney thought [Charest] was a great guy, always ready to go into the trenches. Mulroney liked him much more for that than for his ministerial skills," says Lapierre. "Mulroney enjoyed having a Praetorian Guard of young French-speaking ministers who were always itching for a fight," says Charest.

As time passed, however, Charest would calm down. So thick-skinned was he to become that, a few years later, after Lucien Bouchard blew up in the House when Newfoundland MP Brian Tobin called him a "coward," Charest advised his colleague from Lac Saint-Jean not to let it bother him.

A REAL CHALLENGE

It was with considerable apprehension that, in the spring of 1988, the members of the Task Force on National Sports Policy awaited Jean Charest, the newly appointed federal minister for Fitness and Amateur Sport. Starting with former Canadian track champion

Abby Hoffman, they were a group of tried and tested experts. The group, set up by Charest's predecessor, had toiled for several months to produce recommendations for the much-needed reform of amateur sport in Canada. And then, at the end of the process, the Prime Minister had foisted a new minister on them, adding the portfolio to Charest's existing responsibilities as minister for Youth. Worse yet, it came at a time in Charest's life when his diet seemed to consist primarily of hot dogs. "Sports policy didn't seem like a natural fit. Just looking at his body and style, he was not the athletic type," remembers one of the committee members, Wilf Wedmann. "Everybody was stunned at how young he was. He had his golliwog haircut and we wondered: how mature is he?" says Roger Jackson, then president of the Canadian Olympic Association. "I didn't fit the profile," concedes Charest.

Like so many others before them, the members of the task force soon fell under Charest's spell. "When we met with him for the first time," says Jackson, "clearly he had read most of the material. He had very practical comments and questions, and he wasn't trying to kid anybody." As usual, Charest had done his homework. Back in Sherbrooke a few days after his appointment, he had called up Jean-Guy Ouellette, a University of Sherbrooke physical education professor and chairman of the board of the Canadian Track and Field Association. Ouellette, an emotional man with a football player's build, spent the day briefing the minister on the ins and outs of amateur sport, with its labyrinth of associations, federations and unions, its governing bodies at the provincial, federal and international levels, its traditions, its players and their epic discontents. Charest took notes with Amélie on his knee.

Charest's deputy minister, Lyle Makosky, recalls their first meeting as if it were yesterday. "I still remember him walking into my office . . . When he approaches you, he looks you straight in the eye and doesn't let go of it for quite some moments. That's quite impactful, because the impression is that here's a person that is confident." He got the full Charest treatment. As performances go, his in Sport was no more spectacular than in his previous portfolios. But he took on the files left by his predecessor, stick-handling them with dexterity, competence and enthusiasm, whether it was drafting the new amateur sport policy proposed by the task force or dealing with international doping negotiations, the participation of disabled athletes in the Commonwealth Games or the organization of the first Jeux de la Francophonie. The Canadian amateur sport community remembers him as one of the best ministers it ever had.

The Department of State for Fitness and Amateur Sport no longer exists, another casualty in the war on the deficit. Federal politicians of the day viewed it as a free ride. In appointing him to the position, Brian Mulroney told the younger man that Sport was "the most extraordinary department." In truth, it was a non-controversial portfolio if ever there was one. The minister could spend his time handing out cheques from sea to sea and enjoying photo-ops with the Ben Johnsons and Sylvie Berniers of the world. "It was an ideal place for building a political network," explains Marcel Danis, who once briefly held the position. Charest handled the job with consummate skill, taking advantage of the opportunity without abusing it: "He was not one who wanted to take the spotlight from the athletes," says Lyle Makosky. "He wanted to stay low-key. He was quite adamant about not wanting to play a prominent role and take away the athletes' limelight."

"When Otto Jelinek was the minister, if there was the slightest bit of a reason to have your picture taken, Jelinek was front and centre and nobody, including the athletes, could get between him and the camera. We had ministers like Steve Paproski . . . Don't get in the way!" says Hugh Glynn, then president of the National Sport and Recreation Centre, who has worked with fifteen different ministers.

"An extraordinary department," Brian Mulroney had told Charest, never once suspecting that his protégé was to encounter two huge controversies. The first would be touched off by a urine sample; the second by a telephone number.

9.79 SECONDS

September 24, 1988. Eyes glued to their television sets, millions of Canadians waited with bated breath for the start of the final in the 100-metre sprint at the Seoul Olympic Games. With the crack of the starter's pistol, Ben Johnson exploded out of the blocks, quickly building up an insurmountable lead over American sprinter Carl Lewis. With breathtaking ease, Johnson powered across the finish line in 9.79 seconds, smashing his own world record. Far across the Pacific, the surge of Canadian pride brought back memories of the delirious public response to the goal by Paul Henderson that won the "Series of the Century" for Team Canada sixteen years earlier. Brian Mulroney hurried onto live television to congratulate the winner. For the PM, who was about to call a general election, Johnson's victory was like manna from heaven.

The minister of state for Amateur Sport, all of six months into his new portfolio, was not in the Olympic stadium that evening. After attending the opening ceremonies and the first few days of competition, he had left Seoul and returned to Sherbrooke to prepare for the upcoming campaign. On September 24, as he and Michèle were dining tête-à-tête in a North Hatley restaurant, the world of sports seemed far away indeed. But that evening, the chef was watching the event on television, between sauces, in the kitchen; so, like so many of his countrymen, Charest witnessed Johnson's extraordinary performance.

On that same night, the International Olympic Committee (IOC) informed Canada's Olympic mission chiefs in Seoul that Ben Johnson's urine sample had tested positive, revealing traces of stanazonol, a proscribed anabolic steroid. A second sample would be examined later the following day. The news spread like wildfire. No one knows who first alerted the minister, but the calls poured in thick and fast from Seoul. Everyone who was around him at the time says he remained calm and collected. With one exception: while he was talking to Makosky, he brought his fist down hard on

First victory. On May 15, 1984, Jean Charest wins the Conservative nomination in Sherbrooke. *Top:* Charest with several of his earliest supporters, including Denis Beaudoin (far left) and Dr. Pierre Gagné (far right). *Bottom:* adversary Claude Métras concedes defeat. *Photos: Perry Beaton.*

The voice of experience. Jean Charest launches his first election campaign on July 14, 1984, with advice from veteran Roch Lasalle. *Photo: Perry Beaton.*

The whites of their eyes. The "Charest effect" in action: door-to-door campaigning in Sherbrooke. *Photo: Perry Beaton.*

Trading robes. Appointed Assistant Deputy Speaker of the House of Commons, Charest quickly learns the parliamentary ropes. *Jean Charest/Michèle Dionne collection.*

"It wasn't me!" Jean Charest uses humour to win over an audience. Laughter is one of the most powerful weapons in his arsenal, say those close to him. *Photos: Perry Beaton.*

Stay in School. Education has always been a top priority for Jean Charest since his first cabinet posting as Minister of State for Youth. *Photo: Perry Beaton.*

Say "cheese." Jean Charest and Marcel Masse didn't always hit it off as fellow ministers in the Mulroney cabinet. *Photo: Perry Beaton.*

Mystery photo. Jean Charest, camera-shy? *Photo*: La Tribune.

Star sprinter. Charest gets his baptism of fire with the controversial suspension of sprinter Ben Johnson at the 1988 Seoul Olympics. *Photo: Canadian Press.*

Where's Lucien? May 17, 1990: Jean Charest tables the report of the Special Committee on the Meech Lake Accord. Several days later Lucien Bouchard resigns in protest to the "Charest Report." *Photo: Reuters* — La Presse.

his kitchen counter. "I made a dent," recalls Charest. "It's one of the few times I've lost my temper." In front of Jean-Guy Ouellette, he worried aloud about the embarrassment the incident — the Johnson affair, not the dent in the counter — might cause the Prime Minister.

In the hours that followed, the initial test results were confirmed. The IOC moved quickly to strip Ben Johnson of his gold medal. "It was as if the sky had fallen on our heads," Charest said later. The episode set off a tidal wave that swept around the world. In Ottawa, the minister's office was inundated with calls from the international media. *Nightline*, the popular American current-affairs television program, requested an interview with the minister. It was up to the chubby Sherbrooke MP to decide what sanctions the Canadian government would impose on the man who, only a few hours previously, had been a national hero.

In fact, no decision was needed. Sport Canada regulations, drawn up in 1985, left little room for interpretation: "Individuals proven to have violated antidoping rules involving anabolic steroids and related compounds will be subject automatically to a lifetime withdrawal of eligibility for all federal government sport programs or benefits."

Two weeks before the Olympics, the rule had been automatically enforced in a case involving four Québec weight-lifters. The athletes, who had tested positive for prohibited substances, had been banned for life from all government financial support, by ministerial decree. When the Johnson affair became public, Jean Charest had little choice, and he knew it: "I had just enforced the rule against the weight-lifters; I could do nothing else in Johnson's case."

"Ben Johnson suspended for life," blared a September 26, 1988, press release. "The Government of Canada is unequivocally opposed to the use of performance-enhancing drugs and will therefore suspend for life all federal financial support to Ben Johnson in accordance with our doping control program." The next day, Jean Charest told reporters outside the House of Commons: "The consequence is a life suspension for Ben Johnson from Sport Canada funding and participation on national teams." But back in Seoul, the Canadian Track and Field Association brass lost no time in contradicting him: they would decide who was and was not a member of the national team. The ministerial regulations applied to government funding only. In other words — the CTFA willing — Ben Johnson might conceivably run for Canada in the future, as long as he paid his own expenses.

Ten years later, some people blame the media for misinterpreting Charest's words. Others point out — not incorrectly — that no consensus existed about how far the policy went, and that the minister had merely adopted the point of view of the majority of his bureaucrats. Lyle Makosky believes that Charest, like many others, did not grasp the subtleties of Canadian policy: "He had only been in this portfolio a few months. There were only three people in the department who understood the policy in its application fully enough to deal with this kind of sophisticated issue, and the three of us were in Seoul. I think the time difference, problems in communications and inexperience meant that his statements weren't quite clear enough. It would have been preferable for him to say that the Government of Canada would be removing its support from Mr. Johnson for the rest of his life and would expect the sports community to do so as well."

In short, though Charest might well have done his homework in the Johnson affair, he got himself into hot water by not taking into consideration the sensibilities of the country's sports federations, each of which was fiercely jealous of its prerogatives. The result was a steady stream of contradictory statements from all sides, culminating in a welter of confusion. Charest had wanted to play hardball by announcing tough sanctions immediately following confirmation of the first test, but he had not anticipated the surge of sympathy for the sprinter. Initial public reaction, egged on by Opposition MPs, sided with the fallen hero. Of course he had cheated, but a lifetime ban seemed excessive. "I would like to ask him under what authority he said that Ben Johnson should be banned from the national team for life. How did he say that, at this time, before any hearing? Should the man not get a fair hearing before he gets a life sentence?" protested Liberal Warren Allmand, indignantly, in the Commons.

Opposition MPs weren't the only ones who objected to Sport Canada's decision. Many Conservatives thought the penalty was too stiff. MPs from the Toronto area, home to a large community of Jamaican origin, were particularly critical. Just as Brian Mulroney was about to call an election, his protégé had provoked an upsurge of ill-feeling in Canada's largest city. Under pressure from the Prime Minister's entourage, Charest began to cast about for ways to appease Johnson's supporters without compromising his principles. "Canadians are sympathetic to the case of Ben Johnson, as all of us are," he told the Commons. "Ben Johnson being a Canadian, with the difficulty of maybe a mistake on his part, I think we are all sympathetic to this cause."

Today, Jean Charest is prepared to admit that there might have been a "breakdown in communication": "My mistake was not taking the time to explain the nature of the decision that had been taken," he says. It was a time when a little more patience and a little more wisdom were called for. In other words, a little more experience. "Jean was in such a rush that he banned Johnson before the urine test!" joked his friend Pierre Blais a few months later.

The incident transformed Jean-Guy Ouellette, who had just returned from Seoul, into an unconditional Charest admirer. No sooner had Ouellette and CTFA president Paul Dupré arrived than the minister summoned them for a meeting. There was tension in the air. Journalists had staked out the building housing the minister's modest offices, which had been locked up tight for security reasons. In addition to Ouellette and Dupré, deputy minister Lyle Makosky, was in attendance. The talks rapidly began to sour when Makosky accused Ouellette and Dupré of being lax about doping control. "We were pointing the finger at one another," says

Ouellette, "but Jean was in charge. He said, 'Wait a minute, we're going to look at this rationally.' That really impressed me, a young minister acting a little precipitously in a crisis like that, then getting on top of things the way he did."

The government extricated itself from the mess by creating a commission of inquiry on doping in sport, presided over by Mr. Justice Charles Dubin. "A fairly typical response when governments are at a loss about what to do," Charest admits. But in this case, the general consensus in the amateur sport community is that the commission's hearings helped clear the air, and that its recommendations led to a more effective doping control system. As for Charest, the Ben Johnson affair undoubtedly had a beneficial effect on his career. Pierre Blais put it best at the Charest roast: "Jean loves Ben [Johnson]. He's the one who put him on the map. Who had heard of Jean Charest before the Ben Johnson affair?"

"The Minister Knew"

As sympathy for Johnson rapidly waned and the media began to pry into the sprinter's questionable entourage — particularly his personal physician, Dr. Jamie Astaphan — it quickly became glaringly apparent that the runner had no adequate defence to offer. Canadians began to accept the idea that their hero had, in fact, cheated. More than once.

Meanwhile, the Opposition and the media continued to hold the minister responsible for the episode. For months, rumours of rampant doping involving the sprint team had been circulating, clamoured the Liberals. "He decided not to do anything about it!" Allmand protested. "The minister could have prevented this sad turn of events if he had taken the appropriate action at this time, and he would have saved Ben Johnson and Canada this terrible humiliation." "Both the Canadian Olympic Association and the federal Sports Minister were well aware of the swirling rumours about this sprinter [. . .]," editorialized *The Globe and Mail* on September 28. "Yet Canada's pooh-bahs did nothing to ensure that their athlete was clean before sending him abroad with all our hopes on his shoulders. How slipshod, how inexcusably reckless." Two days later, the same newspaper ran a front-page story featuring excerpts of a letter sent to Charest by Dr. Andrew Pipe, a noted Canadian doping control specialist. Written a few weeks before the games, the letter warned the minister that "allegations of undetected drug use by athletes undermine the integrity of Canada's drug testing program."

True, doping rumours — particularly some involving Johnson — had been flying thick and fast. Some had even reached the minister's ears. But it is far from clear whether he was well enough informed to insist that the track and field association investigate the allegations. People familiar with the issue deny he was. Dr. Andrew Pipe says, "My letter was misinterpreted. I wanted to bring my concerns to the minister's attention and suggest a meeting to discuss them, but it would be unfair to conclude that he'd received information that would have allowed him to take action to stop what happened." "The minister was relatively far removed from that whole incident," adds Rolf Lund, who, as president of the Ontario Track and Field Association, had tried to convince the heads of the CTFA to investigate the sprinters' training habits. "In this area, Sport Canada had no responsibility whatsoever, absolutely none. They acted as a funding agency and they were several stops away from the athletes. They had no direct involvement with the training," says Roger Jackson, former president of the Canadian Olympic Committee.

The Commission of Inquiry into the Use of Drugs and Banned Practices Intended to Increase Athletic Performance, headed by Mr. Justice Charles Dubin, found the CTFA responsible for Canada's flawed doping control procedures. Despite strong pressure from the Department of State for Fitness and Amateur Sport, the association had taken its own sweet time improving its random testing program.

Jean Charest's name appears not once in the Dubin Commission's report. The minister was not even called to testify. Toronto attorney Bob Armstrong, the commission prosecutor who questioned Charest in private, explains why he decided not to summon him: "He didn't have anything to tell us. He didn't have any personal or direct information on the use of drugs in sports. The government had very little direct control over the organizations that ran the sports. They just weren't a factor. The issue of the minister's responsibility never really got raised at all."

Rumours circulated, but they were only rumours. The people who could have confirmed them were keeping quiet. Organized Canadian sport was prepared to improve doping controls, even if it was dragging its feet. Jean Charest had performed well at the first international conference on anti-doping in sport, held in Ottawa two months before the Seoul Olympics. At home, his civil servants applied pressure where necessary. In short, there was no reason for the minister to believe the situation called for direct intervention. In any case, had he attempted to impose his views, "the sports organizations would have rebelled," says Paul Dupré, former head of the CTFA.

"It's great to hear all this information, that everyone knew all about this. Where were you when Ben Johnson tested positive? Before it happened, did you know he was using drugs? I certainly didn't. It's great to be wise after the fact!" adds Dubin Commission prosecutor Armstrong.

OUT OF THE FRYING PAN INTO THE FIRE

The Johnson affair was still front-page news when Jean Charest got involved in a race of his own. The election was set for November 21 and Charest's re-election was not a foregone conclusion. This time, his Liberal opponent would be Dennis Wood, a well-known businessman and former president of the Sherbrooke Chamber of Commerce.

The local election debate reflected the mood of the country. One issue dominated the campaign: the free trade agreement Canada had signed with the United States the previous year. The comfortable lead enjoyed by Brian Mulroney's Conservatives at the beginning of the campaign began to disappear after the leaders' debate, which saw John Turner don the mantle of defender of Canadian sovereignty. Charest's lead in Sherbrooke began to melt away. "When Turner's support soared, it showed up right away in our tracking polls," recalls Conrad Chapdelaine, Charest's Sherbrooke campaign manager that year.

Many had been surprised at Charest's choice of Chapdelaine as chief organizer. An attorney, he was well known for his sovereigntist views and was even a member of Péquiste Raynald Fréchette's organization. Needless to say, provincial Liberals working for Charest were less than enthusiastic about the appointment. But it was dictated by strategic considerations: Charest needed to hold on to the PQ supporters who had voted for him in 1984.

The Turner surge turned out to be short-lived. The Conservatives quickly recaptured their lead, in Sherbrooke and throughout the rest of the country. His adversary's lack of experience made Charest's task all the easier.

The two debates with Wood marked Charest's introduction to Jean-Bernard Bélisle and Claude Lacroix, communications and marketing experts with Everest, a Sherbrooke public relations firm. For the prideful young man, the experience was a painful one. During a session at Bélisle's house, Charest was subjected to a hail of criticism. "Jean, that just isn't the way!" the advisers kept repeating. "You sound like you're reading from a book. It doesn't come from the heart!" The minister stalked out in a huff, humiliated. "Suzanne," he told his aide, "don't ever drag me to a meeting like that again!" He slept on it, however, and the next day asked to see Bélisle and Lacroix before the first debate. It would prove to be a wise decision. "He ate him alive!" is how Bélisle describes his candidate's performance against the businessman. Charest and his two advisers have been inseparable ever since.

The Blunder

—⟋⟋—

In the early afternoon of January 23, 1990, Québec Superior Court Justice Yvan Macerola was munching on a sandwich while he put the finishing touches to a decision that would determine the fate of track and field coach Daniel Saint-Hilaire, dropped by the Canadian amateur sport establishment from the Canadian team at the Commonwealth Games getting under way in New Zealand that same day.

The telephone rang: it was a call from Auckland. "Hello, this is Jean Charest, minister for Amateur Sport. It seems there's something you'd like cleared up?"

It was an unusual call, but Judge Macerola wasn't unduly surprised. Someone from Charest's office had already tried to contact him earlier that day. The magistrate had instructed his secretary to tell the caller that it was impossible for him to speak to a politician. He had the same message for Charest. "I'm sorry, Mr. Charest, but I cannot talk to you. I'm trying a case in which you are involved. The best of luck to you and to the Canadian athletes in New Zealand."

The judge hung up and returned to Room 208 of the Montréal courthouse to bring down his verdict. For a few long moments, he wondered how he should react to Charest's call. It would have no influence on his decision; that had already been written. But should he make the minister's initiative public? Justice Macerola decided he had no choice. "I was torn, because I could imagine the consequences for him," the magistrate explains. "But a judge is bound to make it known when a member of the executive has contacted the judiciary. If I hadn't done it, I'd have been the one in hot water." Not to mention that the judge's secretary had already mentioned the call from the minister's office to other people in the courthouse.

When the court resumed, Justice Macerola briefly informed the parties that "the minister called my office but I refused to talk to him." Then the judge brought down his verdict, attempting in it to minimize the consequences of the incident for Charest. The court had felt "neither bound nor influenced" by the minister's opinions, he explained, and they "have not undermined the impartiality of the judiciary."

La Presse legal correspondent Yves Boisvert, who was attending the session, immediately grasped the significance of what had taken place. He phoned Liberal MP Jean Lapierre in Ottawa to get his reaction. Within minutes, Lapierre and colleague Stan Keyes had convened a press conference to demand Charest's resignation.

PRECEDENTS

Lapierre knew a political gold mine when he saw one. But he also knew a thing or two about the relationship between partisan politics and the judiciary. In 1976, when André Ouellet had been forced to resign under similar circumstances, the minister had instructed his youthful aide to study the legal precedents. The aide's name was Jean Lapierre. Ouellet, the minister for Consumer and

Corporate Affairs in the Trudeau cabinet, had been accused of contempt of court. In an attempt to muffle the affair, the minister asked his colleague Bud Drury to contact the judge who was going to hear the case. Drury had a lengthy discussion with the judge to find out whether Ouellet could avoid a trial by apologizing. In his investigation of the highly irregular approach taken by Drury and Ouellet, Québec Superior Court Chief Justice Jules Deschênes had described the evidence as "serious."

Just as the Ouellet affair was breaking, it emerged that, in 1971, minister of Indian Affairs Jean Chrétien had spoken with a judge to ask when there would be a ruling in a case involving a resident of Chrétien's riding. The judge later said, "While I did not regard the telephone call to be proper practice," it could not be considered "interference or intervention calling for formal protest." Chrétien kept his job. Given these revelations, Prime Minister Trudeau laid down guidelines for cabinet behaviour. "In future," he announced in the Commons on March 12, 1976, "no member of the cabinet may communicate with members of the judiciary concerning any matter which they have before them in their judicial capacities, except through the minister of Justice, his duly authorized officials or counsel acting for him."

Charest's case was certainly less serious than Ouellet's, where an attempt had been made to protect the minister's personal interests. Jean Charest's call might even have been less unethical than Jean Chrétien's, since no conversation between the politician and the judge had taken place. But the Liberal Opposition could not be bothered with legal niceties. Besides, the guidelines laid down by Prime Minister Trudeau fifteen years earlier could not have been clearer. "The rule is quite simple. A cabinet minister does not call a judge," the Liberals told reporters.

The Grits had another motive for demanding Charest's resignation. Lapierre hadn't gotten over a cutting remark made by the minister for Amateur Sport in the Commons. To a Liberal member who suggested that he talk to Justice Dubin (the chairman of the commission of inquiry on the Ben Johnson affair), Charest shot back arrogantly: "The Honourable Member should be cautious about communicating with judges. He would do better to consult some of his colleagues in that regard!" Lapierre says, "There was no doubt about it. I said to myself, 'Well, well, look who's lecturing us! That just about takes the cake!' No way he was going to get a break from us after that."

"WHY RESIGN?"

When news of the tempest in Ottawa reached Auckland, Charest adopted a defensive stance. "There has been absolutely no interference in the case," he told a press conference. Resignation was out of the question. But in the hours that followed he began to grasp the magnitude of the affair. First, he received a call from Stanley Hartt, Mulroney's chief of staff. Hartt's job was to break the news to Charest. The minister was thunderstruck. "But why should I resign?" Next, Charest chatted with deputy prime minister Don Mazankowski, a wily veteran who had a particular liking for the Sherbrooke MP. "Hold on, Jean. Listen to the news. *The National* is just starting." Charest's blunder had been given top billing. "This is a no-no. You won't be able to withstand the pressure in the House and outside the House. So you should probably do the right thing. Or else your image will be tarnished forever. You have a great future in politics, better pay the price for your mistake and get on with it."

"Tell the Prime Minister to do what he thinks is best," sighed Charest.

At noon on Wednesday, Ottawa time, Prime Minister Mulroney called his protégé. Charest was still hoping the storm would abate, but his arguments made little impression on his boss. Brian Mulroney had seen nine ministers leave cabinet under a cloud of scandal. The Conservative government's image was badly stained. The Prime Minister did not intend to let Charest tarnish it further.

Besides, the older man was much less naive than the youngster. Mulroney knew that the Liberals would never back off. "I was afraid Charest would lose his shirt," the former prime minister confides. "'Jean,' I told him, 'I want your resignation before I go down for Question Period. If you don't do it, your career may be seriously compromised. It's a question of living to fight another day.'"

The minister's resignation was clearly far less spontaneous than he would have us believe. "I offered my resignation to the Prime Minister. I didn't wait for him to ask for it," he repeated during one of our meetings. But that's not Stanley Hartt's, Don Mazankowski's or Brian Mulroney's version.

Charest wrote his letter of resignation. Mulroney's reply left little doubt about his future intentions: "You have been a valuable adviser and an excellent minister, and I know that you will have the opportunity to serve your fellow citizens in the future." After the Prime Minister wrote the letter, he called Red Charest. "Jean has to resign from the cabinet, but he has done excellent work, Red, and I am going to make sure that he comes back one day. And I assure you that when he does, it will be at the top."

Tears flowed freely in Jean Charest's Sherbrooke office. But not from Red. The great oak stood unbending, just as he had done when his beloved Rita had died. There was no outpouring of maudlin sentiment, no speeches. Just a few well-chosen words: "It's dangerous when things are going up all the time. You've got to have ups and downs." Life goes on.

CATASTROPHE

When the Prime Minister entered the House of Commons, it was dawn in Auckland. Sitting in a hotel room with Michou by his side, the young politician watched his dreams turn to ashes. "It was a catastrophe," he says. "With one silly blunder, I had just ruined my political career." He thought of everyone he had let down: Red,

Robert and his sisters — everyone who had helped him since 1984. He called some of them, particularly George MacLaren and Denis Beaudoin, to offer his apologies. Adding to his woes, the journalists were closing in, hounding him in the hotel corridors until he agreed to hold a press conference. Worse yet, foreign journalists covering the Commonwealth Games, attracted by the smell of scandal, turned up as well. It's difficult to imagine more abject humiliation. "It was a little embarrassing to explain all that to the [Austrian journalists] . . ."

Despite his discomfort, Charest handled the press conference skilfully and persuasively. But his face bore the marks of a sleepless night. Emotion welling in his voice, he said, "I understand the rules, I respect Parliament and the judicial system. And that is why . . . I've offered my resignation, and that is why it has been accepted." Jean-Guy Ouellete, who had first led Charest into the labyrinth of amateur sport, was looking on from the mezzanine: "I cried like a baby!"

For Jean and Michèle, the worst was yet to come. On their return to Canada they would face humiliation, not long distance but in person. They stopped over on the Fiji Islands for three days to catch their breath. Their first stop was Toronto, where their friend Bruno Fortier joined them to face the music on their arrival at the airport. "When we stepped out of the hotel room, it seemed as if the corridor would never end," says Charest.

Nearly one hundred friends and supporters greeted the Charests when they landed at Dorval. The heart-warming welcome helped ease the pain. Standing proudly right in front was Red. "Tears were flowing freely," wrote *La Tribune*. "It was one of the hardest and yet one of the most moving moments in my life," Charest was to say a few years later. The fallen minister had considered giving up his seat, but quickly made up his mind to serve out his term as MP for Sherbrooke. As soon as he returned to Ottawa, he apologized to the PC caucus. When he entered the House for Question Period, he took a seat alongside the Tory backbenchers. He'd been sent to the back of the class. "There was silence in the House when I entered," says Charest. "I took my seat and I thought: 'Well, that's over and done with!'"

The ensuing few months in purgatory proved beneficial. The Charest family, including its newest member, their third child, Alexandra, were able to spend some quality time with the pater-familias. But he was already dreaming about returning to cabinet. Luc Lavoie, who worked in the PMO, recalls that his friend plied him with questions on the subject. "The day I hinted that it might be about to happen, Jean went goggle-eyed!"

THE FAX AND THE SHAVING CREAM

How could Jean Charest have made such a colossal miscue, "that silly blunder" as he describes it? How could a cabinet minister, a lawyer by profession, actually pick up the telephone and call a judge to discuss a case involving his department? Just a few weeks earlier, Charest had declared that the independence of the judiciary was one of the most sacred principles in the Canadian system of government. Wrote Superior Court Chief Justice Jules Deschênes: "It is of the utmost importance that this independence of the judiciary, achieved through great effort during the course of the last three centuries, be jealously guarded against all attacks. More particularly it must remain protected from interventions from Members of the Cabinet, whatever may be the quality of the intentions that inspire them."[*]

Some sleuthing is required in order to piece together exactly what went wrong — what happened in Montréal and in Auckland, minute by minute, according to all the witnesses. But reconstructing events is a tough job. Witnesses contradict each other, and Charest's testimony is extremely vague. The story is a complex one.

First, the stage setting and the actors. In the Montréal courthouse, Justice Yvan Macerola hears a request for an injunction by track and field coach Daniel Saint-Hilaire. Saint-Hilaire had been

---

[*] *House of Commons Debates*, March 12, 1976, pp. 11776–79.

passed over when the Canadian Commonwealth Games team was put together. He promptly sued, accusing the CTFA and the Commonwealth Games Association of Canada (CGAC) of discriminating against French-speaking Québeckers. What made the case even more touchy, politically, was an earlier claim by high jumper Michel Brodeur that he had been kept off the team because of discrimination.

Jean-Laurier Demers, a fire-breathing Sherbrooke solicitor, represented the CTFA in court. Why did a pan-Canadian association go all the way to Sherbrooke to hire a lawyer? Chalk it up to the friendly advice of Jean-Guy Ouellette, CTFA chairman, University of Sherbrooke professor and close friend of Jean Charest.

Meanwhile, the Commonwealth Games Association of Canada, which has the final say in selecting the national team, had managed to persuade the Québec Court of Appeal to declare that Québec courts had no jurisdiction over it. Meaning that when Mr. Justice Macerola took up the Saint-Hilaire case once more, the coach had no hope of victory. The magistrate, lacking authority over those who had made the decision, would have no alternative but to reject Saint-Hilaire's petition. Daniel Caisse, the coach's lawyer, knew his case was lost. It was all Demers could do to keep from celebrating a victory that was in the bag.

So far, so good. As Justice Macerola was hearing the attorneys' final arguments, 25,000 kilometres away, in Auckland, New Zealand, the Honourable Jean J. Charest, the minister of state for Fitness and Amateur Sport, was attending the opening ceremonies of the Commonwealth Games. His chief lieutenants and Canadian amateur sport dignitaries, including his friend Ouellette and Paul Dupré, also of the CTFA, accompanied Charest. The heads of the CGAC, the very same people who had excluded Saint-Hilaire and Brodeur from the national team, were also in Auckland. Charest took the opportunity to meet them to discuss the Brodeur case, which the minister saw as a flagrant example of injustice. They told the young minister to take a hike. One of them, Ken Smith, maintains to this day: "The minister has no say in the selection of athletes. The sports associations will defend this prerogative to their death. They don't like outsiders telling them what to do." The case of Saint-Hilaire didn't even come up.

After the meeting, Charest sent a letter to Michel Brodeur's lawyer, Daniel Caisse, who was also representing Daniel Saint-Hilaire. He admitted that he had failed in his final attempt to help Brodeur. Then he concluded: "With regard to Mr. Saint-Hilaire's case, the Commonwealth Games Association of Canada will comply with the decision of the Québec Superior Court without pursuing the matter before another court." In other words, after winning an appeal court ruling removing the CGAC from the jurisdiction of Québec courts, the association was now ready to bow to their authority. No one remembers how or why the sentence got there. Jean-Guy Ouellette's words reflect the general feeling of the people involved: "We always wondered why that damned letter was sent!"

When Caisse got to his office on January 23 and found the fax from Auckland on his desk, he could hardly believe his eyes. Hurrying over to the courthouse just as Justice Macerola was about to bring down the verdict, he asked for the "investigation to be reopened" so that he could produce Jean Charest's letter. Jean-Laurier Demers was appalled, then furious: "If Charest had wanted to sink me, he couldn't have found a better way to do it," says the lawyer. "That letter of his completely undermined my case!" A case he seemed on the verge of winning now looked hopeless. Demers got an adjournment until mid-afternoon, claiming "I have to talk to my people."

Fit to be tied, Demers stalked back to his hotel. Then he swung into action. His first call was to Paul Dupré, president of the Canadian Track and Field Association, in Auckland. It was six o'clock in the morning in New Zealand. Demers explained the situation. Then, dictating almost word for word, he outlined a second letter he felt the minister should send him. He could use the second letter in court to undo some of the damage caused by the first. Dupré and Jean-Guy Ouellette called Charest's aide, Lane MacAdam, inviting him to a meeting in Sport Canada's rented offices near the Hyatt Hotel, where the minister was staying. Why there? Because the place was equipped with a fax machine. From the start, their objective was perfectly clear: to fax Jean-Laurier Demers a letter that he could submit to Justice Macerola.

In Montréal, Demers got a call from MacAdam and Dupré in Sport Canada's New Zealand offices. Time was short; court was scheduled to resume at any moment, he told them. Maybe the minister should speak to Justice Macerola directly. No one knows who was the first to make this bizarre suggestion. Some appear to recall that it came from the lawyer. "I never asked him to call the judge," insists Demers. "I would never dream of the idea." Jean-Guy Ouellette thinks it more likely the suggestion came from MacAdam, the minister's young assistant.

One thing is certain: it was MacAdam who obtained the judge's telephone number and gave it to the minister over the phone. MacAdam and Ouellette then went to Charest's room. The minister opened the door, his face lathered with shaving cream. He had just hung up the phone: "The judge didn't want to talk to me. He didn't seem very happy." He went up to Ouellette, slapped him on the shoulder and opined, "I think I've just put my foot in it." Until that moment, no one had so much as wondered whether it was a smart idea to approach a judge directly. "We were buddies, we were trying to solve a problem," says Paul Dupré. Surrounded by his buddies, Charest didn't think twice. "It never even entered my mind that what I was doing violated the ethics guidelines, because I had the impression my call had been requested [by the judge]."

THE SET-UP

Charest loyalists in Sherbrooke have long believed — and some believe it to this day — that their man was set up by two Liberals, Jean-Laurier Demers and Yvan Macerola. But the theory doesn't hold water. Demers would have risked losing an important case, and Macerola, a respected magistrate, would have jeopardized his career just to bring down a junior minister — highly unlikely.

Charest himself gave this piece of fantasy credibility when he returned from New Zealand. "They handed me the judge's telephone number. I wasn't the one who called all the way to Canada to get it."

"Do you think someone tried to set you up?" reporters wanted to know.

"Draw your own conclusions. It's hard to tell what really happened, but I was under the impression the judge wanted me to call him."

When he heard that, Jean-Laurier Demers exploded. He demanded, and obtained, a meeting with the outgoing cabinet minister. The two met over breakfast the day after Charest's return to Sherbrooke. It was vintage Charest. He dislikes conflict or enduring animosity and is skilled in the art of defusing political time bombs.

When he arrived at the restaurant, Charest quipped, "Look, Jean-Laurier, no more limousines, no more expense account."

"If that's the way it is, I'll buy you breakfast, but it'll be bacon and eggs, not eggs Benedict, like in Ottawa."

Demers describes the rest of the meeting: "I looked him right in the eye and said, 'Jean, there's one thing I can't stand: people are saying that I talked to you, that I asked you to talk to the judge and that I set you up.'" The meeting was productive. Charest contacted the local media and dismissed the conspiracy theory: "I don't believe there was a plot against me," he told *La Tribune*.

"It wasn't in my interest to get involved in a lot of finger-pointing," says Charest. "It was my fault. It doesn't matter what Demers did. He wasn't the one who dialled the number. I did. So I'm the one responsible."

Yet, for a long time, Charest remained rather vague about the episode. Though he was pointing no fingers, it was as though he were trying to slough off some of the blame. The first time I asked him about the matter, seven years later, he had just discussed it with Jean-Guy Ouellette. Charest, Ouellette had reminded him, had not spoken personally to Demers when he was in New Zealand. All the same . . .

"I got a call . . ." Charest told me.

"Was it Demers?"

"Yes."

[. . .]

"Did you talk to Mr. Demers?"

"That's my recollection."

When I told Jean-Louis Demers this, he reacted just the way he had in 1990: "Do you know what we should do? We're going to sit down together, the three of us, and I'll look him in the eye [and say]: 'Jean, I NEVER talked to you!'" In the event, the confrontation wasn't necessary. Demers later ran into Charest in Sherbrooke, spoke to him face to face and convinced him to change his version of the events.

To sum up, these are the facts of the case. First, Charest did call Justice Macerola. Second, nothing faintly resembling a conversation took place between the two men. Third, the bright idea for the call seems to have been the brainchild of one of his advisers in Auckland, probably Lane MacAdam. Fourth, Charest did not volunteer his resignation after he had committed the blunder, contrary to what he has maintained. And fifth, Charest was not the victim of a conspiracy. He was the victim of his own carelessness.

POWER TRIP

Reaction in the sports community to Jean Charest's forced resignation was all but unanimous. In Auckland, the team was stunned. One athlete said, "Tell Saint-Hilaire to stay home. Give us back Charest!" Dick Pound, Canadian International Olympic Committee representative, summed up the general feeling: "It's a bitter blow for Canadian sports. Charest was an intelligent, ambitious and well-prepared young minister. His departure is our loss." All the same, Pound couldn't get over the fact that the minister had made such a blunder. "Attempting to speak to a judge when a trial is in progress is a very delicate thing, and it's difficult for me, as a lawyer, to conceive of how a lawyer and a minister like him could have made such a mistake."

There can be little doubt that Charest's blunder was due to a peculiar set of circumstances: the early-morning hour, communication problems, not to mention his lack of experience as a lawyer and a politician. At the same time, Charest was discovering the power a cabinet minister possessed, and he did not hesitate to wield it, sometimes unwisely. Put bluntly, he was on a power trip.

When a trucker from the Eastern Townships was arrested in the United States in December 1989 following a traffic accident, Charest didn't hesitate to intervene. Given the reluctance of the American authorities to release the trucker, Richard Bilodeau, the minister called the district attorney in charge, giving his word as a guarantee that the truck driver would return to New Hampshire to stand trial. It was a commitment made in the name of the Canadian government . . . without the authorization of the government. His action might have been imprudent in the extreme, but considering the intense media coverage in Sherbrooke he was happy to take the credit. "My word and my reputation are on the line," Charest told local media. Once again, Charest had trumped François Gérin, who had taken a much more active role in the issue until then. Hoping to gain political advantage, Jean Charest had taken the risk of intervening with the legal authorities of another country on behalf of the government, when he had no mandate whatsoever to do so. "I realize I could have been in a tough spot if Richard [Bilodeau] had refused to return to the United States," he admitted at the time. That was barely one month before the call to Justice Macerola.

TELL ME WHO'S ADVISING YOU . . . ?

Privately, Jean Charest had apparently already held some of his entourage partially responsible for his resignation. Many of his supporters have accused his aides of getting him into hot water, or, at any rate, of not warning him about the possible consequences. In the opinion of his closest advisers, as well as the bureaucrats who have worked with him, Jean Charest's greatest weaknesses are his propensity for surrounding himself with the wrong people and his inability to get rid of incompetent staff.

During his tenure as a cabinet minister, Jean Charest's advisers were as young as, if not younger than, he was. Nothing unusual about that: cabinet ministers' political staffers are often in their twenties or thirties. For modest salaries, these people are ready to work countless hours and do what they are told without asking questions. For seasoned ministers, the combination is ideal. But when the minister is almost as young as his advisers, it can cause problems. At various times in his career, Jean Charest could have benefited from wiser voices, who would have advised him to think twice before banning Ben Johnson for life. Someone who would have grabbed the receiver from his hand when he was about to call Justice Macerola. "Jean Charest's biggest weakness," reluctantly confides longtime friend and organizer Denis Beaudoin, "is the way he manages his staff. Jean has a hard time choosing people who will work for him, using them the way they should be used and appreciating them the way they should be appreciated. That's one thing he doesn't like. He doesn't like dealing with people. Telling them to work a little harder, or a little less hard."

Friend and political aide Robert Dubé says that when Charest returned to cabinet in 1991, he took forever to settle conflicts among his staff in the Environment department. "Two people, whose personalities were just the opposite of Jean's, were hauling everyone and everything over the coals. I told Jean, 'This is ridiculous. It's just not like you.' He found it very difficult . . . It's not easy to fire somebody, and he respects people." Toby Price, who worked as Charest's chief of staff at Environment for a few months, recommended someone with a good deal of experience as his successor. Charest chose Philippe Morel instead. Morel was talented, but very young. "He was wet behind the ears," says Price. "If he had won the leadership race [in 1993], would Charest have named Morel chief of staff to the prime minister?" Not unlike other Charest aides over the years, Morel earned a reputation for arrogance. "It's a trip!" says Price. "You're close to power, maybe close to the next prime minister!" Arrogance was precisely the wrong attitude to have when it came to piloting a file like the Green Plan, since to implement the program, as we shall see later, Environment had to co-ordinate the activities of several other departments.

The Johnson affair, the call to Justice Macerola, Green Plan management problems, the 1993 leadership race and the 1997 election campaign all revealed weaknesses that led people to question the competence of Charest's closest advisers. "That's the problem in politics," veteran Denis Beaudoin points out. "In political life, your staff is three-quarters of your life, three-quarters of your decision-making. Your staff decides what you're going to do tomorrow morning, what you're going to do next Sunday." Surrounded by the wrong people, even the most resourceful politician would make a poor prime minister. In the coming years, the people Jean Charest chooses will certainly have a decisive effect on his career and, perhaps, on the future of Québec and Canada.

The Report

—ᴠᴠ—

"Camille, help me convince Charest to chair the Meech committee!" said Lucien Bouchard as he strode into Camille Guilbault's
house, little Alexandre cradled in his arms. The occasion was a dinner party thrown by Ms. Guilbault, who handled relations between
the Québec caucus and the Prime Minister's Office, for Audrey
Best, Bouchard's wife. It was to be her first step back into the
social whirl after giving birth a few months earlier. But the evening's main dish turned out to be politics. The guests didn't realize
it at the time, but the meal would mark a turning point in Jean
Charest's career.

It was late March 1990. Charest, relegated to the lowly status of a
backbencher following his blunder, had been enjoying life for two
whole months. His family was in high spirits. Michèle's eyes sparkle
when she thinks back to those days. "It was an extraordinary time. We
entertained friends and spent much more time with the children!"

Meanwhile, Canada was in the throes of political crisis. Hopes
had been raised that the Meech Lake Accord, signed by the

country's eleven first ministers, would finally smooth the way for Québec to endorse the 1982 Constitution. But Meech was in jeopardy. The legislatures of every province had to ratify the accord before it became law, but two provincial elections had taken place since the signing ceremony, and the newly elected premiers — Frank McKenna of New Brunswick and Clyde Wells of Newfoundland — were avowedly hostile, withholding assent and insisting that the accord be reconsidered. Wells and McKenna, both Liberals, found aid and comfort in Pierre Elliott Trudeau's virulent attack on the agreement. Meech, trumpeted the former prime minister, "would render the Canadian state totally impotent." Jean Chrétien, about to be elected leader of the Liberal Party of Canada, shared this view. Manitoba premier Gary Filmon, aboriginal leaders and women's groups were flocking to the anti-Meech camp. Adding to the suspense, the accord had a built-in deadline: June 23, 1990.

It was three months before the deadline. Meech was Prime Minister Mulroney's masterwork, and he swung into action to save it. In Montréal and Ottawa, secret negotiations got under way between his representatives — chief of staff Stanley Hartt and former deputy minister of Justice Roger Tassé — and the future Liberal leader's representatives, Eric Maldoff and John Laskin. Initiated by tycoon Paul Desmarais, the discussions focused on the clause recognizing Québec as a distinct society. Jean Chrétien feared the article would limit the scope of the Charter of Rights. "The discussions were very long and sometimes hard," says Tassé. "They [Liberal representatives] implied that Québec might be less democratic, that it risked being more authoritarian than the other provinces." Meanwhile, Senator Lowell Murray, the federal minister responsible for the Constitution, and Norman Spector, cabinet secretary for Federal-Provincial Relations, cobbled together a solution with New Brunswick premier Frank McKenna. For months, McKenna had been calling for a parallel agreement to mollify the groups hostile to Meech. Ottawa had rejected the idea. But with the deadline fast approaching, the federal government indicated that it would not oppose a "Companion Resolution" adopted by the nation's legislatures, providing it took nothing away from Meech. Although federal representatives energetically denied it at the time, they admit today that every comma of the Companion Resolution presented by McKenna in March had been negotiated with Ottawa. Says Norman Spector, "Once we agreed on the principle, we sat down and began to discuss the nature of that parallel accord. There was very close collaboration between the governments of New Brunswick and Canada."

Voyage to Article 2 Country

The text of the McKenna resolution covered two pages and consisted of eleven articles. One of them, Article 1 (2), refers to article 2 of the Meech Lake Accord, which reads as follows:

2. (1) The Constitution of Canada shall be interpreted in a manner consistent with:
(a) the recognition that the existence of French-speaking Canadians, centred in Québec but also present elsewhere in Canada, and English-speaking Canadians, concentrated outside Québec but also present in Québec, constitutes a fundamental characteristic of Canada; and
(b) the recognition that Québec constitutes within Canada a distinct society.
(2) The role of the Parliament of Canada and the provincial legislatures to preserve the fundamental characteristic of Canada referred to in paragraph (1)(a) is affirmed.
(3) The role of the legislature and government of Québec to preserve and promote the distinct society of Québec referred to in paragraph (1)(b) is affirmed.

The McKenna resolution would have added an Article 2.1 to this part of the Meech Lake Accord, which recognized Québec as a distinct society. It reads: "The role of the Parliament and Government of Canada to promote the fundamental characteristic of Canada referred to in paragraph (1)(a) is affirmed."

The shade in meaning was subtle indeed. Under the Meech Lake Accord, the government of Québec was assigned the role of *protecting* and *promoting* Québec's distinct society, while the government of Canada could only *protect* the two linguistic groups throughout the country. In the McKenna resolution, Ottawa would be given the task of *promoting* linguistic duality. This would mean, according to many Québec analysts, that the federal government would be free to *promote* the development of the English-speaking minority in Québec.

The McKenna resolution proposed other additions to the Meech Lake Accord, all of less consequence for Québec. The federal scenario called for public hearings across the country by a parliamentary committee struck to discuss the resolution. Essentially, the initiative would be an educational one, intended to acquaint Canadians with the idea of a Companion Resolution. Québec Tory nationalists, among them Lucien Bouchard, were cool toward the idea. Bouchard was particularly miffed: he had found out about the committee through the media while on a trip to Vancouver. But once the decision had been made, the "minister responsible for Québec" defended the decision in caucus, over the energetic objections of future Bloc Québécois MP François Gérin. The day before the Charest Committee was set up, a few MPs conferred with Bouchard in his office. The meeting wound up in a shouting match between Gérin and the minister.

"Lucien, you're opening the box, even though we said we wouldn't!" Gérin shouted.

Bouchard was furious. "Listen, the committee will just serve to calm down English Canadians. Meech will stay the same."

A torrent of insults ensued, fuelled by Lucien Bouchard's antipathy toward the MP for Megantic-Compton.

GUESS WHO'S COMING TO DINNER!

No one knows for sure whether it was Lucien Bouchard or Brian Mulroney who first thought of Jean Charest to chair the controversial committee. At the time, professional relations between Bouchard and Charest were cordial. With the birth of Alexandre, the Best-Bouchards' first child and Alexandra, the Dionne-Charests' third, relations became even warmer. It is surprising, nevertheless, that Bouchard considered Charest the "ideal choice" for the position.* If Bouchard was already worried about how the whole process would end, as he has always maintained, why was he willing to assign the responsibility to a man he knew to be a devoted Mulroney loyalist and a strong believer in compromise?

In addition to Lucien Bouchard and Audrey Best, Camille Guilbault's guests on Sunday, March 25, 1990, included the Charests and Pierre Blais and his wife. The meal was interrupted by a telephone call from the Prime Minister, which Lucien Bouchard took in another room. The two men discussed the choice of a chairperson for the committee. Charest's name came up. According to Mulroney, Bouchard sounded enthusiastic about the idea: "In fact, he's here this evening!"

"Well, set it up."

"When I approached him on behalf of the Prime Minister, he readily accepted. He showed so little surprise that I have always wondered if he was tipped off," Bouchard recounts in his autobiography.** The other guests contradict Bouchard's version. Charest, they say, seemed both astonished and reluctant. "Jean is the soul of caution, he rarely says yes or no. But I had the feeling he didn't want to do it," says Pierre Blais. "Jean said, 'I've just gotten over a very unpleasant experience. I don't need the exposure,'" Camille Guilbault recalls.

---

*   Lucien Bouchard, *On the Record*. (Toronto: Stoddart, 1994), p. 228.
** Ibid., pp. 228–29.

Why would an ambitious young man like Jean Charest hesitate at the chance to step back into the limelight earlier than anticipated? Today Charest pleads the difficulty of the task, and the happiness he'd rediscovered with his family. His real motives, however, lay deeper down. Charest feared he would be turned into a sacrificial lamb. Getting involved in something with a substantial risk of failure might permanently compromise an already shaky career. In the notes he took at the time, he refers to the conversation presumed to have taken place that evening.

Charest: "You don't think it's risky?"

Bouchard: "No, it's not."

In short, Charest's hesitations were career-motivated. He rushed to consult longtime friend George MacLaren, who would eventually act as his adviser throughout the committee's public hearings. "The day the report is released, you'll be putting a target on the table. The Péquistes will have to destroy it immediately, so will the provinces if they have doubts about the content. And in all that, you'll be the scapegoat," warned MacLaren. Charest also knew that if the report were rejected, Prime Minister Mulroney would be forced to dissociate himself from it. "It was like walking on thin ice," says Charest. "'You lead the way, and we'll see if the ice is still thick enough.' If you make it across the lake, wonderful. That means you can walk on water. Bully for you! If you sink like a stone, well . . . he was a nice guy." Asked whether it wasn't a great opportunity to get back into the action, Charest demurred. "That was the other way of looking at it. But, from my perspective, I didn't need to expose myself to that."

While Bouchard used his immense gifts of persuasion to get Charest on board, he also let the younger man know he had serious reservations about the McKenna resolution concerning the promotion of linguistic duality. In reply, Charest quoted an article published in *Le Devoir* that weekend by Senator Gérald Beaudoin, an expert on constitutional matters. The senator held that "the function of promoting linguistic duality is applicable only in the federal domain." In other words, the new article would give no new powers to the federal government beyond the current Official Languages Act.

"Lucien, I don't know whether you've read Gérald's text? I agree with him. I don't think there's any problem," said Charest. Already the two men had begun to go their separate ways.

Charest could live with the notion of a Companion Resolution. The approach presented no particular risks as far as he was concerned. He remembered studying the American Constitution back in law school. Though the Constitution was ratified in 1789, some states refused to adopt it until a series of amendments was added. These amendments, or "companion resolutions" in Canadian parlance, became the basis of the American Bill of Rights.

By next morning, Charest had made his decision: he would make the sacrifice . . . to advance his career. Loyalty to the PM and to Lucien Bouchard, he concluded, was his best insurance policy for the future. At lunch time, in the parliamentary restaurant, Robert Charest, then Lucien Bouchard's aid, carried notes about the composition of the committee back and forth between his boss's table and his brother's. That afternoon Charest met Mulroney. The next day the PM tabled an order of reference in the House of Commons, creating a fifteen-member committee. Representing the three recognized parties in the Commons, the committee was to study the McKenna resolution and to present a report "no later than May 18, 1990." Public knowledge since late March, the May deadline was to become a key element in the story.

FOREWARNED IS FOREARMED

The Charest Committee's task was to be as cumbersome as its name: The Special Committee to Study the Proposed Companion Resolution to the Meech Lake Accord. It had two months to set itself up, tour the country and write a report on the issues that have divided Canada from its beginning. "We had very little time to work," says one of the committee's clerks, Jacques Lahaie. "The logistics had to be put in place very quickly, which meant making fifty decisions in one evening!"

At the outset, few believed that Charest's politically diverse committee could bring down a unanimous report. Tory David Macdonald, the vice-chair and a social democrat at heart, was primarily interested in international issues. Charest aside, the committee's Conservative heavyweight was Newfoundlander Ross Reid, an affable, intelligent man who would have been in the cabinet long before, had it not been for that other influential Newfoundland Tory, John Crosbie. Other Conservatives included Gabriel Desjardins and André Plourde from Québec, cautious men who kept a low profile in the constitutional debate.

The Liberals picked two heavy-hitters, André Ouellet and Robert Kaplan. Ouellet might have been a Meech supporter, but his job would be to act as liaison between the committee and the Liberal caucus with its many Trudeau loyalists, outgoing leader John Turner, and his probable successor, Jean Chrétien. The NDP named two representatives, Lorne Nystrom and Svend Robinson, known for his sympathies for the demands of aboriginal peoples and women's groups.

While Commons bureaucrats were bustling about setting up the committee, Senators Solange Chaput-Rolland and Gérald Beaudoin offered to share their experience with Charest. Fifteen years earlier, the two had been members of the Pépin-Robarts Task Force on Canadian Unity. Ms. Chaput-Rolland told Charest that the Royal Commission's public hearings had degenerated "into dark nights full of shouting and demonstrations."* Such was the climate of intolerance that the one-time journalist burst into tears during a public hearing in Montréal. "I cracked. Two days earlier we had been grossly insulted in Winnipeg. I was hoping, naively I can see

---

* Solange Chaput-Rolland, *De l'unité à la réalité* (Montréal: Pierre Tisseyre, 1981), p. 23.

now, that Montréalers would display their usual courtesy toward the members of our Commission . . ."* Protesters "grabbed the microphones to vent their anger, their frustration, their demands" and "marginal individuals put on a show for the television cameras," Ms. Chaput-Rolland told Charest.** Finally, she reminded Charest of how painful the experience had been for André Laurendeau, co-chairman of the Royal Commission on Biculturalism and Bilingualism in the mid-1960s. "It was like facing machine-gun fire," the eminent journalist had noted in his journal. "It's easy to see why the weakest among us give way immediately, and why even the strongest go through periods of extreme emotion. This treatment is hard on everyone."***

"I'd been warned," Charest says. He had also been told in no uncertain terms about the importance the government attached to the undertaking: no blunders this time around. Norman Spector, cabinet secretary for Federal-Provincial Relations, didn't mince words. Early on, after a committee meeting held behind closed doors, Spector took Charest aside and uttered these words: "Jean, don't fuck up!"

KEEPING THE SHOW ON THE ROAD

Frank McKenna, the official author of the Companion Resolution formula, was the first witness to appear before the committee. "For us, passing Meech Lake as it is is unacceptable. We believe it would represent a significant shock to the stability of Canada in its present form. It would make it very difficult for Canadians to embrace this Constitution as their covenant if it were forced upon them without changes or without improvements." Turning to his most

---

*   Ibid., p. 25.
** Ibid., p. 24.
*** André Laurendeau, *Journal tenu pendant la Commission royale d'enquête sur le bilinguisme et le biculturalisme* (Outremont: VLB editor/Le Septentrion, 1990), p. 173.

controversial suggestion, that the federal government promote linguistic duality, McKenna explained, "The maintenance of the French language and culture throughout Canada can only be assured through active promotion. [. . .] We must never forget that somewhere in the vicinity of one million francophones live outside the borders of the province of Québec and that they, much more than francophones within the province of Québec, face the constant danger of assimilation every day." In other words, the new article concerning the promotion of linguistic duality was aimed at French-speakers outside Québec, not English-speaking Québeckers. "Thus, the promotion of Canada's linguistic duality becomes a national objective, and it is essential that a national government have a constitutionally affirmed role to play in such promotion within its sphere of jurisdiction. I repeat, this is only within the sphere of jurisdiction of the Government of Canada." This was the view expressed in *Le Devoir* by constitutional expert Gérald Beaudoin, whom Charest had quoted to Lucien Bouchard at Camille Guilbault's dinner party.

Following McKenna's testimony, Charest reiterated the argument, trying to convince McKenna to accept changes that would answer Bouchard's concerns. "Would you agree that an article should be added to a Companion Resolution that would clearly state that the promotion clause is restricted to federal government jurisdiction and federal government institutions?" The premier of New Brunswick left the door ajar. "If there are words that could improve the certainty of the objective without subtracting from the objective itself, I would be prepared to entertain them, yes." But when it later turned out that francophone representatives from outside Québec were hostile to the idea, the Liberals threw their support behind them and the committee backed down.

After McKenna, the committee heard 159 other witnesses in thirty-one public meetings held from April 9 to May 4. Committee members crisscrossed the country at a dizzying rate, visiting Yellowknife, Whitehorse, Vancouver, Winnipeg and St. John's. In the course of their peregrinations, the committee members heard:

- John Amagoalik, an Inuit leader: "A promise from Bourassa carries absolutely no weight with our people. Here is a premier who is bent on destroying the Inuit homeland in northern Québec without any regard for us."
- Keith Lay, a resident of the Yukon, described the skepticism felt by aboriginal peoples over promises that future amendments would be forthcoming once the Meech Lake Accord had been adopted. "If you go to a car dealership and want to buy a new car and the dealer says to you, well, you can buy the car, but the heater does not work, but buy the car and we will fix it later, you are not going to accept a deal like that."
- Claude Castonguay, a businessman and the chairman of a pro-Meech group: "If the Meech Lake Accord is reopened, obviously there will be a long period of uncertainty. We fail to see how a premier of Québec could return to the constitutional negotiating table in good faith when most people in Québec feel that the Meech Lake Accord is the least that can be done."
- Don Lanskail, the mayor of West Vancouver: "I support Meech Lake. It is not a perfect instrument but I think it is something we can live with."
- Alex B. MacDonald, a Simon Fraser University political science professor: "The Meech Lake Accord blocks for all time federal fund-matching for social programs that have in the past helped every Canadian spread a measure of social equality from coast to coast and contributed to our sense of pride in being Canadians."
- John McCabe, a resident of British Columbia: "Everybody knows Québec is a distinct society. But it does not have to be written into the law of the land. It would then be more than distinct; it would be very special. This can apply to all

groups in Canada. It would be stupid to cater to such an attitude. This would create discord. The top priority for any person in this country should be to be a good Canadian citizen and to be thankful to be living in such a wonderful country."

- Joan Saxon, another British Columbian, asserted that the Meech Lake Accord offered "nothing but the potential to suppress the linguistic rights of other Canadians."

In short, like André Laurendeau, Solange Chaput-Rolland and so many other French-speaking Canadians before them, the Québec members of the Charest Committee ran into a wall of prejudice. "It was a very painful experience," recalls Gabriel Desjardins. "When you're an MP for Témiscamingue and you go to Vancouver and you have to listen to that . . . sometimes Plourde and I would look at each other . . . We even left the table a couple of times because we found it hard to hear how badly people in the West misunderstood Québec."

At times, even Charest could hardly believe his ears. When the committee reached Winnipeg, attorney Mona Brown opined that the distinct society article might limit "reproductive freedom" in Québec. "The character of the distinct society accommodates a predominantly Roman Catholic community, and that could be used in arguments to the Supreme Court to justify discrimination on that basis. One can use the distinct society clause to say that we need to keep our population up in Québec," asserted the co-chair of the Manitoba Association of Women and the Law. Charest recalls, "I listened to that and I thought, 'It's completely ridiculous for her to come here to say that!' And I looked around me — there must have been hundreds of people in the room — and I saw perfectly sane people — lawyers, engineers, public servants — nodding their heads. They agreed with her! The climate was so tense, the debate had gotten so far off track that we'd reached the point where some people were spouting nonsense and others were agreeing. I thought about history, about other events, the Second World War, all kinds of times and places where people had let themselves get carried away . . ."

When Charest heard such statements before the committee, he sometimes remained silent. At other times, after Ms. Brown's testimony, for instance, he felt obliged to set the record straight. "I think you would want to give careful thought to what you have said about reproductive freedom. I do not agree, and I think that is one thing you would want to think about very, very carefully before entering into it again." The chairman also reacted when an aboriginal leader objected to the presence of "separatists sitting in the federal cabinet." "I think we would want to make it very clear that all the people of Québec are citizens of Canada, and whatever choice or whatever vote they may have cast in 1980, being a citizen of Canada gives them all the privileges and rights afforded all citizens in this country, and those people who may have voted yes in the 1980 referendum of course could fully expect to be part of any national government we represent today," said Charest.

Some would say that the commissioners had gone straight to the heart of the Canadian problem: mutual ignorance and intolerance. "The crisis in Canada is not the result of the uncouth behaviour of a minority, but of the ill will of the majority," Solange Chaput-Rolland had concluded. But the lessons Jean Charest took home had less to do with Canadian dysfunction than with the dangers inherent in public consultations. "I don't think it's peculiar to Canada. The exercise lends itself to that sort of thing, because what we're getting is people's gut reaction."

The Chairman Sums Up

It's generally considered that Jean Charest handled the public hearings with aplomb. When things got tense, he stayed calm, in full control of his emotions and of the situation. A generally harmonious atmosphere prevailed among committee members, with the urgent nature of the situation acting as a catalyst. This was particularly true of the key players: Charest, Ouellet, Nystrom, Reid, Kaplan and Robinson, who spent long hours negotiating over the list of witnesses the committee would hear.

But Opposition MPs found one of Charest's habits particularly irritating: the chairman had taken to summing up the testimony of each witness, a practice unheard of in Ottawa, where parliamentary committee chairpersons are expected to be self-effacing. Robert Kaplan and Svend Robinson often expressed their displeasure during the public hearings. "It is not necessary to have a summary. This is an abuse of the powers of the chair," Robinson accused. "We did not come to Manitoba to listen to the chair," Kaplan bristled. "And you ought to try following the precedents of the House of Commons itself to restrict the amount of time you allocate to yourself." "I don't know why he did it. [. . .] I kind of thought it was a bit of a chance for him to show how smart he was," says committee vice-chairman David MacDonald. Other members of the group were of the same opinion. Jean Charest would not chair such an important committee, whose hearings were broadcast live from one end of the country to the other, without seizing the opportunity to show how brilliant he was. Charest, of course, says he acted out of the noblest of intentions. "It forced committee members to listen much more attentively than usual," Charest explained somewhat pretentiously. "When you're sitting on a committee, it's easy to read a newspaper, but when the chairman sums up a witness's testimony the committee's members are forced to listen, because every time he does so, it's a test of accuracy. It was a way for me to assert my control over the committee," he adds, "and to make sure I kept events on course and kept the debate focused on the issues we wanted to resolve, instead of constantly being sidetracked by other issues."

Charest's summaries enabled him to bask in the spotlight, while giving some witnesses a chance to articulate their thoughts. And the whole thing ended in laughter. A certain Garry Williams was the one-hundred-sixtieth and final witness. His presentation was totally incoherent: "The Mulroney-Bourassa agreement is an unacceptable document. Why? The principle of equality for all . . . Mr. Parizeau, call off the wolves." That was the preamble. Some minutes later he concluded, "I believe no province should be much larger than the island of Newfoundland."

Jean Charest politely thanked Mr. Williams. And New Democrat MP Philip Edmonston asked slyly, "On a point of order, Mr. Chairman, could we have the benefit of your summary of our witness's presentation, as you have done in the past?"

"Adjourn the meeting," said Robert Kaplan, who saw little to laugh about. "Let's get to work."

It was May 4, and the Charest Committee had fourteen days to draft its report. "It is my hope that the report of this committee will contribute to the future of our country," said the chairman before the members went into closed session to negotiate.

MEMORY LAPSES

So much murky constitutional water has flowed under the bridge since then that the participants recall the events rather dimly. When I interviewed him, Ross Reid kept saying, "Wait a minute, that's what I think, but maybe it happened in another committee . . ." The recollections of Lorne Nystrom, Svend Robinson, David MacDonald, Robert Kaplan, Gabriel Desjardins and André Plourde are equally vague. André Ouellet refused requests for an interview: "I've been involved in so many of those things, you know . . ."

Over lunch, Charest, Kaplan and Nystrom quickly agreed on the general form the report would take. "We decided to do a very brief report focusing specifically on the contentious issues," Charest says. The chairman gave Gary Levy, the former parliamentary library researcher who was to draft the report, the following instructions: "I want the report to be no longer than a dozen pages. It should address the concerns of the provinces that are hesitant. First, New

Brunswick's Companion Resolution should constitute the most important part. Then the issues raised by Manitoba and Newfoundland. Finally, I want an introduction, a brief conclusion and that's all." Charest categorically rejected Levy's suggestion that the committee address the other issues that had dominated the public hearings. *Stick to the point* was the watchword. Levy and Jacques Rousseau, another researcher from the parliamentary library, set to work. A lawyer by profession, Rousseau was responsible for the French-language version and the legal aspects of the document. They devoted the first weekend in May to their task.

While Rousseau and Levy were toiling away, Conservative senators and MPs were gathering for what would be a tense meeting at Mont Tremblant. On Saturday, newspapers reported that several Tory MPs had conferred with Parti Québécois vice-president Bernard Landry, who had urged them to abandon the Conservative ship if Meech failed. Brian Mulroney read the riot act to François Gérin and other MPs who were thinking of following him. "Québec MPs are in complete agreement with my position and the government's. If any MPs, for personal reasons, find themselves torn, they can go and sit elsewhere than with us."

Tension was running high when Levy returned from his weekend retreat to hand the draft report to Charest. On May 8, in Room 200 of the Ottawa Conference Centre, where so many constitutional meetings had been held and the 1981 agreement sealed, the fifteen-member committee was handed the draft. If we are to believe Levy, the fifteen pages submitted by him and Rousseau remained essentially intact. "The introduction and the structure weren't changed. The debates were over a few words in a number of paragraphs. Days and days! We'd redraft and redraft. The paragraphs would stay the same — only those few words would have changed."

During the ten days of debate, there were times when the machine would grind to a halt. On the afternoon of Thursday, May 10, Charest was forced to suspend the plenary session to consult with the key players of each party, who were themselves in

consultation with their respective leaders, caucuses, provincial government representatives and various pressure groups. When this
happened, the other committee members would gather together in
the rooms earmarked for each party group. "There were long times,"
recalls Conservative Gabriel Desjardins, "when we drank coffee and
sat there staring at each other!"

It has been all but impossible to get to the heart of the horse-
trading that went on at the time, and to assess the exact influence
of every player, starting with Jean Chrétien. What is known is that
Jean Charest and Ross Reid regularly consulted Senator Lowell
Murray and senior bureaucrat Norman Spector. Robert Kaplan met
Jean Chrétien twice while the committee was at work. He also
conferred with Pierre Trudeau. "I thought it was important that Mr.
Trudeau know what was going on," says Kaplan. Among other
things, Kaplan acted as liaison between the committee and the
secret negotiations conducted by Stanley Hartt. The committee's
drafts were forwarded to Hartt, Tassé, Maldoff and Laskin, who
studied them and sent their comments back to the Liberal MP.
"Every morning, Kaplan was informed of the results of our work the
previous night," explains Hartt. "When Charest tabled his report,
there wasn't an item that hadn't gotten Chrétien's approval." Jean
Charest might have been vaguely aware of these manoeuvres, but
he did not have a hand in them.

Québec kept close tabs on what was going on: Norman Spector
regularly reported the latest developments to Robert Bourassa's close
adviser, Jean-Claude Rivest, and Diane Wilhelmy, a provincial civil
servant in the Intergovernmental Affairs department. "They were
very nervous throughout the whole process. On the one hand, they
didn't tell us to stop, but on the other hand they weren't saying yes.
Because recall they were saying [publicly]: No changes to the Meech
Lake Accord," says Spector. "It was really pretty much our assessment
of how much flexibility there might be in the Québec position." "We
were making very certain that we had Québec on side," maintains
Senator Murray. "I knew that there would be some problems when

the report came out, but Bourassa wasn't going to bolt. There was nothing in the Charest Report that would cause Bourassa to burn his bridges." According to Rivest, the Québec premier, like Lucien Bouchard, was particularly concerned about the idea of handing Ottawa the responsibility for *promoting* linguistic duality and had ordered experts to prepare several legal opinions on the subject.

THE REID REPORT?

Oddly enough, Québec-related issues were not the most intractable problems the committee had to deal with. The MPs had little trouble agreeing to support Frank McKenna's proposal to include in the Constitution the Canadian government's role to *promote*, and not only to *protect*, linguistic duality. "Testimony from constitutional experts," the final report explained, "is unanimous in affirming that the promotion of linguistic duality as proposed is limited to federal jurisdiction."* However, the committee was careful not to propose that the point be added explicitly, as Charest himself had contemplated. The recommendation that was to enrage Lucien Bouchard more than anything else, caused so little controversy among the members of the group that it never even reached shadow negotiators Hartt, Tassé, Maldoff and Laskin.

The mysterious quartet did, however, solve the issue of the relationship between the distinct society article and the Charter of Rights. In fact, the committee went further than the McKenna resolution, recommending "that First Ministers affirm in a Companion Resolution that the operation of the fundamental characteristic clause, recognizing the linguistic duality/distinct society, in no way impairs the effectiveness of the Charter of Rights. [. . .] That Companion Resolution should affirm that the clauses providing roles for Parliament and the provincial legislatures do not

---

* For the full text of the committee's report, known as the "Charest Report," see pp. 303–17.

accord legislative powers." Constitutionalists had already made the point; the committee wanted the first ministers to assert it even more clearly: the distinct society clause would add nothing to Québec's rights and powers. It was a step that had to be taken to get Chrétien's and Wells's support. But as Robert Bourassa would remark when the report was made public, "When an amendment is proposed to the effect that the Charter should not take into account the distinct society, or when absolutely no other power is granted, something already relatively limited is further reduced."

On Thursday, May 10, these were not the issues that caused a stalemate. Liberals and New Democrats insisted on a guarantee that, once the Meech Lake Accord was adopted — in other words, once the June 23 deadline had been successfully met — Ottawa would not drop the other issues raised in the report, especially those concerning Senate reform and aboriginal rights. In other words, the Opposition parties wanted to make sure the Companion Resolution would produce concrete results. After lengthy discussions, the parties agreed to dump the hot potato right into the premiers' laps. "Your committee recognizes," said the report, "that if the elements of the Companion Resolution we have proposed are to provide an opportunity to break the Meech Lake impasse, the question of 'certainty' will have to be addressed and unequivocally resolved."

Once agreement had been reached on this point, Jean Charest began to see the possibility of producing a unanimous report, something that had seemed quixotic a month earlier. A few last-minute manoeuvres were undertaken to bring recalcitrant MPs like Svend Robinson, Bill Rompkey and Ethel Blondin on board. Committee members also had to convince their respective caucuses. For the Liberals and New Democrats, the task was a particularly onerous one. "Occasionally you felt closer to the people in other parties [in the committee] than to people in your caucus. You'd feel you had a common cause with them because of the importance of what we were trying to achieve," says Robert Kaplan, "and that some members of our own caucus just didn't see it."

The two NDP representatives, Lorne Nystrom and Svend Robinson, presented their caucus with competing recommendations: Nystrom favoured the report; Robinson opposed it. Nystrom's proposal carried the day. "I recall that, when I left the Wellington Building [opposite Parliament Hill, where the committee had set up for business], I wondered whether I had done the right thing by signing the report," Robinson says.

So, the report was unanimous. How much credit does Charest deserve? It's difficult to say. All the members of the committee praised him. But several also point to the very active role Newfoundland MP Ross Reid played during negotiations in the final days. "Ross was an absolutely essential player for the government," says Svend Robinson. "He did a lot of the brokerage, the nitty-gritty detail work, on actual wording and that kind of thing. Charest was involved, but it was more in terms of the broader picture, trying to put the thing together." "At that stage, Ross Reid played more of a role than Charest," insists Lorne Nystrom. "Charest was more important during the public debates." "Jean had a perception of the bigger picture," Reid says. "There were clearly times when it was Nystrom, Ouellet and I, and that had to be. It was the appropriate way to do it." Maybe it should have been called the Reid Report. Charest himself might not be offended.

WHERE'S LUCIEN?

At 6:30 p.m., Tuesday, May 15, the agreement was sealed. All that remained were a few adjustments, the signatures and a six-thousand-copy printing. In French, the report, at fifteen pages long, was two pages longer than in English. "We have tried to address the problems to the best of our ability," wrote Levy and Rousseau in the introduction. "Having done so we acknowledge that, in practical terms, the solution to the present impasse is in the hands of others, and we respectfully submit the following report for consideration."

It was what Charest repeatedly called "setting the table for the first ministers." "By the end," laughs Gary Levy, "I never wanted to hear that phrase again!"

Aside from the points already mentioned, the report supported the essence of the McKenna resolution, and suggested a few additions that could be counted on to displease the government of Québec. On Senate reform, for instance, the committee recommended that, after three years, the unanimous consent rule be replaced by "a less restrictive formula," meaning the Senate could possibly be modified without Québec's consent. The committee encouraged the first ministers to recognize the aboriginal peoples and Canada's multicultural heritage "in the body of the Constitution." Finally, the report expressed the wish that the Companion Resolution provide reassurance "that the federal spending power to promote equal opportunities for the well-being of Canadians will not be impaired by the Meech Lake Accord."

When Svend Robinson left the Wellington Building, all the committee members had signed. Everything was in place for the report to be officially tabled in the House of Commons. There was just one detail. Wouldn't it be a good idea to get the approval of the minister responsible for Québec, Lucien Bouchard? But where was Lucien?

The Environment minister was in Bergen, Norway, taking part in a high-level international conference on greenhouse gas emissions. The Bergen Conference on Sustainable Development was scheduled to end on May 16, two days before the special committee was to publish its report. Did Mr. Bouchard return to Ottawa as fast as he could to keep an eye on the last-minute wheeling and dealing? No, he joined Audrey and Alexandre in Paris, where they had planned to spend the weekend. "The tabling of the Charest Committee report was scheduled for Friday, the 18th," Bouchard wrote in his autobiography. "I believed I would be back in Ottawa at the right time to find out what was happening and join with my colleagues in deciding what position we would take." It was a curious decision for a man who claimed great concern about the way things were developing and who later complained he hadn't been given the chance to "block the manoeuvre."* Well aware that the denouement was close at hand, he remained far from the heat of the action, enjoying a few days' holiday with his family. He was to return to Ottawa only after the report had already been released. Didn't he realize that in politics, to quote George MacLaren, "it's always better to be where the action is. That's why African heads of state rarely leave their countries?"

Since Bouchard refused interview requests, it is impossible to clarify further his attitude at the time. Also, there is reason not to take at face value the views of people who, having felt betrayed by Bouchard, now consider him the devil incarnate.

In the testimony I have gathered, including that of MPs who subsequently joined the Bloc Québécois, nothing would indicate that the minister for the Environment was contemplating jumping ship before leaving for Norway. In the Québec caucus's Meech Lake meeting in mid-March, he had sounded out each of the fifty-six MPs to assess the risks of resignation and to identify the caucus's weakest links. He ended the meeting with a ringing appeal for solidarity. At the national caucus meeting at Mont Tremblant in early May, he had pleaded with François Gérin not to make a scene. Then, on May 8, he'd presented a draft of the Charest Report to federal ministers from Québec. In a word, Bouchard had played his role as the minister responsible for Québec to perfection.

On the other hand, some people have let it be known that, in private, there were hints that Bouchard was becoming dissatisfied. Journalist Michel Vastel describes a long conversation he had with the Environment minister in mid-February, a conversation in which Bouchard, "speaking in the past tense, looked back on his term in Ottawa. In other words, he was making a break."** Former Mulroney speech-writer Paul Terrien relates that, at the same time, Lucien

---

* Lucien Bouchard, *On the Record* (Toronto: Stoddart, 1994), p. 318.
** Michel Vastel, *Lucien Bouchard: En attendant la suite* . . . (Outremont: Lanctôt éditeur, 1996), p. 136.

Bouchard sent him the text of a speech on the Meech Lake Accord that he was going to make in Toronto. When Terrien ventured that it sounded more like a speech by a representative of the Québec government than the words of a federal minister, Bouchard is supposed to have said something like, "You know very well I won't be a federal minister much longer — I'm heading for Québec!"

Jean Charest was startled to learn that Lucien Bouchard would be in Europe when the report was published. "It makes me nervous," he confided to MacLaren. In fact, he was so alarmed that he phoned the Prime Minister: "He can't be absent when the report is tabled! It just isn't possible! Somebody has to carry the ball. I'll give you twenty-four hours after the report has been made public. I'll work with the media for twenty-four hours. After that, I'll disappear from the scene. I don't intend to commit political suicide defending that report."

Charest's comments, as he reports them, show that he was well aware of the political damage he could suffer from the document. While he had accepted what looked like a suicide mission, he was determined to do everything in his power to reduce the risks and save his skin. But his words also show that Charest had nothing to gain from attempting to trick Lucien Bouchard about the contents of the report. On the contrary, if the minister responsible for Québec were to be his ally and "carry the ball," Charest would be safe and sound. If not, the Tory MP would have to shoulder the blame all alone. When he handed the now unwanted baby to federal minister Lowell Murray, Charest told the senator: "Lowell, let me give you a bit of advice I got when I set off on this adventure: 'Don't fuck up!'"

Many Tory MPs were worried when they were told of the report's contents in the Tuesday caucus meeting. They were so concerned that Benoît Bouchard took it upon himself to call the premier of Québec. "Mr. Bourassa, don't give in!" he implored. Bouchard considered the moment so crucial that his wife taped his side of the conversation!

Two days later, Jean Charest tabled in the House of Commons the report with which his name will be forever associated. "In the committee's opinion," he told the MPs, "a Companion Resolution which adds clauses to the Meech Lake Accord, without eliminating anything whatever, is probably the best way to resolve the constitutional dilemma."

His worst fears, however, quickly materialized. The provinces that had been dragging their feet over Meech until then saw the report as a good basis for negotiation. But Québec was up in arms. The Péquistes, to no one's surprise, tore into the document tooth and nail. Jacques Parizeau called it "insulting." Robert Bourassa himself spoke of "unacceptable demands": "We have kept our word; we would like others to do the same." Even the staid Claude Castonguay denounced the report, asserting that it "removes the content from the concept of the distinct society."

As Charest had promised, he spent a whole day, Friday, May 18, doing the rounds in the Québec media. "It was a sad day," recalls George MacLaren. "We went by taxi from one place to another. All the Québec ministers were keeping out of sight; Charest was the only target. I felt a little bit like I was his only friend."

The task completed, Charest fled to the Eastern Townships. The family had planned to spend the Victoria Day weekend visiting Michèle's parents in North Hatley. But the report pursued him.

On Friday evening, Prime Minister Mulroney called:

"Did you manage to get in touch with Lucien?"

"No, Mr. Prime Minister, we've been trying for several days, but he hasn't returned our calls."

"Try again!"

Jean Charest spent Saturday trying to get in touch with the Environment minister, who was lying low at the Canadian ambassador's residence in Paris. A storm was brewing, that much was clear. That same day, Bouchard — a federal cabinet minister — fired off a telegram to Parti Québécois workers meeting in Alma, in his home riding, to commemorate the tenth anniversary of the

1980 referendum. It was, wrote Bouchard, "another occasion to remember the openness, the pride and the generosity of the Yes vote that we fought for alongside René Lévesque and his team. René Lévesque's memory will unite us all this weekend, for it was he who led the Québécois to discover for themselves the inalienable right to decide their future for themselves." In Ottawa, the telegram had the effect of an atomic bomb. From that moment on, Charest no longer had any doubt: Lucien Bouchard was going to resign.

On Sunday, the Sherbrooke MP asked Camille Guilbault to call a meeting of all the ministers from Québec the next evening. In the end, Charest himself issued the invitations. On Monday, the Charest family returned to Ottawa. The children were screaming in the back of the car, Jean had the cellular glued to his ear while Michou was behind the wheel, fuming because the long weekend had been ruined.

As soon as he reached Parliament, Charest headed straight for Lucien Bouchard's office. Bouchard wasn't there, so Charest left a message for the Environment minister to call him. The call never came. When Pierre Blais went to Bouchard's office a little later, Bouchard had already left to announce his resignation to Paul Tellier, the clerk of the Privy Council. When Blais entered the office, he spotted the text of the letter of resignation on the computer screen: "I reject the report and I refuse to give it tacit approval with my silence. [. . .]" Blais waited. In the early evening, the Environment minister returned from meetings with Paul Tellier and Bernard Roy, a mutual friend of Bouchard's and Mulroney's. Tellier and Roy had tried in vain to dissuade Bouchard. Blais described what followed: "We went into his office, and Lucien told me he was resigning: 'They've concocted a report with Chrétien: Meech Lake is dead.' It was high drama, straight out of Racine, a Greek tragedy!"

Blais tried to change his friend's mind. "Wait until June 24 at least. Trust the Prime Minister. If things don't work out by that date, you can go your own way! If you don't wait, it'll look like you're leaving the ice because you're losing 3 to 1 after two periods!" All for naught. "I felt like I'd just lost the most important trial of my life," Blais says. His plea was interrupted at 7:25 p.m. when the Prime Minister summoned Lucien Bouchard to his residence. But even Brian Mulroney couldn't persuade his minister to stay.

That evening, the Québec ministers met at Camille Guilbault's house. The atmosphere was funereal. Benoît Bouchard was perhaps the only one who believed the other Bouchard would stay on. "Poor Benoît!" sighed his colleagues inwardly. Then Bernard Roy joined the group and brought them up to date on his unsuccessful efforts. Lucien Bouchard resigned the next day, Tuesday, May 22, 1990. "This report should not have existed. I am against it," he explained in the Commons. "And I find that I will have to leave the government with pain and with sadness."

So powerful was the shock that Prime Minister Mulroney burst into tears at that evening's Québec caucus meeting as he called upon his MPs to reaffirm their loyalty. Benoît Bouchard had to take over. Mulroney appointed him minister responsible for Québec; in the blink of an eye, his nationalist scruples had vanished.

GENTLY INTO THAT GOOD NIGHT

The next three weeks were among the most eventful in Canadian political history. No one had expected the triumphant welcome that was given to Lucien Bouchard by the Montréal Chamber of Commerce. Rumours of large-scale resignations rippled through the Conservative caucus as Brian Mulroney and Benoît Bouchard laboured feverishly behind the scenes to prevent them. The first ministers met behind closed doors for seven days, cobbling together a complex agreement aimed at rescuing Meech. Elijah Harper, a native MP from Manitoba, blocked the agreement. On June 23, 1990, the Meech Lake Accord was dead. Québec premier Robert Bourassa responded with a declaration that fanned nationalist sentiments across Québec: "Let them say, let them do what they will, Québec is, and will always be, a distinct society, free and capable of shouldering its own destiny and its own development." The next day, one million people took to the streets in the annual Saint-Jean Baptiste Day parade marking Québec's national holiday.

The hero of this story, however, was nowhere to be seen during those eventful days. It must not be forgotten, of course, that Jean Charest was only an MP — the key decisions were being made at a much higher level. But if Charest was withdrawing from the battle, he had his own reasons — personal and political — for doing so. He was crushed by Lucien Bouchard's attitude toward him. "Out of basic decency, he should have looked me straight in the eye and told me what he intended to do," Charest says seven years later. "After all, he asked me to take on the job!" And he was concerned as well about the political price to be paid for carrying out the Prime Minister's mission. Lucien Bouchard's resignation had the potential to touch off a fire storm of nationalism that could burn Charest badly.

Perhaps that possibility was troubling Charest on the evening of June 9, 1990, following the signing ceremony attended by Canada's eleven first ministers. Senator Lowell Murray was getting into his car when he saw Jean Charest walking by himself, an expression of concern on his face. "He certainly didn't look like a very happy man. He looked almost dejected. I yelled at him and called him over to the car and shook his hand and told him how important his role had been," recalls Murray. "He was not in a ecstatic frame of mind. I think he felt that he might be the fall guy if the deal didn't go through."

"CHRÉTIEN'S LITTLE PILE OF SHIT"

These were the words Lucien Bouchard used to describe the Charest Committee's report.* What charges did the resigning minister lay

---

* Michel Vastel, *Lucien Bouchard: En attendant la suite . . .* (Outremont: Lanctôt éditeur, 1996), p. 149.

against his former colleague, the member for Sherbrooke?

First, Charest had kept his colleague badly informed about what was going on. "I had reason to believe," wrote Bouchard, "that [the committee] would not propose any modifications affecting the substance of the accord. In fact, two or three weeks earlier, toward the end of April, as I was observing the debate in the Commons, Jean Charest came and sat beside me. From what I recall of the conversation, the committee would make propositions in keeping with the essential propositions of Meech, but some concession would have to be made concerning Aboriginals, as there was considerable pressure from that side. In short, things seemed to be going rather well."*

Second, many of the recommendations of the Charest Committee had changed "the essence of the accord itself." The distinct nature of Québec society had been "trivialized" and "weakened."

Third, Charest had "secretly concocted" the weakening of the accord with Jean Chrétien.

The first charge. In his autobiography, Lucien Bouchard mentions a conversation with Charest about the draft report. According to Bouchard, the conversation took place in the Commons on April 27. Charest's notes show that Bouchard was handed a copy of the draft report one week later and that the two men discussed the document in the Commons on May 7. "L. Bouchard satisfied with project," reads Charest's diary. Furthermore, Robert Charest, Lucien Bouchard's political aide, kept the minister informed of developments on a daily basis. All that remains is to ascertain whether the Environment minister was given accurate and complete information. Lacking evidence to the contrary, there is every reason to believe that he was.

Most of the key players in the drama, including a number of Bloc Québécois supporters, feel the Charest Report was little more than a "pretext" for the minister's resignation, which had been precipi-

---

* Lucien Bouchard, *On the Record* (Toronto: Stoddart, 1994), p. 309.

tated by a set of frustrating circumstances brought to a head by a conflict with Prime Minister Mulroney's new chief of staff, Stanley Hartt. Luc Lavoie, who was close to both Lucien Bouchard and Brian Mulroney, had observed the face-off from the front-row seats: "I'm not alone in believing that Stanley Hartt was the reason Lucien left." The Charest Report, says Lavoie, was just the straw that broke the camel's back.

On the substance of the second charge, no one can deny that the Charest Report proposed changes to the Meech Lake Accord to win the consent of those who opposed it, Jean Chrétien included. But were these changes major or minor? The question becomes one of interpretation, which depends in turn on ideological considerations. The tabling of the Charest Report did not mean game over. Final decisions were not going to be made by the Charest Committee, but by the first ministers themselves. "The game's score would be decided by Bourassa and Mulroney," points out Senator Jean-Claude Rivest, then chief adviser to the Québec premier. "Charest could write whatever he wanted in the report, I was the prime minister!" says Mr. Mulroney. In fact, the eleventh-hour agreement hammered out by the first ministers in June, though it kept some of the Charest Committee's suggestions, rejected others, especially the controversial article on the promotion of linguistic duality. "If there had never been a Charest Report, it would have changed nothing. Trudeau would have kept right on putting on the pressure, the native peoples too . . ." says Mr. Rivest.

The heart of the matter would seem to be this: once the Charest Committee had been set up to study the McKenna resolution, was it not inevitable that the committee suggest additions to the Meech Lake Accord? What did Lucien Bouchard hope would happen? Did he imagine that Jean Charest, having agreed to chair the committee — "An instrument of dialogue," in Bouchard's words — would forbid any changes or additions to Meech? If so, why set up a committee in the first place?

The third charge — that Jean Charest was conducting secret

negotiations with Jean Chrétien — is overstated. The chairman was not involved in direct negotiations with Chrétien, and played a relatively secondary role in the affair. Certainly Charest sought the agreement of the three parties represented on the committee, including the Liberal party, and it was obvious that André Ouellet and Robert Kaplan would never sign a document without Chrétien's approval. Lucien Bouchard should have understood this as well as Charest from the moment the committee was set up.

Jean Charest took the crucial step when he agreed to chair the committee, not while drafting the report. Need it be added that Lucien Bouchard was particularly ill placed to criticize Charest for taking this step? Bouchard was absent, and refused to talk to his friend in the final stages of the process. In so doing, he left the door open for a compromise, which he was in a much better position to thwart than Charest because of his personal influence with the Prime Minister. Lucien Bouchard, the Québécois, played his cards badly. Jean Charest, the Canadian, obediently played the cards Bouchard and Mulroney had dealt him.

WHAT'S LEFT?

Ottawa, November 1994. The Charests were among the dinner guests at the home of *Globe and Mail* reporter Susan Delacourt. But no one was in a party mood. A few hours earlier, Québec had been shocked to learn that Bloc Québécois leader Lucien Bouchard had been hospitalized, stricken by terrible flesh-eating bacteria. Just back from the CBC studio, Chantal Hébert of *La Presse* reported an even more frightening rumour: Bouchard might soon succumb to the disease.

When he heard the news, Jean Charest got up and leaned against the wall. Exactly what happened then depends on who you talk to. Some say that Charest, then the Conservative leader, began to bang his head softly against the wall. When Ms. Delacourt asked Charest if he was all right, he is alleged to have mentioned his mixed feelings about Lucien Bouchard, the former friend who had become his political adversary. Charest then supposedly voiced regret that he wouldn't have the chance to take revenge if the Bloc leader died. Some cite the episode as proof that, after Meech, Charest and Bouchard had developed nothing less than hatred for one another. According to *Globe and Mail* reporter Rhéal Séguin, the animosity between the two men "is visceral, matched only by a profound desire for mutual revenge."*

Guessing what a man as secretive as Jean Charest might be thinking is difficult at the best of times; plumbing his emotions is impossible. Charest makes no secret of the fact that he was deeply hurt by Bouchard's attitude during the Meech negotiations. Resigning at such a critical moment went against Charest's principles. That was bad enough. But accusing Charest of deceiving him was an outright insult. Doing it all without so much as speaking to Charest face to face was a betrayal of friendship, something that cannot be forgiven: "I never took seriously or accepted his accusations . . . If he thought that, if he really believed that, I don't know why he never had the courage to say it to my face! It was hard to take, very hard. Not only did he take a position with which I disagreed, but the way he did it revealed a side of Lucien Bouchard I had never seen before."

True, Jean Charest's public remarks about Bouchard have been particularly virulent. But to speak of hatred and a thirst for vengeance might be an exaggeration. It is unlikely that Charest either hates Bouchard or seeks revenge. Back to Susan Delacourt's November 1994 dinner party: Chantal Hébert does not remember seeing Jean Charest bang his head against the wall. She certainly does not recall him saying that Bouchard's death might deprive him of an opportunity for revenge. The Tory leader's feelings were probably ambivalent ones. According to Hébert, Charest said,

---

* *The Globe and Mail*, March 28, 1998, p. D1.

"There are two Lucien Bouchards," to which Chantal Hébert replied, "There are also two Jean Charests." And Michèle Dionne chimed in, "She's right."

"We were all in a state of shock," Charest says, "but I didn't bang my head against the wall. That's not the way I am." As for his alleged hatred of Lucien Bouchard, he claims, "It's not in my nature to stoop to hating anyone. I don't have the time. I'm not made that way. Sure, I felt let down [after Bouchard's resignation], but I didn't feel any hatred or any profound animosity. I didn't like it, I was disappointed, I was angry with him for doing it, but I said to myself, 'What goes around comes round. We'll meet up again one day.' I never had it in mind to get even with Lucien Bouchard."

Loyalty is one of the fundamental values in Jean Charest's philosophy. Few things hurt him more than betrayal and humiliation. He can bear a grudge. But Charest does not allow himself to be ruled by his emotions; in fact, he makes every effort to keep them under tight control. Bitterness, with him, is not forever. Few things hurt him more than his friend Pierre Blais's refusal to support him in the Tory leadership race in 1993. But today Charest and his former colleague are on good terms.

On the subject of Charest's feelings, Pierre Blais describes an encounter of his own with Lucien Bouchard, eight years after the split. "It was very cordial. He asked me about my children. I had the impression he was glad to see me . . . And I can tell you I was glad to see him. Listen, this guy had come to our house for dinner. His wife and mine had been very close." In other words, over and above the vicissitudes of political life, friendship and respect can prevent bitterness from turning into hatred. "Someone really has to give you a low blow for you to hate him for the rest of your life!" says Blais. In the same breath, however, he likens Bouchard's attitude toward Charest over Meech to a swimmer "who would step right on someone else's head to get out of the water."

Hatred or no, feelings of hurt and resentment remain. "Certainly, Jean took Lucien's departure very hard, very personally," says Gabriel

Desjardins, who was a member of the special committee on Meech. "It was very profound and deep-rooted." How deep-rooted, really? George MacLaren is a longtime friend of Bouchard's, Mulroney's and Charest's. He set up the first meeting between the Sherbrooke MP and Bouchard, in 1988, in a downtown Montréal restaurant over *steak pommes frites*. "Jean Charest sees Lucien Bouchard as a political adversary, but he has nothing against him personally," MacLaren insists. "He was upset with Bouchard, and he would like to beat him [in the next provincial elections]. But waging a personal vendetta against him? I don't think he has the time."

When Brian Mulroney talks about Lucien Bouchard, the anger and the scorn are palpable. "There are so many myths about Bouchard — he's a balloon that's about to lose its air," he's been heard to say in private. Comparing hurts, Mulroney's was far more serious than Charest's. Brian Mulroney had known Lucien Bouchard since their university days. The friendship they lost was much older, much deeper. Jean Charest had known Bouchard for less than two years when the split over Meech occurred. Theirs was more a working relationship than an intimate friendship.

Politics changes people. PR consultant Luc Lavoie, a mutual friend of both men, believes that the animosity between the two developed out of political disagreement. Forced to face off in the political arena in a kind of "mortal combat," the two men might well end up hating one another. Says George MacLaren, "If that's what people want, that's what they'll get: two gladiators fighting to the finish."

At the Summit

—ɯ—

It was the kind of toast that caught people's attention.

Daniel Green was riding high. In 1991, *Affaires* + magazine had dubbed Québec's best-known environmental activist "the man who cuts corporations down to size." His attacks on government policy could just as easily have earned him the sobriquet "the man who cuts cabinet ministers down to size." In June 1992, hard on the conclusion of the Earth Summit in Rio de Janeiro, this same Daniel Green invited the assembled guests at a reception hosted by the Government of Canada to raise their glasses to the Environment minister, Jean Charest. "When I met the senior bureaucrats in the department," said Green a few years later, "they told me the new minister was very good. But I thought, 'So what?' Then I saw him at work in Rio, from six in the morning to midnight, and I knew they were right."

Three events have shaped the public's perception of Jean Charest the politician: the 1995 referendum campaign and the 1993 Tory leadership race, of course — but it was the Rio Summit in 1992 that saw his emergence as a political figure of substance, capable of handling complex issues, bringing honour to Canada at the international level, reconciling widely divergent interests and even charming hard-bitten journalists. And he was still two weeks shy of his thirty-fourth birthday.

Charest had been named Environment minister on April 21, 1991. At the same time, the Prime Minister had appointed him to the cabinet's powerful Priorities and Planning Committee, the P and P. Brian Mulroney had kept the promise he'd made Red a year and a half earlier.

"Today," explains Brian Mulroney, "the environment is a dead issue in Ottawa. But back then, Environment was one of the most important departments." With ill-concealed pride, Mulroney recounts the swearing-in ceremony that signalled the end of Jean Charest's sojourn in purgatory. "Charest was there with his family. After the ceremony, Red told me, 'You're a man of your word, all right. I call that starting right at the top.'"

When Mulroney handed Jean Charest the Environment assignment, the time was ripe. It had been Lucien Bouchard's portfolio until his sensational resignation in 1990. Bouchard had conceived and convinced the cabinet to adopt a wide-ranging environmental agenda called the Green Plan. The five-year, $3-billion program consisted of scores of research, pollution-abatement and public awareness projects. When Bouchard bolted from the Tories to found the Bloc Québécois, Brian Mulroney named as his replacement Robert René de Cotret, a respected economist. But far from fulfilling his potential and becoming the standout many people had expected him to be, de Cotret slipped quickly into insignificance. In fact, most people felt that his term at Environment was an outright disaster. At a press conference in Toronto to announce the first Green Plan initiative, a Great Lakes clean-up program, Greenpeace protesters badgered him so persistently that he finally exploded and called environmentalist Gordon Perks a "son of a bitch."

The Green Plan was quietly shelved until a better salesman could be found. Environment Canada bureaucrats looked forward to working with the new minister. "Charest was the perfect person to sell this stuff!" says Len Good, who was deputy minister at the time. And the Green Plan suited Charest to a T. "The plan included a large number of initiatives, so that he was in a position to go to the public with initiatives on a regular basis over the next two years, which of course is a minister's dream!"

"We were making a new announcement almost every two weeks," says Philippe Morel, Charest's chief of staff at Environment.

True to form, Jean Charest wasted not a moment and began boning up on his new assignment. He contacted childhood friend Robert Dubé, a biologist by training and the director-general of the Fondation québécoise de l'environnement (The Québec Environment Foundation). "He read the thick files the bureaucrats had prepared for him. Then he asked me questions about CO_2 and such-like," relates Dubé. "Even I couldn't always remember all those concentrations and figures. In press conferences, he would trot this stuff out as if he'd known it all his life."

Charest's greatest strength is his brain's sponge-like capacity to absorb a phenomenal amount of information in record time and spill it when needed, coherently and with conviction. Sly tongues wonder whether this is proof of a phenomenal *intelligence* or of a phenomenal *memory*. Undeniably, Charest has the memory. But true intelligence involves more than recording information; it entails understanding that information, combining it with other information and using it to solve problems and to devise new ideas. A law student might know the Civil Code by heart and never become a brilliant lawyer. "Charest can pick up a thick file, read it once and make a speech on the subject. He and Fidel Castro ought to hold a speech-making contest!" quips businessman Dennis Wood, the Sherbrooke MP's one-time Liberal opponent. Memory or intelligence? Image or content? Department bureaucrats, more than Charest loyalists, have the answer — and the civil servants who worked under Charest are convinced their minister was far more than a particularly gifted parrot.

It was not long before Environment Canada officials soon fell under their new boss's spell. "It took about a month," Len Good swears, "before he had the whole department saying: 'This is the most wonderful minister we've ever had.'" Unlike Lucien Bouchard, who was brilliant but cold to his civil servants, Jean Charest made his departmental staff feel as though they were all part of a team. Whenever he met a group of employees, he would introduce himself with a dig at his deputy minister: "Hi! I'm Jean Charest and I work for Len."

"He used this line many, many times and it always worked," laughs Len Good. "They would all crack up, and he would have them in his pocket, just like that!"

The Green Plan presented Charest with two challenges: to persuade the cabinet to approve financing for each initiative, and to ensure that the steady stream of plan-related announcements put the government in a good light, despite the breast-beating of the environmental groups. The minister had learned from his experience at Youth how to prepare the ground before cabinet meetings. "He was extraordinarily good with his colleagues in cabinet," says Len Good. In cabinet, Charest was on top of his files, confident and firm, but always calm and respectful of other ministers' opinions. The contrast with Lucien Bouchard was striking. "Bouchard didn't think it was very important to win the agreement of the people around the table," former minister Pierre Blais explains. "He seemed to be thinking, 'If it stalls somewhere, all I have to do is make a phone call [to the Prime Minister] and the problem will be solved.' Jean took the trouble to convince his colleagues."

Charest quickly learned that throwing millions of dollars around wasn't enough to appease the tree-huggers. His first announcement, $100 million to protect the environment in the far north, was lambasted by militant environmentalists. The freshman Environment minister couldn't believe his ears. "I had to fight in cabinet to get the $100 million. Then I turned on the TV and heard the ecologists calling it ridiculous. I couldn't get over it!" In cabinet the next day, colleague Jake Epp didn't miss the chance to tease him about it. "Good work, Jean. Let me get this straight: we just spent $100 million and, listening to the news last night, we're a bunch of . . . ?"

The Environment minister handed Robert Dubé the task of setting up briefing sessions with the key players before each Green Plan press conference. Charest might not have won the environmentalists' unconditional support, but at least he won their respect. When Gordon Perks, the Greenpeace activist who had goaded de Cotret into blowing his stack, tried to disrupt one of Charest's conferences, the minister defused the situation by offering Perks the mike. "If you've got something to say, come up and say it on the stand!" This was the approach that earned him such success at the Earth Summit, the United Nations Convention on Biological Diversity, an immense political and media happening attended by close to one hundred heads of state.

VOYAGE TO THE EARTH SUMMIT

The "Charest effect" was in full evidence in Rio. Charest charmed the socks off everyone, from Daniel Green to Bill Reilly, director of the U.S. Environmental Protection Agency, and Liberal environment critic Paul Martin. Every morning, the minister briefed the Canadian delegation on negotiations and fielded questions. At noon, he met with representatives of non-governmental organizations (NGOs). "For three hours, he fielded questions about the conference and about all the various issues," recalls Christian Simard, then president of the Union québécoise pour la conservation de la nature, an environmentalist group. "He stood alone in front, trading views with specialists from the various organizations — lawyers, environmentalists and toxicologists from all over Canada. And he didn't miss a beat." Len Good was impressed with the minister's performance. "I'd never seen that before!" he says. "You had every Canadian at that conference saying: 'I know Canada's strategy, and even though I might not agree with this or that part of it, the fact that I was part of that meeting this morning and had the strategy explained to me is enough to make me a supporter.' So, you've got all supporters, whereas if you don't have that kind of a meeting, you could have some Canadians running around and saying 'I disagree with this.' There's no consensus."

Brian Mulroney, who arrived in Rio a few days after the opening of the conference, was proud as a peacock of what his protégé had accomplished. "He did an extraordinary job. And I had comments from Mitterand and Bush: 'My people tell me that your Environment minister is an exceptional young man.' It was obvious he had made quite a breakthrough. When I got there, I could see how skilfully he handled himself at the international level."

At the Rio Earth Summit, Canada announced that, unlike the United States, it would sign the United Nations Convention on Biodiversity. Canada was also a signatory to the United Nations Framework Convention on Climate Change, undertaking to reduce its greenhouse gas emissions to 1990 levels by the year 2000. Finally, to everyone's astonishment, Jean Charest announced that Canada would boost foreign aid to 0.7 percent of its GNP, which meant additional expenditures of $1.7 billion.

The Canadian government presented itself as a world leader on environmental issues. In fact, it was only joining an already widespread movement; in Rio, nations were vying for the title of "greenest." Ninety-eight nations had already approved the Treaty on Biodiversity before Canada declared its intention to sign it. Canada's commitment to reduce greenhouse emissions matched the policies already adopted by many European countries. Many of the nations attending the conference made similar announcements about foreign aid.

Canada's promises in Rio enhanced its image — but were they really anything more than a public relations exercise? Charest himself admitted that he did not know how Canada would meet its greenhouse gas objective. "We knew we didn't have a plan," he explains. "Nor did any of the other countries. They all said, 'First we have to take an inventory. Then we'll have to make a plan.' That must have been in 1993. Then came the elections and things changed." "The contention was that we would be able to get there by increasing the efficiency of energy usage," insists Bob Slater, the senior civil servant in charge of the Rio Summit for Environment Canada. "There was a sense at that time that people knew what it was that needed to be done. But did we have all of the instruments in place to get there? No, we didn't."

Today, it is clear that Canada will not attain its objective. In 1997, greenhouse emission levels exceeded the 1990 figure by 13 percent. Jean Charest blames the Liberal government. Would the situation have been different had the Tories been returned to power in 1993? Not likely. As the economy deteriorated in the mid-1990s, the environment lost its sparkle. And governments, whatever their hue, made deficit reduction and economic growth their priorities. The words "sustainable development," on everybody's lips in 1992, were hardly being uttered two or three years later.

If the commitment to greenhouse gas emission reductions was ambitious, to say the least, the promise to raise Canada's foreign aid contribution to 0.7 percent of GNP was simply preposterous. True, Charest had taken care not to set a date. As promises go, it was not too compromising. In fact, it was hardly credible, as the Mulroney government had singled out foreign aid as one of its main budget-cutting targets. The decision to make such an extraordinary announcement had been made over Charest's head, by Prime Minister Mulroney and his representative in the Rio negotiations, Arthur Campeau. The commitment, Campeau says, was designed to protect foreign aid against future cuts. In cabinet discussions to pinpoint where savings could be made, it would be important to remind ministers that foreign aid could not be drastically reduced because Canada had publicly committed itself to a target figure. A vain hope; from $2.515 billion in 1992, Canada's foreign aid dropped to $2.4 billion the following year.

CHAREST IN YOUR LIVING ROOM

Jean Charest worked hard in Rio. Though negotiations had already been under way for several months, they were not quite completed. Discussions continued night and day. Charest and Prime Minister Mulroney had the last word on the Canadian position. Charest also spent a good deal of time making sure that the government would get as much political capital as possible out of the conference. Enter David Small and his satellite dish. Environment Canada had hired Small to manage communications for the Canadian delegation. The same age as Charest, he was already considered a seasoned political organizer. In 1983, when he was only twenty-four years old, he had played a key role in organizing the defence of Joe Clark's leadership against the assault of the Mulroneyites. He and Charest met in 1990, when Small had been hired to handle press relations for the Parliamentary Committee on the Meech Lake Accord.

Small wanted more than the coverage provided by the national media that could afford to send reporters to the Earth Summit. He rented a portable satellite dish, which enabled him to offer interviews with the Environment minister to local television stations in Canada. The aim was "to get Jean Charest in the living room of every household in the country. He was on the six o'clock supper newscast from one end of the country to the other, live," Small explains. At the end of every afternoon, the minister went up to the roof of a hotel in Rio. "The background was beautiful, with the palm trees and all," says Small. "And we would just do interviews — *bam, bam, bam!* The stations just wanted more!"

Some people believe to this day that Charest was one of the big stars of the Earth Summit. True enough, from a Canadian standpoint. But in international terms, hardly. *The New York Times*, for example, mentioned his name not one single time during those weeks in June 1992. A *Times* story on the outstanding figures of the conference listed the Environment ministers of Germany, India, Singapore and Malaysia. Anyone remember Lian Ting?

BACK TO EARTH

The Environment portfolio gave Jean Charest an undreamed of opportunity to put his 1990 blunder behind him and gain the stature that only international exposure could provide. He also plunged once more into the murky waters of the Canadian Constitution. No longer was it a matter of principles and constitutional theory, as had been the case a year earlier with the McKenna resolution committee. Charest now found himself dealing with something concrete. In fact, he was up to his hips in cement.

At the time, Québec premier Robert Bourassa was dreaming of a second James Bay project, a $22-billion hydro-electric development on the Great Whale River. The native peoples of northern Québec wanted nothing to do with the project and had won the support of Canadian and foreign environmentalists. To get work under way as soon as possible, the Québec government had decided to speed up environmental impact studies by splitting the project in two, dealing first with the access roads to the site, then the hydro-electric plant itself. As road construction posed no particular environmental problems, it could get under way relatively quickly, without waiting for environmental impact studies on the dams.

Ottawa believed it had a say in the project, given that the protection of certain fish and bird species fell under its jurisdiction. Two Supreme Court decisions on similar projects had reminded the Canadian government of its obligations. From a legal and political standpoint, Jean Charest felt he had no choice but to set up a commission to study the ecological consequences of Great Whale. The work of such a commission could well last two years, and in

Charest's mind there was no question of studying the two parts of the project separately.

Aware of the support Great Whale enjoyed among employers and unions — Québec was in a deep recession — Brian Mulroney instructed his young minister to explain the federal decision to premier Robert Bourassa. For someone who aspired to the highest office, it was a unique opportunity to rub elbows with the very embodiment of the politician's craft. "It was fascinating," recalls Charest.

On the evening of July 9, 1991, the premier of Québec awaited the federal minister in his office in Complex J in Québec City, known as "the Bunker." Charest was struck by the informal atmosphere, in marked contrast to the protocol-ridden PMO. Bourassa took off his jacket and loosened his tie as he always did when he was off camera. It was late in the evening, and milk had given way to wine. Charest, who had come armed with the latest issue of *Time* magazine, pointed to a two-page spread on Bourassa's pet project. "The world's most extensive hydro-power project has already disrupted rivers, wildlife and the traditions of Québec's Indians. Is it really needed?" blared the headline. Intensive Cree lobbying efforts in the United States were showing results. "I don't think the Québec government really understood what was happening in the United States," Charest maintains. Ottawa was convinced that a complete environmental assessment, involving all the parties concerned, was the best way to defuse the Cree campaign.

"You see that?" said Charest, pointing to the magazine cover.

"Well . . . you know, Jean, there's no point worrying about things like that . . ." And Bourassa related to Jean Charest how, in the 1970s, he had overcome the Cree and Inuit resistance to build the James Bay project.

"It's a story I didn't know much about," Charest admits. Small wonder; in 1970, Charest was twelve years old. "What he told me essentially was that he was ready to do the same thing," recalls Charest. "It was a bit like bulldozing. Except that times had changed."

The future would prove the younger politician right, and Great Whale would be shelved. But at the time, it was the premier's baby, the linchpin of his government's economic strategy. The meeting was cordial; neither Bourassa nor Charest was given to banging his fist on the table. When the federal minister left the meeting, however, he knew that his decision would touch off a strong reaction in Québec. "[Charest] had to have a whale of a lot of courage," says Michel Dorais, a top federal bureaucrat. "Things were far from clear, and in the end he found himself quite alone." The next morning, Jean Charest announced the federal government's decision at a press conference in Montréal. "When he stood up in front of the eighty or so people attending the press conference, he wasn't any too sure of himself, and neither was I," Dorais says.

The Québec government's reaction was strong indeed. "We will not submit to the directives or procedures of a federal commission," Energy Minister Lise Bacon declared. "There was no necessity for him to go about it like that. It's nothing but another useless constitutional quarrel," protested Richard Le Hir, the head of the Québec Manufacturers' Association. But the environmentalists were jubilant. "Ottawa had no choice. It had to go ahead," said David Cliche, a future PQ minister. "It is clear that the project falls under Québec's jurisdiction, but it is my duty to do an assessment of all aspects under federal jurisdiction," the federal Environment minister insisted.

By taking a hard line — and by taking the heat — Charest would force Québec to be more reasonable. Three months later, the two governments agreed to harmonize their environmental assessment processes for Great Whale. "Thanks to him," says Michel Dorais, "everyone fell into line: the native peoples, Québec, Hydro-Québec. Everyone said, 'Okay, we'll stop fighting in the courts and we'll do the damned assessment!'"

FOLLOWING IN LUCIEN'S FOOTSTEPS

Hard on the heels of the decision, Ottawa tried to put its environmental assessment process in order. When and how should a project be the subject of a federal study? The decree governing the issue — the *Environmental Assessment Guidelines Order* — was being challenged in court, and no one was capable of interpreting it.

In 1990, Environment minister Lucien Bouchard had introduced legislation to clean up the mess — Bill C-78 — but the government had let it die on the order paper. When Jean Charest took over, he introduced what was essentially the same legislation. Bill C-13 called for the federal government to carry out an environmental assessment of all projects it promoted, issued permits for or funded. If the project was to undergo a provincial environmental assessment, C-13 enabled a joint evaluation process, providing it conformed to the conditions laid down by Ottawa.

Québec opposed the rehashed federal bill as vehemently as it had rejected the original bill. But its opposition was distinctly low key, and the issue got little media coverage until March 1992. The House of Commons was about to adopt the bill when Québec Environment minister Pierre Paradis tore into it in the National Assembly: "Everything in the industrial and commercial fields will be blocked by this federal government intrusion into matters that are strictly a matter of provincial jurisdiction!" The remarks, from an MNA known for his unshakable faith in federalism, did more than raise eyebrows. Paradis's outburst could only hurt the federal government's image in Québec. "The fact that Québec disagreed wasn't surprising, but the virulence was," says Michel Dorais.

What had piqued the Québec government? A few days earlier, when he met with Charest, Pierre Paradis believed he had understood that Bill C-13 would not be passed any day soon. Suddenly, it was about to become law in two or three days. "Pierre has always maintained that I sent him the wrong signals," Jean Charest said a few years later. "I don't think so, but it could be. In the brouhaha, sometimes you think you've said things a certain way. I don't know . . ." The day after his tirade, Paradis stepped up the attack. "Someone has to wake up in Ottawa to stop this bill that rides roughshod over Québec's jurisdiction from being bulldozed into law."

Much more than provincial jurisdiction over the environment was at stake, however. At issue was Great Whale, and the underlying fear that the new federal process would jeopardize Robert Bourassa's pet project. "Politically, that's what was stirring up the government people," says André Trudeau, who was Pierre Paradis's deputy minister at the time. "Besides, the government of Québec was already committed to environmental assessment. So why would Ottawa want to invade this area of jurisdiction? But behind it all, what really was at stake, what really drove us to the barricades, was Great Whale."

In a virtually unprecedented move, Mr. Paradis appeared before the Senate committee examining the bill. Sounding like Jacques Parizeau, he spoke of a "domineering and totalitarian" process and of "enforced uniformity." But he did manage to win over Conservative senators from Québec, who hoped their government would wait until the fall before adopting C-13. Appearing the next day before the same committee, Jean Charest was unable to convince senators who were lukewarm about the bill, including constitutionalist Gérald Beaudoin, former Liberal cabinet minister Thérèse Lavoie-Roux and former senior provincial bureaucrat Roch Bolduc. "I've been a deputy minister for long enough to understand what was behind it all," said Bolduc. "The federal bureaucrats are simply attempting to expand their jurisdiction as far as they can at the expense of the provinces, without a thought about the mess they are creating."

BAD TIMING

The bitter dispute between Québec and Ottawa could not have come at a worse time: Canada was in the thick of a new round of constitutional talks. The country's first ministers had concluded the

Charlottetown Accord, designed to repair the damage caused by the Meech debacle. Taken up with his own department, Jean Charest had no involvement in the talks themselves. But out of loyalty to the PM, he flung himself with his customary zeal into the campaign leading up to the October 30, 1992, referendum on the agreement. The national media took little interest in his speeches, as Yes side blunders (the lack of a formal text, the intercepted telephone conversation between two Québec civil servants, etc.) monopolized the spotlight.

Federal strategists showed how highly they regarded Charest's talents, however, when they floated the idea of a debate between Bloc leader Lucien Bouchard and the young Tory in a last-ditch effort to save the Yes campaign. Bouchard refused to square off with someone who had not played a leading role in the Charlottetown negotiations. But there could be little doubt that one day the two best debaters in the country, the two sides of the Québec mirror (to use the expression political scientist Gérard Bergeron applied to Trudeau and Lévesque),* would meet.

QED?

Some say Jean Charest's environment policy decisions point to a penchant for centralizing. The penchant might have been in evidence when he was the minister for Youth, but his tour of duty at Environ-ment proved inconclusive.

The British North America Act of 1867 is mute on the environment. Is it a federal or a provincial concern? According to constitutionalist Gérard Beaudoin, it is both. "Environmental protection cannot, in our opinion, constitute one subject under one authority in Canada. It is, on the contrary, an aggregate of matters without the necessary uniqueness and specificity to assume a single shape. It

---

*   Gérard Bergeron, *Notre miroir à deux faces* (Montréal: Québec/Amérique, 1985).

is diffuse; it touches on many areas of activity. In a federal regime like ours, it must be shared."* Clearly a grey zone exists. Therefore, the legislators must "show dexterity in drafting legislation," writes Senator Beaudoin.** Unfortunately, where dexterity was required, the Canadian Environmental Assessment Act was all thumbs. First, the legislation gave Ottawa the right not only to assess the environmental impact of the project but also to evaluate its raison d'être. At Great Whale, the new law would have authorized the federal government to rule on the advisability of Québec's building new hydro-electric installations, an area that was simply none of Ottawa's business. The legislation might also have been more considerate of provincial processes already in place. Says Michel Yergeau, a Québec environmental law expert: "Harmonizing the federal and Québec processes wasn't possible, because Ottawa took the position that 'we're prepared to harmonize, providing Québec changes its law.' But Québec's own environmental assessment legislation dated back to 1978!"

True, the provincial mechanisms were not always up to the task. Québec might boast that it was in the vanguard of environmental protection, but at the time it carried out no environmental assessment of major industrial projects. "We evaluated marinas, but not aluminum plants," ecologist Christian Simard points out. For the Great Whale project, Québec was apparently ready to ride roughshod over the concerns of environmentalists and native peoples. Québec environmental groups, such as the Union québécoise pour la conservation de la nature, headed by Simard, a longtime sovereigntist, were of two minds about Bill C-13, while everywhere else in the country, the "greens" pleaded with Ottawa not to give an inch.

In short, the federal initiative was praiseworthy from an environmental standpoint. Michel Yergeau called it "a very good law." It

---

*   Gérald Beaudoin, *Le Partage des pouvoirs*, 3rd ed. (Ottawa: Éditions de l'Université d'Ottawa, 1983), pp. 483–84.
**   Ibid., p. 493.

was for a good cause; who can blame Jean Charest for offending Québec sensibilities?

Meanwhile, court decisions — especially in the Supreme Court — about a dam project in Alberta had left the federal government little choice. "Fundamentally, the mechanism was established by the Supreme Court, not Jean Charest's law," adds Yergeau. "The Supreme Court was much guiltier of encroachment [in provincial jurisdiction] than Charest."

Finally, if the Great Whale and Bill C-13 controversies reveal in Charest a centralizing tendency, what is to be made of Lucien Bouchard, who had taken precisely the same position two years earlier? In his autobiography, Bouchard speaks of "an interventionist policy which the judiciary had compelled the department to adopt. [. . .] No one can argue with the fact that Ottawa has an obligation to assess . . . the consequences of the release of mercury into the waters which was triggered by the flooding of the land. This also applies to the impact of ecological changes on the marine mammals of Hudson Bay."

"A sovereign Québec should come to some agreement with its American and Canadian neighbours on the assessment and mitigation of the impact of such projects," Bouchard added, referring to Great Whale.* Was this proof of a centralizing reflex, or was it a legitimate exercise of the Canadian government's authority?

Politicians cannot help but be influenced by the culture of the government they serve. Parliamentarians in Ottawa tend to view issues from a federal perspective — but move them to Québec and they gradually view the same issues from a provincial perspective. Jean Lesage is a case in point. He made the leap to provincial politics in 1958 after labouring in Ottawa for thirteen years. Critics labelled him a centralizing federalist, but that didn't stop him from becoming the father of the Quiet Revolution and a fierce defender of Québec's jurisdictions.

---

* Lucien Bouchard, *On the Record* (Toronto: Stoddart, 1994), p. 214.

A BIRD IN THE HAND IS WORTH TWO IN THE BUSH

Bill Reilly, former head of the United States Environmental Protection Agency, vividly recalls a conversation with Jean Charest during negotiations concerning the North American Free Trade Agreement (NAFTA). NAFTA was then a hot issue in the United States. Among its most resolute adversaries were environmental groups that feared the agreement would reduce American environmental norms to the level of Mexican laissez-faire standards. The White House was convinced that it needed at least some support from the green movement to steer the treaty through Congress, hence Bill Reilly's active role in the negotiations. Reilly says that as he and Charest were wrapping up their discussion, the Environment minister chuckled, "Well, fundamentally, I'm very grateful to you for telling me what Canada's position is. They won't let me in on it here! I have no idea!" It was clear that the minister had less clout with Canadian negotiators than Reilly had with their American counterparts.

In the end, the 1993 treaty dealt more thoroughly with environmental issues than had any previous trade agreement. But this was due much more to pressure from American environmentalists than to Jean Charest's influence. The preamble of the treaty commits the governments of the United States, Canada and Mexico to act "in a manner consistent with environmental protection and conservation" and to "promote sustainable development." Article 1114 stipulates that "it is inappropriate to encourage investment by relaxing domestic health, safety or environmental protections." The three signatories would also conclude a parallel agreement, the North American Agreement on Environmental Cooperation. Says Montréal lawyer Pierre Marc Johnson, an expert in international environmental law, "It was no small matter for Charest and Reilly to persuade their respective departments of international trade to consider environmental issues. It was one hell of a job, and they did it." "This was the first time that trade and environment were ever linked in the public eye," adds Len Good. "So in one sense, it's a vanguard situation to be building environment into NAFTA."

But if we are to believe the book written later by Johnson and his colleague André Beaulieu,* the two agreements leave a good deal to be desired in terms of environmental protection. NAFTA relies on exhortations, not sanctions, to discourage countries from lowering their environmental standards to attract foreign investment. The environmental co-operation agreement calls for sanctions only when a country fails to enforce its own laws, which it is free to dilute if it so chooses. "The solutions presented by those who drafted the agreements are somewhat half-hearted," Johnson and Beaulieu conclude. The inclusion of environmental issues in NAFTA would appear to be mostly a symbolic gesture. But public pressure could turn these symbols into a very real influence on the behaviour of the three countries. "So we were patriating a role that a few years ago would have been considered absolutely impossible for a department of Environment to play," maintains Len Good. "It's more a measure of making progress rather than getting as much as we wanted."

IF I ONLY HAD THE MONEY . . .

Jean Charest could not have arrived at Environment at a better time. But the wind was already beginning to shift. Environment still ranked high on the government's agenda, but the deficit was rapidly becoming an obsession. The Environment minister had to fight tooth and nail to defend his budgets against Finance minister Don Mazankowski's axe. All things considered, Charest did rather well.

Environmental groups vehemently protested projected cuts to the Green Plan. They also objected to the slowness with which

---

* P. M. Johnson and A. Beaulieu, *The Environment and NAFTA: Understanding and Implementing the New Continental Law* (Washington, D.C.: Island Press, 1996).

many projects got under way. No final accounting of the plan was ever made public, and the Chrétien government scrapped it. But one bit of information is still available through Environment Canada: of the $3 billion announced by Robert de Cotret, $2.6 billion was spent. How? Where? What was accomplished? How much new money was really injected into the environment? "It's like looking for a needle in a haystack," says ecologist Christian Simard. Few would disagree. Nonetheless, if the $2.6-billion figure is accurate, most of the $3 billion must have survived the cuts. "A Conservative government injecting $3 billion into the environment! We're a long way away from that now!" Simard says.

Under Charest, the environmental protection budget grew from $358 million (1991–92) to $399 million (1993–94). A more modest increase than predicted, but an increase all the same. "We're gonna break faith with constituencies that are just now starting to embrace us," Charest complained to Mazankowski.

"Jean," replied "Maz," "if we don't do some scaling back right across the board, we won't be around to experience that."

THE LAWYER

Like the amateur sport community, Environment Canada bureaucrats and environmental groups considered Jean Charest one of the most outstanding ministers to hold the portfolio. Not that he had left his mark on the environment through his imagination or by bringing in innovative programs. What impressed the environmentalists were Jean Charest's personal qualities: his grasp of the files, the enthusiasm he brought to the job, his skills as a communicator, his ability to bring people together. He convinced everyone, from bureaucrats to Tory party workers, that he respected them; he won from them the same respect.

A pervasive, discordant note lingers. An ex-bureaucrat put it this way: "He wins you over so much with his enthusiasm and convinces you so much in his belief and passion for the subject matter . . . Then, when he's wearing a different hat, the subject of the environment never comes up, and you start to say: 'Oops! Did he really mean that?' Was he sincere? When he was running for the leadership [of the Conservative Party], you didn't hear the word environment once."

In 1997, the election platform of Jean Charest's Tories was only marginally more expansive. One proposal was to slash the environment department budget by 9 percent and to create, in the name of economy, a super-ministry of Sustainable Development, combining Environment, Agriculture, Natural Resources and Fisheries. Worse, a Charest government would have sliced $473 million from Canada's foreign aid budget, a 25 percent reduction. What had happened to the Jean Charest of Rio fame? "He's a professional politician," says the former civil servant. "When he's wearing the environmental hat he's the best minister of the Environment you've ever seen, and when he's in Industry he's the best minister of Industry you've ever seen, and when he's a leadership candidate he does whatever is required for a politician to be successful at that. And if the environment is not on the radar screen, then so be it."

Charest is a politician's politician. More precisely, he's a lawyer. A trial lawyer. When he was young, he turned to criminal law so that he would be able to win over juries. Ever since he entered politics, he's been trying to win over voters.

Lawyers, however, do not choose their cases based on ideology or personal conviction. They simply defend the cases their clients bring them. No need to smoke to be a lawyer for the tobacco industry; no need to believe a client is innocent to help him avoid a prison sentence. Jean Charest is built that way. As minister for Sport, he defended athletes passionately. If he had been Fisheries minister, he would have done the same for the fish.

Which leads to the oft-repeated dismissal of Charest as "just a good talker"; "He has no substance." The shoe fits, but not precisely. Charest is vitally interested in content. As a minister, he steeped himself in the files until he knew them inside out. Jean Charest is no young Ronald Reagan.

But he is no Trudeau, no Lévesque, either. They had time to reflect, to form convictions, to develop a system of intellectual references before they entered politics. More often than not, Charest prefers to go with the flow. He was a nationalist when he arrived in Ottawa — a photograph of René Lévesque hung on his office wall. He then absorbed the vision of Canada that is prevalent in Ottawa. He started out as a lawyer defending widows and orphans; later he crusaded for middle-class taxpayers. After pleading for the state to spend billions of dollars on youth and the environment, he sang the praises of deficit reduction. Not long after entering provincial politics, he ventured that balancing the budget wasn't so urgent after all. Some would argue that Charest is an opportunist. It would perhaps be more accurate to call him a pragmatist, like so many politicians before him. Like Robert Bourassa, for instance. Bourassa's success suggests that voters may not mind leaders who vacillate, providing they don't lose sight of their priorities.

For a long time, Jean Charest did not know what he really stood for. He knew he had leadership ability, but where should he lead the people? "Jean has realized, maybe in the last two or three years, why he's in politics, aside from the sheer fun of it," says Charest's long-time friend and adviser Denis Beaudoin. Jean Charest is in politics to work for the survival of Canada, "a country of tolerance, diversity and mutual respect," a country that is "different from all other countries in the world." Jean Charest believes that Québeckers can and must find their place in Canada. A few hesitations aside, he also feels that if Québeckers happen to decide otherwise, the rest of Canada should respect their will.

On other issues, such as the notion of a distinct society, the deficit or gun control, his position depends on which way the wind is blowing. Does that make Jean Charest an opportunist? Opportunism, as defined by *Webster's Collegiate Dictionary*, is "the art, policy, or practice of taking advantage of opportunities or circumstances, esp.

with little regard for principles or consequences." The first part of the definition fits Charest perfectly. However, though Jean Charest doesn't adhere to a specific political doctrine, he does have principles. Integrity and openness are values with which he makes relatively few compromises. In a world peopled with Pinocchios, Red Charest's son has a normal-sized nose. He has another principle: he respects adversaries and institutions. In general, Charest prefers not to stoop to vulgarity and cheap tricks. In his last session in the Commons, he did everything he could to discourage his MPs from adding to the circus atmosphere created by the MPs in other parties — the insults, the temper tantrums, the flag-waving and the raucous nonsense. He may be ambitious, he may be a politician to his fingertips, but he is a man of integrity. Is he just a good talker? It would be more accurate to call him an accomplished advocate.

The Stronghold

—◊—

On the right, halfway up the road leading to the University of Sherbrooke, lies a huge vacant lot. The billboard erected by Energy and Natural Resources minister Jean Chrétien on May 24, 1984, has vanished. No trace remains of the ground-breaking ceremony that took place on this, the proposed site of the new Canadian Institute of Cartography, a $35-million building that was to house four hundred specialists. In Sherbrooke, the university, the municipality, the CEGEP and the Chamber of Commerce had a dream: the Institute would anchor a research and development park. "Laboratories run by government or by private industry, centres and institutes for applied research and development will attract substantial amounts of capital to the region," the university newspaper explained. A few months later, the Liberals were voted out of office. Chrétien's sign survived for several months, but the Institute of Cartography never saw the light of day, and the dream of the Sherbrooke elite went up in smoke.

In fact, Sherbrooke now boasts a Geomatics Canada facility,

which employs about one hundred people. The centre's projects have earned it an excellent reputation. (Geomatics is the collecting, managing and interpreting of information derived from geography.) But the federal government installed the centre in an office building owned by a group of local businessmen. One of them, Denis Berger, is a leading Charest fundraiser. The research and development park is nothing but a distant memory. There are still persistent whispers in Sherbrooke that "Charest gave it to his cronies." No wonder. Until recently, the building at 2144 King Street West housed the office of the MP for Sherbrooke, Jean Charest.

The fate of the Institute mirrors two aspects of Charest's political career. First, despite his enormous popularity in the region, his contribution to Sherbrooke's economic development can be described as modest. Second, he has strong links with his local "clan." These ties may well be based on sincere friendship, but they often seem to veer in the direction of favouritism. Anyone who wants to find out about the real Jean Charest will have to do more than admire his performances on the national stage. He will have to visit his stronghold, walk around the offices at 155 King Street West, eat lunch at Da Toni, *the* restaurant for the lawyers, accountants and businesspeople who make the city's economy go round. As Jacques Fortier, Charest's former organizer, says, "It all starts in Sherbrooke." Remember that two of these influential Sherbrookers — Jean-Guy Ouellette and Jean-Laurier Demers — played leading roles in the drama that led to the Tory golden boy's forced resignation.

"Sherbrooke is a village," its residents readily admit. As the years went by, the frightening efficiency of the "Charest gang's" organization made it the dominant force in the village. A well-developed sense of paranoia makes it hard to distinguish between fact and fantasy, but Charest and his people undoubtedly run a tight ship. Their readiness to play hardball has riled many people. Not only does Charest's well-oiled political machine, in place since 1984, virtually guarantee him a seat in Parliament, it also hands him enormous leverage at many levels of society: he has a say in hospital management, he can influence the political process in surrounding ridings, and his presence is felt in the mayor's office. Just one example: when a former Charest organizer, Conrad Chapdelaine, a sovereigntist, ran for the PQ nomination against Marie Malavoy prior to the 1994 provincial election, Jean Charest got into the act. He offered the opinion that Chapdelaine was the more federalist of the two candidates. It would be difficult to find a better way to trip up a candidate seeking the support of the PQ faithful. Chapdelaine lost to Marie Malavoy who, as Sherbrooke's MNA, would not be likely to overshadow the federal member.

A COUPLE AND THE EVEREST GROUP

Around Sherbrooke, more than a few people complain about being pushed around by two of Charest's closest advisers, longtime aide Suzanne Poulin and Everest Group vice-president Claude Lacroix. Poulin and Lacroix are like one another in many ways. Though they are unfailingly courteous, they will not hesitate to defend their boss tooth and nail. The political adviser and the image-maker have been living together for several years, adding to the aura surrounding them. The facts are few, but opinions are easy to come by. Insurance adjuster Claude Métras, a keen observer of Sherbrooke economic and political life, sums up the feeling: "Claude Lacroix is a bit of a bully. He'll come calling, taking it for granted that you'll work with him. If you refuse, he has ways of making people feel cool toward you. People don't much like it because they say, 'Some day we may need Jean Charest, and if Lacroix tells him, "Watch out for that guy, he didn't deliver for me . . ."' You know, it's a small community — it's you scratch my back, I'll scratch yours.

"That's as much as you can say because there's no proof. There's nothing in writing. It's a kind of grey zone," says Métras. "If you don't like Jean Charest or don't share his ideas, you can bet there'll be some getting even," insists a disenchanted organizer.

Claude Lacroix met Jean Charest through Jean-Bernard Bélisle, Charest's friend and adviser. In 1976, Bélisle founded Everest, a small marketing firm. It soon became one of the largest advertising agencies in Québec. A few months after the 1984 election, Bélisle offered Charest his services and joined the Club de la Relève, the group of young businessmen and professionals who backed Charest. When Everest hired on Claude Lacroix as a graphic artist, he was naturally drawn into the new MP's orbit.

In one of their first meetings, Lacroix told Charest he needed more exposure in Sherbrooke. "You're like a paint merchant who has a sale and puts all his signs up inside the store," he said. "You do a lot of good things, you work hard, but nobody knows about it." Ever since, thanks to Lacroix, Jean Charest's local organization has become known for its colourful events. And the Everest Group slogan reflects Lacroix & Co.'s work for Sherbrooke's star politician: "The name Everest reflects our ability to do what it takes to help our clients climb to the top."

Suzanne Poulin had worked as an event co-ordinator at the Sherbrooke arena before joining the Charest team a few weeks after his election in 1984. A tireless worker, matchless organizer, with a reputation for unwavering loyalty, she quickly became indispensable to the MP. "If Jean Charest has gotten this far, it's 50 percent thanks to Suzanne Poulin," people say. Before his leap into provincial politics, Ms. Poulin's official task was running the Sherbrooke office, but her influence has always extended well beyond the Eastern Townships. Suzanne Poulin organizes Jean Charest's life. There's no one he speaks to more often, no one he confides in more.

As a single-minded woman who serves a demanding boss, Suzanne Poulin has made a fair share of enemies. Many complain she is overprotective of Charest and makes it all but impossible to get access to him. "Everyone has to report to Suzanne Poulin or Jean-Bernard Bélisle. In a political party, this is just not acceptable," grumbles a former Charest organizer. "We felt that to get things done, we had no choice but to go through Suzanne Poulin first. It shows a lack of respect for people." An aide who worked for Jean Charest when he was a federal minister claims that dealing with Suzanne Poulin was "a form of purgatory," that she was a control freak. Tory riding workers have long resented Suzanne Poulin's attitude toward them. When the leader was displeased, they say, it fell to her to handle the offending volunteer, something she rarely did with kid gloves. "She doesn't absorb the stress," another Tory organizer says ruefully. "She amplifies it. If Charest isn't happy with the turnout at a public appearance, she'll call the organizers and chew them out. How do you think they feel, after they've worked two weeks to fill the room?"

Once again, it is difficult to distinguish between fair criticism and jealous carping. In their entourage, leaders must have an alter ego, someone who makes decisions in their name, steers them away from sticky situations and handles the political dirty work: refusals, criticism and bad tidings. It's a nasty job, but somebody has to do it. "I must insist on the same rigour Jean Charest demands of us," says the woman whom some have called the real MP for Sherbrooke. "People who join his team must be disciplined. Half measures just won't do. Jean Charest intends to be successful, and he wants a team that will help him attain that objective."

Poulin bears an additional burden: because her boss wants to be Mr. Nice Guy, he never says no. He never turns down an invitation or a request. Even when asked to do something he detests he cannot bring himself to refuse. He leaves it hanging . . . and lets his assistant deliver the bad news. "I have a tough job," she admits. "It's not that I don't want people to meet him, he just doesn't have the time. What makes it seem like I'm hard-boiled, as if I'm refusing access to Jean, is that he says yes to everybody! Quite sincerely, he wants to please everyone!"

Few question Suzanne Poulin's extraordinary abilities. But her lack of tact, abrasive tone and excessive loyalty have damaged her reputation. Jean Charest is not perfect, and people have a right to tell him so. It might even help him if they did. Suzanne Poulin doesn't seem to see it that way. Apparently, neither does her boss.

THE DIVORCE

Jacques Fortier, a claims adjuster from Sherbrooke, pulls a photograph from a file. "That's my wife in the middle with Mila and Michèle . . ." His voice trails off, a sob catching in his throat. "It was during Brian Mulroney's visit to Sherbrooke. Denise works at the hospital centre, and Jean arranged for Mila to go and meet her . . ." He breaks down again. "For ten years, my wife and my daughter Caroline gave me their support, although I wasn't home very much . . . They couldn't understand why Jean treated me the way he did."

Jean Charest never had a more dedicated political organizer than Jacques Fortier. He toiled long and hard for the man and for the friend, never expecting anything in return. For four years, he organized the annual golf tournament to raise funds for Charest's Sherbrooke organization. In the aftermath of the fateful call to Justice Macerola in 1990, Fortier helped organize the welcoming committee at Dorval Airport for the fallen cabinet minister. In the 1993 election, Fortier had the responsibility for "D Day" in Sherbrooke, running the machine that got out the vote. After the victory, Charest wrote, "I can't tell you how proud I am to have you on my team. Your personal qualities combined with your organizational abilities, dynamism and dedication have always impressed me." A year later, Jean Charest would cruelly betray their friendship, wounding a man whose sensitivity he knew well. "It was like a divorce," Fortier sighs.

Like many political organizers, Fortier worked on several levels. In 1994, he ran Sherbrooke mayor Paul Gervais's election campaign. But the Charest troops had thrown their weight behind an adversary of the mayor and a member of the Club de la Relève,

Jean Perrault. That was hardly surprising. The surprise was seeing Jean Charest, who had never become openly involved in municipal politics, line up behind Perrault. The move was seen as a turning point in the campaign; Perrault was elected mayor of Sherbrooke by 757 votes. Jean Charest never thought it necessary to make his decision known to his loyal supporter, Jacques Fortier. When Fortier heard the news on television, he felt humiliated, devastated. "It didn't bother me that he was supporting Perrault; he's entitled to do what he wants. But I would have liked him to call and let me know, out of respect, out of friendship." Richard Miquelon, an influential local businessman and longtime Conservative, agrees. "It wasn't the thing to do. Jean Charest upset some of his organizers and they've never gotten over it. It was one thing too many. Some of Charest's friends, including me, didn't agree with what he had done. We were all witnesses to everything Fortier had done for him, and that's why we thought it was wrong. He wasn't some third-rate organizer. He was Charest's number-one man."

It was definitely not the thing to do, but Charest was responding to the desires of his closest organizers, people like Jean-Yves Laflamme, who was to become the new mayor's chief of staff after the election. Some say that the Charest clan acted out of revenge because Paul Gervais had refused to support the favourite son during the 1993 leadership race. "Suzanne Poulin told me over the phone that Paul Gervais got what he deserved," reports Liberal lawyer Martin Bureau.

The net result is that the Charest clan now controls City Hall. And though the MNA is a member of the Parti Québécois (for the time being), Charest has always been able to count on the unconditional support of the Liberal MNAs from neighbouring ridings, Monique Gagnon-Tremblay (Saint-François) and Robert Benoît (Orford). Over the years, Gagnon-Tremblay and Charest have shared organizers, including Denis Berger, Albert Painchaud and Jean-Yves Laflamme. Clearly, in Sherbrooke, it takes courage to oppose Jean Charest openly. Or Suzanne Poulin for that matter.

Or Claude Lacroix. "There's nothing overt, and it doesn't have to be," says Jacques Pronovost, editor-in-chief of *La Tribune*. "People are aware that these ties exist. They know that Jean Perrault is Jean Charest, that Everest is Claude Lacroix, meaning Jean Charest, that Monique Gagnon-Tremblay is Jean-Yves Laflamme, meaning Jean Charest."

Nothing overt, no scandals, just a certain atmosphere. In Sherbrooke, people are cautious when they criticize Charest. News travels fast, and they worry that one day they'll be called on the carpet. "I'm always careful about what I say *in front of* or *about* Suzanne Poulin, because it could definitely prove fatal," confides a high-profile Sherbrooke resident. Over the years, Suzanne Poulin has set up an extremely efficient communications network. Everyone in the Charest camp whom I met in the course of my research immediately reported to Suzanne Poulin. She knew almost as well as I did to whom I had spoken and what questions I had asked. And Poulin has a very effective way of letting people know she's keeping an eye on them. "Well, you do get around! Seems you're interested in a certain file?"

INCORRUPTIBLE . . . JUST ABOUT

Jean Charest isn't a corrupt politician. By nature, he's honest; he has integrity. But politics has its rules and requirements that ambitious politicians ignore at their peril. Don't expect Jean Charest to reform Canadian political morality. He can be tough. He knows how to reward friends and, when necessary, how to punish enemies. Charest might be relatively young, but he is a politician in the traditional mould. Since he entered politics, several allegations of patronage have surfaced. In some of these cases, Charest is blameless. In a few others, his innocence is less apparent.

The first case involves the never realized Institute of Cartography. Here, critics find fault with Charest on two counts. First, they claim that he was willing to settle for a dwarf version of the original project, with no real impact on the region. Second, they accuse him of favouritism toward his cronies. The facts, as far as can be ascertained today, point to Charest's innocence on both counts.

In the early 1980s, the Institute was a controversial subject, not only in the Eastern Townships but also across the province and even the country. Jean Chrétien's plan irritated many, especially Ottawa-based civil servants who didn't want to hear about moving to Sherbrooke. On the hustings, Charest had promised to complete the project, but at the Department of Mines and Resources, people hoped the Tory victory would bury the Liberal obsession. "Everyone in the department was opposed to it," recalls Pierre Perron, who had just arrived in Ottawa as an assistant deputy minister. "The union was against it, and Minister Pat Carney didn't want to hear of it." The decision would be made after the new government had reviewed all programs in an effort to trim expenditures. It took two years of effort by Charest, the Sherbrooke economic establishment, the Québec Conservative caucus and the Québec government to reach a solution that would give Sherbrooke a consolation prize without uprooting federal bureaucrats or depleting the Treasury. The "Queen of the Eastern Townships" would be host to a facility dedicated to geomatics, the cartography of the future. Ottawa bureaucrats could choose to work there, but no one would be obliged to leave the federal capital.

It was a more modest project than anticipated — one hundred employees instead of four hundred — but under the circumstances, it wasn't half bad. "I was impressed with Charest's pragmatism," says Perron. "He realized it was going nowhere, and that a bird in the hand is better than two in the bush. He was ready to compromise. He knew the art of the possible when he saw it."

Once the solution had been found, Ottawa had to choose the site of the new centre. The building chosen belonged to a group of accountants, including Guy Savard, who was a provincial Liberal close to Charest, and Denis Berger, the minister's principal fundraiser

— hence the accusations of favouritism levelled against Jean Charest. A few clues do exist, but not enough to prove anything. To begin with, the first unit of the Institute had already been established in the controversial building at 2144 King Street West in Jean Chrétien's day. "All the figures are there. People can look at them and judge for themselves whether or not it was a good decision," Charest now says defensively. In fact, the figures are available because the tenant was chosen after a call for tenders. Public Works Department documents on the subject are unequivocal: the proprietors of 2144 offered a much lower rent than an ad hoc group of local dignitaries, who were keen to build a new facility on the site of their planned research park. The competitors believed the government should have chosen their bid, despite the difference in rent, because of the potential spin-offs for the area. But Charest is right: the gap between the bids (almost $200,000 a year) was too great and the local establishment's scheme was far too hypothetical for the government to pass over the lowest bidder.

More damaging to Charest is the fact that he opened an office of his own in the building. The move was, apparently, a little gift to his friends. "Setting up his office there didn't help much," businessman Richard Miquelon admits. "Jean's very good, but he's not perfect."

GREEN PATRONAGE

The next "affair" surfaced when Charest was Environment minister. Under the Green Plan, the federal government launched a program called "Partners for the Environment" to help environmental groups carry out a variety of projects. In 1991, the largest grant was given — coincidentally — to a group from Sherbrooke, the newly created Eastern Townships branch of radio host Louis-Paul Allard's FQE (Fondation québécoise de l'environnement — The Québec Environment Foundation). The group got $188,000 for its project, a "multimedia campaign encouraging people to take action on the environment." The project boiled down to a large-scale promotional campaign, complete with an opinion poll, media advertising, billboards, a play and a gala.

The announcement of the grant infuriated local environmental groups. In their view, the FQE was too close to the business community. Moreover, the Sherbrooke section of the FQE didn't have a proven track record, they argued. And finally, they could smell patronage. Indeed, the FQE branch president was Guy Fouquet, a well-known Sherbrooke engineer. The former head of the FQE, Robert Dubé, happened to be a Charest childhood friend — now part of the minister's staff. On top of that, the promotional campaign was awarded to none other than the Everest Group. Everyone involved in the deal, including Guy Fouquet, Jean Charest and the Everest people, deny there was any form of patronage. But it's safe to say there is more to the story than meets the eye.

A consultative committee made up of civil servants and representatives from environmental groups evaluated project applications. The list of the projects rejected by the committee in December 1991 includes project QUE-561, Project Enviro-Info of the Fondation québécoise de l'environnement — Eastern Townships section. "The committee," the report reads, "considers that the methods envisaged are unrealistic, considering the realities of the region. The plan is too vague and the budget is overvalued." One month later, however, the minister's office approved the project. Of all the projects refused at the time, it was the only one in which the minister overrode the committee's recommendations. It is difficult to avoid the impression that the Environment minister and/or his staff favoured a project spearheaded by people they knew. "You'd have to be crazy not to think that [the people in Jean Charest's office] didn't give a little push," concedes FQE president Guy Fouquet. "Charest must have looked at the list to see what there was in the region, in his constituency in particular."

"They were non-profit organizations. The idea was to give something back to the community," adds Fouquet. He is certainly right about that. Someone might have acted inappropriately, but it's far from clear that anyone benefited financially. Everest was paid to organize the campaign but, if the documents submitted to the Environment ministry are to be believed, the amounts were relatively small, and Everest provided a number of services free of charge. At best, the individuals and companies concerned benefited from being associated with a good cause; their participation enabled them to make contacts. As scandals go, it was a minor one.

A FAMILY AFFAIR

L'École de langue de l'Estrie has been operating in Ottawa since 1990. The school is doing well — so well that, in the fall of 1997, it was forced to rent extra classrooms to accommodate the civil servants who study French there.

L'École de langue de l'Estrie belongs to Jean Charest's eldest sister, Louise, and her husband, Stanley Mardinger. A week before the 1993 Conservative leadership convention, reporters, tipped off by a competitor, learned that apparently, following Charest's return to cabinet, the school had been raking in the contracts.

Had favouritism reared its ugly head? According to the Charests, Jean has scrupulously respected government guidelines. But here, there's no need to take anybody's word for it. The figures speak for themselves.

Each year, Public Accounts Canada publishes, for each government department, a list of professional service suppliers who have signed contracts of more than $100,000 with the government. In fiscal 1990–91, its first year of operations, L'École de langue de l'Estrie received $632,461 from such large contracts. It was an exceptional start — but can its success be attributed to Jean Charest's influence? That year Charest resigned his cabinet seat after the call to Justice Macerola. He was a mere backbencher.

The number of lucrative contracts awarded by the government to Louise Charest's school fluctuated from year to year, but nothing points to undue influence. When Jean Chrétien's Liberals came to power it was business as usual. And in 1996–97, L'École de langue de l'Estrie recorded its best year ever, winning more than $1.1 million in major contracts.

YOU SCRATCH MY BACK, I'LL SCRATCH YOURS

It came as no surprise to regulars at Da Toni, the Sherbrooke power restaurant, when Léo Daigle, Jean Charest's top organizer, and Paul-Marcel Bellavance, a former president of the Sherbrooke Tory association, were named to the Québec Superior Court on July 11, 1991.

People in Sherbrooke were saying Justice Daigle owed his appointment to Jean Charest.

"So what!" says the judge. "Even if I tried to deny it, what difference would it make? But let me tell you how it happened. He came to see me. 'Listen,' he said, 'you're the only one who hasn't asked for a judge's appointment.'

" 'Why are you telling me this?'

" 'There are some spots opening up.'

" 'Jean, I told you before, I always wanted to be a lawyer.'

" 'Anyway, think it over.'

"He gave me two weeks to make up my mind."

The advice Daigle got from a judge tipped the balance: "If someone gives you a train ticket, you take the train."

When Justice Bellavance is asked whether he owes his nomination to Jean Charest, the discomfort is thick enough to slice. "Ask him . . ."

"What do you say?"

"The way I see it, someone who used to belong to a political organization shouldn't be prevented from performing a particular function."

"Are you any less talented just because you've been involved in politics?" asks Conrad Chapdelaine, a lawyer and sovereigntist organizer. Chapdelaine goes on to tick off a number of well-known Liberals in the region who were appointed to the bench by Liberal governments. It's a hoary tradition, accepted in both legal and political circles. As a rule, each party appoints the most competent lawyer . . . from its own camp. Lawyer and politician Jean Charest was merely respecting tradition.

THE STAR OF SHERBROOKE

Jean Charest was the member for Sherbrooke from 1984 to 1998, when he became the provincial Liberal leader. In 1993, he survived the Bloc Québécois tidal wave, winning by more than eight thousand votes. In 1997, he crushed his opponents. Charest now appears unbeatable in his constituency. And yet, even his supporters find it difficult to list his accomplishments on the local scene. "It's hard to point to any major projects," says Conservative businessman Richard Miquelon. "There haven't been any in Sherbrooke. Not that there were any before him, either." Claude Métras puts it more bluntly. "That's his problem. He hasn't done anything for Sherbrooke. He hasn't brought anything to the town. [. . .] Businesspeople are still waiting for a large-scale investment."

"He's never done a goddamn thing for Sherbrooke," says businessman Dennis Wood, Charest's former Liberal adversary. "Handouts, that's all he's good at, $100 or $500 cheques . . . the welfare bums love him, *Les filles d'Isabelle* [a charitable organization], that kind of people. He does all the parties, the bingo nights. Oh yeah, and he named a couple of judges."

The criticism is harsh, but inaccurate. During his years in cabinet, Jean Charest was instrumental in bringing several key projects to Sherbrooke, including the Institut de pharmacologie de Sherbrooke, the Centre de recherche clinique de l'Université de

Sherbrooke and the Enviro-Accès centre. The years between 1991 and 1993, when Charest and Gagnon-Tremblay were ministers on the federal and provincial level respectively, were particularly fertile. "We were lucky enough to have Monique Gagnon-Tremblay as minister in Québec and Jean Charest, whose party was in power," says Sherbrooke industrial commissioner Pierre Dagenais. "Not because it was Jean Charest. Anyone with an influential position in the government would have gotten the same results."

Why the harsh criticism levelled by some businessmen? There can be no doubt that, despite both governments' best efforts, the regional economy has suffered considerably in recent years. Unemployment soared from 7.2 percent in 1988 to 11.8 percent in 1997. But is Charest to blame? During the same period, unemployment rose throughout Québec. In 1987, the first year in which Charest's influence as a minister could have been felt, the Sherbrooke unemployment rate was 0.4 percent higher than that of the province. Ten years later, the gap still stood at 0.4 percent.

On the other hand, Charest's role in these projects should not be exaggerated. They were mostly the result of local initiative. "Politicians can help, but there are limits to what they can do," the industrial commissioner for Sherbrooke points out. "Charest or no Charest, things wouldn't have been much different." The new leader of the Québec Liberal Party, says Dagenais, was a good MP. "Having been a minister, he has the contacts, and he is ambitious — he wants to be liked."

Charest maintains a constant presence in the region, thanks to tried-and-true practices and a remarkably efficient staff. As External Affairs has no Sherbrooke branch, Charest's office handles passport applications. At first he would carry the paperwork to Ottawa himself and bring the passports back the following weekend. Now, the operation is conducted using a courier service, with the help of volunteers.

Volunteers also scan local newspapers for announcements — weddings, obituaries, and prizes — worthy of the MP's attention.

Since he started out in politics, Jean Charest has spent untold hours signing letters of condolence or congratulations, gestures that are always much appreciated. But Canadian political history is replete with electoral landslides that have swept away good MPs. If Charest survived in 1993, despite a questionable record and a blunder or two, if he seems unbeatable today, it's because he has become a national figure. "He has put Sherbrooke on the map," says Miquelon. "I travel all over Canada, and whenever I say I'm from Sherbrooke, people ask me right away whether I know Jean Charest."

Charest has always understood the importance of stroking his fellow citizens' egos. Every important announcement of his career has been made in Sherbrooke, focusing the whole country's attention on the Eastern Townships. In Sherbrooke, in 1993, he declared his candidacy for the Progressive Conservative Party leadership. He announced his intention to get into provincial politics in Sherbrooke. "All eyes were on Sherbrooke," ran the proud headline in *La Tribune* the day after the latest announcement.

"Jean's popularity in Sherbrooke has nothing to do with what he has accomplished," says Justice Daigle. "It's a personal relationship. He's like everyone's son." And people are always ready to forgive everything of a son who is successful.

The Tortoise

—⚋—

Like many Québeckers, Tory organizer Pierre-Claude Nolin was spending the winter break on the ski slopes. February 24, 1993, was dawning when the telephone rang in his room at the Mont Sainte-Anne resort: it was Environment minister Jean Charest.

"Pierre-Claude? Today's the day."

"No kidding."

"The deal's still on?"

"It sure is."

It was Charest's way of telling Nolin that Prime Minister Brian Mulroney would announce his resignation later that morning. Still on was the agreement the two men had made two months earlier. Nolin would head up Jean Charest's leadership campaign in Québec. It was the day Charest had been waiting for.

The Sherbrooke MP had never concealed his ambitions. In 1986, he and his friend Léo Daigle had found themselves strolling in front of the Parliament Buildings. "Léo," he said, "I'm going to tell you something I've never told anyone else. Ever since I was thirteen,

I've been dreaming that one day I'd be the boss." When he hired Philippe Morel as his chief of staff at Environment in 1992, he put him on notice. "That's where I'm headed," he said, pointing skyward. There was no doubt in Morel's mind that Charest meant he intended to become Prime Minister of Canada one day.

After the collapse of the Charlottetown Accord, rejected by a majority of Canadians in October 1992, the federal capital had been rife with rumours of Prime Minister Mulroney's resignation. Behind the scenes, would-be successors began to jockey for position. Or, if they were not doing the jockeying themselves, others were doing it for them. Longtime Tory organizer Jules Pleau, a vice-president with Bombardier, pledged Jean Charest his support and advised him to name Pierre-Claude Nolin his chief Québec organizer. During the Clark-Mulroney contest in 1983, Pleau and Nolin had found themselves on opposite sides of the fence and, like so many participants in the "Battle of Québec," they had emerged shaken from the experience. In the next leadership campaign, they swore, Québec Tories would unite behind one candidate. In 1993, only one Québecker could hope to rally the Tories: Jean Charest. "Our plan was to make Jean Charest the king-maker," says Pleau. "We were certain that if Québec backed Charest, he would determine the next leader."

Expectations — at least in Brian Mulroney's mind — focused on a hard-fought leadership race, involving many candidates. "My last two cabinet shuffles were carried out with that in mind," says the former prime minister. "I put Charest at Environment so he'd be a candidate. I removed Michael Wilson from Finance to 'purify' him so he'd be a candidate. I named Barbara MacDougall to External Affairs, Bernard Valcourt to Human Resources and Kim Campbell to Defence for the same reason. They were all practically on the same level and on the cabinet priorities committee. I thought we'd see eleven or twelve candidates."

Jean Charest had made up his mind to be part of the pack. During the Christmas break, well before Mulroney's resignation, Charest had contacted Nolin. About the same time, Charest invited Jodi White, Joe Clark's chief of staff and a good friend of George MacLaren's, to his home in North Hatley and asked her to head up his national campaign. Philippe Morel went looking for people with political smarts to beef up Charest's office staff, including PMO staffer Marie-Josée Bissonnette. "We weren't aiming to win the leadership. We wanted to carve out a place for ourselves in the party establishment and give Jean Charest a higher profile," says friend and adviser Jean-Bernard Belisle.

On the English side, David Small joined the fray. Small was the man who operated the satellite dish in Rio, and he had been a senior Clark strategist in the 1983 leadership campaign. After the Earth Summit, he had landed a new contract with the Environment department, this time to pilot the Green Plan. The contract would later generate considerable controversy. Small, contended the Liberals, was cashing cheques from Environment Canada at the same time he was working on his minister's campaign. The allegation would never be proved, and Small swears to this day that, prior to Brian Mulroney's resignation, he worked on the leadership race strictly "in my own time." "I was doing this at night. In the office, I was surrounded by bureaucrats. I was not in a position to be actively engaged in those things." When the leadership race got under way, Small wrote a letter to his deputy minister, requesting suspension of his contract. "Generally, I work for free," he says. Free? How professional political organizers earn a living is one of the best-kept secrets in Canadian politics. Some are paid by the organizations that employ them. How well? Mum's the word. Every election campaign, scores of consultants and lawyers abandon their jobs for weeks and even months, pursuing their passion "for free." Payment will come later, in the form of contracts or jobs.

By January 1993, the political infighting among the contenders was driving Brian Mulroney to distraction. Hugh Segal, the PM's chief of staff, warned his colleagues in the ministerial offices, "Cool it, he's not going anywhere." "But we're not campaigning," Morel

"*When Irish Eyes . . .*" Michèle Dionne and Brian Mulroney at a Conservative Party function, 1987. *Photo: Perry Beaton.*

Fathers know best. Jean Charest flanked by "godfather" Brian Mulroney and biological father Red. *Claude Charest collection.*

Feuding brothers. Jean Charest with François Gérin, former Conservative MP for a neighbouring riding. Gérin resented the younger man's success. *Photo: Perry Beaton.*

Blood brothers. Ministers Jean Charest and Pierre Blais at a public meeting on free trade, 1987. Despite the age difference, the two men became fast friends. *Photo: Perry Beaton.*

The alter ego. Suzanne Poulin has been Jean Charest's top aide since his election in 1984 — and an important part of his success story. *Photo: Perry Beaton.* Bottom: Poulin with the author as Charest announces his move to provincial politics. *Photo:* La Tribune.

The image-maker. Marketing Jean Charest: Everest Group vice-president Claude Lacroix. *Photo:* La Tribune.

Two Grits and a Tory. While a Conservative, Jean Charest built ties with Liberals like MNA Monique Gagnon-Tremblay and federal Finance minister Paul Martin. *Photo: Perry Beaton.*

Make yourself at home, Ralph. September 1994: Alberta premier Ralph Klein pays Jean Charest a call in Sherbrooke. Between them, businessman and Charest confidant George MacLaren. *George MacLaren collection.*

"You gotta go for it." Denis Beaudoin convinces Charest to run for the Conservative leadership in 1993. Convention weekend found Beaudoin in the Charest box. *Photo: Bill McCarthy. Jean Charest/Michèle Dionne collection.*

From Clark to Charest. Jodi White, Joe Clark's former chief-of-staff, took over the Charest leadership campaign in 1993. "We lost in the last week," she says. *Photo: Bill McCarthy. Jean Charest/Michèle Dionne collection.*

"Who will pay?" George MacLaren, Robert Charest and Jean Charest at the PC leadership convention. Charest sent the photo to MacLaren with a note: "George, the question is: who will pay?" *George MacLaren collection.*

Joe who? After flirting with the idea of running, former PM Joe Clark throws his support behind Jean Charest in the 1993 PC leadership race. *Photo: Bill McCarthy. Jean Charest/Michèle Dionne collection.*

protested. "We're not even letting the minister appear in public any more for fear that it might be misconstrued." Morel promptly handed the message to Small, who said "Thanks" just like everyone else and kept right on phoning. "I didn't care," he admits. "There was this huge Campbell-mania thing in the media. Their tank was going much faster than anything I was driving. As long as there was someone in front of me on the track, I wasn't gonna pull out of the race!"

TIDAL WAVE

Brian Mulroney resigned on a Wednesday, and by the following Saturday, lawyers Jean Riou and Marc Drouin and the other Big Blue Machine bosses from the Québec City region had convened Conservative organizers from Eastern Québec to a hotel in the provincial capital. They had no difficulty lining up support for Defence minister Kim Campbell, although she had not even announced her candidacy. "There was a consensus that running a woman from the West could be very interesting," Drouin explains.

Beginning in early March, the most influential Tory organizers and fundraisers in Québec and the rest of the country threw their support massively behind Campbell as polls showed her rapidly gaining popularity. In English Canada, Tory strategists hurriedly concluded that the Vancouver MP was the only Conservative capable of making people forget Brian Mulroney, who was despised everywhere but in Québec. But Kim Campbell was a relatively unknown quantity who had entered federal politics only five years earlier. True, she had risen rapidly and earned plaudits as Justice minister for her skilful handling of controversial issues like abortion and gun control. But who could have anticipated "Campbell-mania"?

The Charest camp was caught flat-footed. That first weekend, Nolin had decided to stay in Mont Sainte-Anne with his family until Sunday — an error he would regret. In Ottawa, Charest's young staff swung into action. Philippe Morel and Marie-Josée

Bissonnette joined forces with an old friend, Martin Desrochers, and other former Young Conservatives: this group would become the core of the Charest organization. And what of the future candidate? "It took Jean a while to get going," recalls Bissonnette.

Charest waited until two days after Mulroney's resignation before calling Conservative MPs and senior organizers in Québec to sound out their reaction to his possible candidacy. Charest — a left-hander — jotted down a summary of the conversations, including each MP's position, the names of important contacts in every riding and potential sources of funding. His notes reveal the inroads the Campbell machine had already made in the few hours following Mulroney's resignation announcement: the Defence minister and her supporters had by then contacted a large number of MPs. Junior minister Marcel Danis, who was thinking about becoming a candidate, had also gotten off the mark faster than Charest. Several of the MPs refused to commit themselves. It was too soon, they argued; first they had to consult their local associations. Almost all of the "undecided" MPs would eventually throw their support behind Kim Campbell. Some were surprisingly candid. The member for Portneuf, Marc Ferland, told Charest, "One of the problems with your candidacy is your age. I see you as Prime Minister, but not before 1998–99." Organizer Luc Ouellet gave him a clear assessment of the Québec City meeting: "Ninety percent of the people are backing Kim. It's not the time to choose a Québecker. People see you as a future leader." Charest's notes also reveal that cabinet minister Marcel Masse told him he "didn't intend to get involved" because he was going to "get an appointment in a few weeks." Masse did not get the posting he'd anticipated — Canadian ambassador to UNESCO — and when he did come out it was in favour of Kim Campbell.

Back to Charest's notes. Jean-Guy Guilbault, the member for Drummond, informed his colleague that "[Minister Gilles Loiselle] has promised that Kim will come to my nomination meeting." Loiselle is alleged to have said, "You'll get what you want afterwards." Some MPs displayed amazing powers of clairvoyance. The member for Québec-East, Marcel Tremblay, warned the Environment minister, "If you don't win, Québec will vote Bloc Québécois." François Pilote, the young man who would become one of Charest's chief organizers, told the minister, "I didn't like the Québec City meeting. There was panic in the air."

Charest asked Gabriel Desjardins, the president of the Québec caucus, to tote up the support he could expect from Québec MPs. "I'd need at least twenty MPs from Québec," he told the Témiscamingue MP. The next day, Desjardins brought him the news he wanted: "Twenty-two. At least."

By the time he'd finished his phone rounds in early March, Charest knew that Kim Campbell had built up a sizable lead, even in Québec. The Meech debacle was still hurting him; nationalist MPs from Québec eyed him with distrust. Cabinet colleague Benoît Bouchard made a terse assessment: "I'm a Québecker; Jean Charest is a Canadian." David Small kept putting out feelers in English Canada. Like Charest, Small got a ton of good wishes, but very little solid support. "Would there be a viable campaign? That was a serious question; it was not at all clear," he says. The strength of the Campbell movement made Kim look invincible. "Why should we support Charest when we can support the next leader?" asked party workers when they were approached by Charest's embryonic organization. In Québec, fundraisers Mario Beaulieu, Guy Charbonneau and Fernand Roberge had already "hitched their wagon to Kim Campbell's star," as Jules Pleau puts it. Campbell's organizers couldn't believe their good fortune. "We had sort of expected to get ten or fifteen members of caucus. We could run a neat little campaign, do some interesting things, a little high-tech, a lot of pizzazz!" recalls Ross Reid, who had been campaign manager for the minister of Defence. "It never happened. There was just this unbelievable flood that I never understood."

The other organizations came to the same conclusion: Kim Campbell was the one. One after another, potential candidates — Wilson, MacDougall, Valcourt and Beatty — withdrew in her favour.

Brian Mulroney's grand strategy collapsed like a house of cards. Perhaps Mulroney was to blame. Many observers feel that though the PM liked the idea of a contest, he put his organizers to work for the "Blond Comet," a suggestion Mulroney himself has always vigorously denied. "Hugh Segal, Jean Bazin, Michel Cogger, Bernard Roy, Pat MacAdam, people who are really close to me, all supported Charest. My wife and children were for Charest!" Perhaps. But the PM's entourage support came too late in the race to have any significant impact.

As the Campbell tidal wave bore down on him, Jean Charest found his will had begun to slacken. He was shaken by Perrin Beatty's withdrawal from the race. Charest and Beatty had much in common. Young and ambitious, they had become good friends. In previous weeks, they had talked on a few occasions — "If I go for it, will you?" — and even begun building an alliance that might have been useful at the convention. With Beatty on the sidelines, Charest found himself alone. "If you've got a bunch of people in the race, you can form alliances, the way Joe Clark did when he won, to everybody's surprise," George MacLaren reminded him. But if you are the front runner's only foe, you stand a good chance of being crushed. That's what was troubling Charest. "Above all, I had to avoid getting into a contest in which I would be humiliated," he says.

Worse, Jean Charest had begun to fear that the leadership race might leave him in debt. "I was jeopardizing my family's material security," he maintains. Is he exaggerating? Probably not. The political playing fields are strewn with leadership candidates who took years to emerge from the financial abyss into which their ambition had plunged them. MacLaren, senior fundraiser for the Charest campaign, was deeply concerned: "Remember Donald Johnston. Friends of his were holding fundraisers three years after the convention!" Are candidates really, personally responsible for expenses incurred during a campaign? "After we're all gone, they start phoning the guy, because that's the only name they know," MacLaren adds. The bottom line was that a Charest campaign would cost an estimated $1 million.

Charest gave himself until March 16 to make a decision. His annual Sherbrooke fundraiser was to be held on that date. If there were to be a campaign, it would get under way then.

What Are Friends For?

A few days before the dinner, Charest suffered two nasty setbacks. A poll published by *Maclean's* magazine revealed that 38 percent of Tory voters would support Kim Campbell, while only 5 percent would vote for her younger colleague. The second cut, unkinder still: Charest's friend Pierre Blais, whose support he had never doubted, informed him when they ran into each other at the Toronto airport that he was going over to the Campbell camp.

"Jean, I'm going to support Kim . . ."

"The encounter might have lasted two minutes," says Charest, "but it seemed like two hours — it was hard for both of us." "Blais couldn't look Jean in the eye," says Philippe Morel, who witnessed the scene. "It was as if he'd been stabbed. They were friends. They'd entered cabinet together. Their wives were friends. Pierre Blais's daughter babysat the Charest children!"

Blais hadn't made his decision lightly. Everyone in the Québec City region, which he was supposed to control, had already climbed aboard the Campbell bandwagon. Torn, Blais consulted Brian Mulroney. "Mr. Prime Minister, everyone is lining up for Campbell. Masse, Loiselle and [Michel] Côté have already put their organizers to work for her. I can't support Jean!"

"Pierre," Mulroney replied in the suave tone he likes to affect. "You don't know Kim Campbell. I don't either, at least not as well as I know the rest of you. We've been together for nine years. You never can tell what will happen. Imagine if her campaign collapses. If you haven't supported Charest and he hasn't run on that account, who will be prime minister? Garth Turner?" (Turner was a backbencher who, along with a few other long shots, had thrown his hat in the ring.)

The two men had a good laugh, but Mulroney's moral suasion was not enough to convince Blais to keep the faith with his Sherbrooke colleague. Why jeopardize what had been a solid friendship? Out of self-interest? Because Campbell had promised him an important ministry in her future cabinet? "Do you think that after running six departments I was afraid I wouldn't be in cabinet?" says Blais. "I didn't have to horse-trade. I was doing it for Canada. I had the impression Jean would get his chance another time." But the dagger had done its work. The two men have reconciled since then, but the scars remain. "We don't talk about it," adds Blais, "the subject is taboo." All the more taboo because, during the convention, Charest's organizers verbally attacked Pierre Blais's wife. He has never forgiven them.

The day before Jean Charest announced his decision, he paid a visit to 24 Sussex Drive, the official residence of the Prime Minister of Canada. Not surprisingly, the two men have slightly different recollections of what transpired. Jean Charest would like to dispel the notion that he was Mulroney's puppet, while the former prime minister would have us believe that he was responsible for much of his protégé's success.

When he met the Prime Minister, Charest's mind was not yet made up. "I went to see him to tell him that I felt like running, but that I had certain reservations," says Charest. "He came to see me to tell me that he wouldn't be a candidate," is Mulroney's version. We do know that Mulroney tried to allay his minister's concerns. "Jean, it's March 1993," he said. "In March 1983, I decided to run for the leadership of the party. I was taking on a former prime minister [Joe Clark] who had been leader for seven years and controlled the organization. Even you were sure Clark would win. Why? Because the polls said Clark would win easily, and almost all the MPs and ex-ministers were behind him. If they were right, why have I been sitting here in this house for nine years? If the polls and the MPs are so important, why am I prime minister? Because leadership races have nothing to do with that. What counts is an individual's capacity to display courage and leadership, and to persuade delegates that he can win because he has ideas to champion and a vision for the country that people can accept."

The history lesson must have stung Charest like a slap in the face. "You want to become prime minister of Canada. If you run, you have no guarantee of winning. On the other hand, if you don't run, you have an absolute guarantee: you won't win," the PM concluded.

Was Mulroney in a position to put Charest's mind at ease about campaign financing? Did Mulroney promise to put his fundraisers at Charest's disposal? "I can't remember whether it came up," says the former prime minister. "I know that I reassured him. I don't know whether we went into the details. I did know that Charest would have an immense success, that the coffers would fill up, that there would be no difficulty. At first, I had enormous problems, too," adds Mulroney.

Even after the meeting with Mulroney, both Charest and MacLaren seemed leery about the financial risks of the adventure. It is known, however, that some fundraisers who had been working for Campbell until then, particularly Senator Guy Charbonneau, agreed to help Charest along as well.

Mulroney recalls Charest being "quite shaken" when he left the meeting. But Charest swears that the meeting determined nothing, and rejects the suggestion that he joined the race at the express wish of the Prime Minister so that there would be some semblance of a contest. "Nothing could be more false!" insists Charest. "He told me what he told all the candidates! He told the same thing to Valcourt, to Beatty, to Kim and all the others." Not quite, says Mulroney. The Prime Minister did encourage other potential candidates, but with much less insistence than he showed toward his young protégé. "I gave it my best shot," says Mulroney. Why? Because Charest was the last top-flight candidate still in the race. "He had so many good qualities that I didn't want to see them going for naught. I knew that if he didn't run, the public would never find out about those qualities. If he backed down, it would be the end of his career. What would have become of Charest after the leadership race if he hadn't run? Would he have become minister of Fisheries?"

Still, some Charest loyalists were outraged by the Prime Minister's attitude. David Small says, "The meeting at 24 Sussex was a bit of a joke. The Prime Minister's Office put the party in this position, by setting up a Kim Campbell coronation, and then they realized they had gone too far. And after all the others had backed off, the only hope for putting together an effective leadership process was if the Prime Minister could personally convince Jean Charest to run, which I thought was the ultimate in hypocrisy."

AMÉLIE, DENIS & CO.

Come the morning of March 16, all was in readiness for the grand announcement. Claude Lacroix and his friends had dug up a theme song, printed posters and invited a thousand people to the Delta Hotel in Sherbrooke. They even laid on a bus from Ottawa for the fifteen or so MPs who had decided to back their young colleague. There was only one hitch: the star of the show still hadn't made up his mind whether he wanted to take part.

Before leaving for the Eastern Townships, Jean and Michèle drove Amélie to school. On the radio they heard, "Today we will learn if Jean Charest is to be a candidate for the Conservative leadership . . ."

"Dad?"

"Yes, Amélie."

"Are you going to run?"

"Well, I don't know. What do you think I should do?"

"Would you like to be prime minister?"

"Yes."

"Would you be a good prime minister?"

"I think so."

"Well then, go ahead!"

On the way, Charest phoned some of his advisers. But he could not use his cellular telephone. Ever since a conversation between two Québec bureaucrats had found its way into the newspapers a few months before, politicians had become suspicious of this latest wonder of technology. So the MP stopped off at a McDonald's and commandeered two telephone booths. A woman recognized him: "Are you Jean Charest?"

"Yes," he replied, clutching a receiver in each hand.

"Oh! I'm really so pleased to meet you."

"It's my pleasure, ma'am."

"Could you wait a minute?"

A few seconds later, the woman returned with her daughter-in-law. "Can we take a picture?"

Somewhere in Canada, a woman has a historic photograph of Jean Charest weighing his future.

When Jean Charest and Michèle Dionne reached his King Street office, Jean-Bernard Bélisle, Albert Painchaud, Suzanne Poulin and Maurice Champagne were waiting for them. Charest then held a telephone conference with senior advisers, including his brother Robert, Jodi White, George MacLaren, Denis Beaudoin and a handful of others. Beaudoin, who had managed Jean's first election campaign, had become a close friend. At the time, he was working for the Canadian International Development Agency (CIDA) in Mali. There was a near-consensus that the adventure was too risky. Robert and MacLaren were particularly concerned. Michèle was, for the most part, in favour of going ahead, and Beaudoin was categorical: Jean could not pass up the opportunity. But once everyone had spoken, the decision seemed clear: Charest would not be running. Suzanne Poulin advised the media that there would be a press conference at three o'clock that afternoon. Meanwhile, Charest got another call from Denis Beaudoin.

"What we're doing doesn't make any bloody sense, Jean!"

"What?"

"Fuck all that stuff. Turn your clock back to July 8, 1984. We were going to lose for sure, the polls stank like shit, and we didn't have a cent. We did it on plain old guts. Jean, I'm telling you, you gotta go for it."

Then Michou spoke up. "You think so, Denis?" Beaudoin's plea was so moving that Michèle and Suzanne Poulin couldn't hold back their tears. "Jean, if you don't fight this battle you'll regret it all your life!" he said all the way from Bamako. "Win or lose, if you don't go for it, you'll never live it down. Let's say you lose. So what! You've got things to say you've never had a chance to say. How you would change the country, how you would change the province. It's one chance in a million. You'll never get the chance again. You don't have a million? Big deal. So you'll campaign with $300,000, for chrissakes. Remember Sherbrooke, back in '84? The spiffy little campaign we ran with the cash we had on hand? Well, do the same thing! If you do, I'll help you out. I'll come back for a month. I'll pay the hotel, the plane — it's on me."

"You're right, Denis," said Michèle, breaking into sobs. "It's true!"

Silence. Jean and Michèle were alone. In a few minutes, a shout rang out in the office. "Suzanne," shouted Jean, barging through the door, "hold everything. We're gonna go for it!"

Two hours later, in front of fifteen hundred loyalists and reporters from all across the country, Jean Charest announced he would be a candidate to succeed Brian Mulroney. He presented himself as the defender of the common man, the anti-establishment candidate. "In Ottawa," he said, "they seem to have decided everything. But that's not the way you choose a prime minister, without discussing a single idea. Democratic debate is first and foremost a debate of ideas, which can't be replaced by a contest between organizations."

Yet Charest seemed to have given little consideration to the ideas he intended to put forward. His speech that evening could only be described as predictable: deficit, debt, dropouts and flexible federalism. The speech had been written at the last minute, and it sounded like it. But in it Charest staked out his defensive perimeter against the two arguments most likely to be used against him. First, his age: he was thirty-four years old. "Ten years ago, they told me the same thing," he replied, referring to his first election campaign. "Back then they said I was too young, that it would be good experience for the next time. I refused to believe that ten years ago and I refuse to believe it today." Never had the kid doubted his ability to assume the responsibilities of the prime minister of Canada at such a young age. "He's always had a strong belief in his own abilities," says Jodi White.

The Campbell organization could be counted upon to zero in on a second weakness. After ten years under Brian Mulroney, the party could not hope to win with another leader from Québec. "Nominating only one party leader from Québec in a hundred and twenty-five years wasn't exactly an abuse of the rule of alternation," was Jean Charest's pre-emptive reply.

The meeting might have looked a bit like amateur night, but the campaign launch was a success. In the middle of the night, Jean and Michèle returned to Ottawa in a driving snowstorm. When Charest finally fell into bed around three o'clock in the morning, euphoria soon gave way to the anxiety of the previous weeks: "What have I gotten myself into?" he wondered. "I'll lose my house!"

The new candidate for the Tory leadership got up three hours later and headed for the CBC studios for an early-morning interview. As he slogged through the slush on Wellington Street he spotted the headline of an Ottawa daily: "It's a race!" "We're off," he sighed.

"The biggest mistake my opponents made," Jean Charest maintains today, sounding a little like Red, "was to believe that I was just going along for the ride. A big mistake." His organizers might not have believed it, but Charest had thrown his hat into the ring fully intending to win.

LONG LIVE HAITI! LONG LIVE CHAREST!

In any Canadian political party, a leadership race consists of three distinct phases. First, delegates are chosen. The party members in each riding elect a dozen delegates to attend the convention. Most of the time, each camp presents a slate of delegates. Once chosen, the delegates have a moral obligation to vote for the candidate they represent, at least on the first ballot. This first phase is like trench warfare.

The candidates then get down to wooing the elected delegates, especially those who haven't yet made their minds up. It's also time for candidates to shop around for support in case a leader isn't elected on the first ballot, in which case some candidates will be forced to pull out. Finally, the third phase is the convention. A weekend-long carnival.

When the race got under way, Jean Charest's small team was at a substantial disadvantage. Campbell had much more money and much more support among organizers, cabinet ministers and MPs. "Only at the delegate selection meetings at the very end of the process were we finally able to run Charest slates against Campbell slates," points out David Small. "In each area you had to identify someone who was supporting you, who could line up a slate of delegates and sell enough memberships to prevail. When it came to that, we were in the junior leagues compared to our major competitor."

In Québec the situation was different. Once he'd stowed his skis, Pierre-Claude Nolin had set up a high-powered team of young organizers. Meanwhile, Kim Campbell's Québec ministers tapped two old war horses, Claude Dumont and Jean-Yves Lortie. Some observers were amazed to see Lortie resurface. The Montréal bailiff had been accused of using questionable tactics when he worked for Brian Mulroney in 1983. At any rate, Lortie wasn't taking things very seriously. In the middle of the race, he jetted off to Florida. Dumont, left to carry the ball on his own, seemed to be running himself ragged.

Tactics hadn't changed much since 1983, when a fresh-faced Jean Charest had helped get a pro-Clark slate elected in Sherbrooke. It was a matter of selling as many membership cards as possible in each riding. Organizers targeted young adults and senior citizens, as well as members of ethnic groups. If they could persuade a leader from one of these groups to support their candidate, organizers could automatically add a few dozen votes to their tally. In 1983, Brian Mulroney's organizers recruited homeless people from the Old Brewery Mission to vote for delegates in the St. Jacques riding. The payoff for supporting the Mulroney slate was free beer.

During the Campbell-Charest contest ten years later, the abuses were less spectacular — but there were a few spicy items all the same. In the downtown Montréal riding of Laurier–Sainte-Marie, the Charest camp recruited scores of people from the Chinese community, many of whom had not signed their membership cards and carried no identification. But they were allowed to vote, and Charest's list won. In Jonquière, a hundred and fifty young folks, freshly converted to Toryism, propelled the pro-Charest slate to victory; at the end of the meeting they were handed vouchers for a few rounds at a nearby tavern. In Bourassa, another Montréal riding, Charest's supporters brought scores of Haitians to the meeting. When a reporter asked some of them why they had come, they replied that they had to support Charest "because, as a Haitian like us, he can help us get out of the crisis."

There was nothing original about these manoeuvres. Pierre-Claude Nolin and his ambitious young friends had learned them from Lortie. Overtaken by his pupils, Lortie blew up, denouncing the very tactics he himself had used many a time: "I'm fed up seeing my good name smeared because of a system like this." It was an outburst that provoked howls of laughter in Québec political circles.

Kim Campbell could well speak of a new approach to politics, Jean Charest could well promise to respect a code of ethics, but neither was particularly squeamish about the tactics used by their organizers. Charest could not plead ignorance: "Every evening at eleven o'clock, I gave Jean a blow-by-blow account of what had happened during the day, what we had won and what we lost," says Martin Desrochers, one of his senior organizers. "He knew very well what was happening, and he never gave us any indication [to proceed otherwise]."

"He never told you that he didn't want to hear about certain tactics?"

"He was very happy when we recruited delegates."

The youthful François Pilote was put in charge of the Charest organization in eastern Québec. At the first delegate selection meeting, Pilote, party rule book in hand, noted irregularities committed by the opposing camp. That evening he voiced his frustration to Pierre-Claude Nolin. Nolin's reply was unequivocal: "You've got a choice: keep the rule book and hire a bunch of lawyers, or throw it in the garbage can and get your delegates elected." "So," explains Pilote, "I did what I had to do to elect my delegates."

Money Matters

"They had much more money than we did." Ask people who were involved in Charest's campaign organization why their candidate didn't win the Progressive Conservative leadership race in 1993 and money will come up. Ask for the figures and a straight answer is hard to come by. "I didn't have anything to do with that" or "I don't remember" are the common replies. George MacLaren, who was in charge of fundraising, suggested that reports could be obtained from the Ottawa PC office. The party categorically refused. Yet, at the outset, the Conservatives had promised to make public all donations exceeding $250, and set a spending limit of $900,000. Jean Charest himself had promised to disclose the names of all those who donated more than $100 to his campaign. The campaign over, the fine promises went up in smoke. "A leadership campaign is a private affair," says Jacques Léger, a Progressive

Conservative fundraiser. A private affair financed with public funds, to be exact. Political organizations issue tax receipts that enable donors to deduct the expense from their income.

When he unveiled his code of ethics at the beginning of the campaign, Jean Charest referred to the Royal Commission Report on Electoral Reform and Party Financing published two years earlier. One excerpt from the document makes interesting reading.

> The legitimacy of the leadership selection process is undermined when constituency delegates and supporters are recruited indiscriminately and without due regard to the dignity of individual citizens. The principle of fairness is undermined in leadership selection by the absence of credible or enforceable spending limits.[...] Public confidence is undermined by the absence of full and complete disclosure, particularly when public monies are used and when there is doubt that the rules are enforced.[...] Both delegates and the public should have the opportunity to fully assess the sources and sizes of the financial contributions that a leadership contestant receives.[*]

"What's important," Charest says, "is to avoid extremes. As far as everything else is concerned, the tactics of the two camps pretty well balanced out." "Extremes" is the operative word. Charest, a young politician in a hurry, favours a somewhat elastic definition of the term.

TAKING THE LID OFF THE POT

Reporters, ever mindful of the country's future, got it into their heads to find out whether the prime ministerial candidates had

---

[*] Royal Commission on Electoral Reform and Party Financing, *Final Report*, vol. 1 (Ottawa: 1991), pp. 281–82.

smoked marijuana. A year earlier, during the American presidential campaign, Bill Clinton had paved the way by admitting he had smoked pot, but without inhaling. Kim Campbell owned up, too. She had smoked a joint. But just once. And yes, she had inhaled. The admission was not very damaging.

Carefully cultivating his image, and fearful that his wild-oats adolescence might come back to haunt him, Charest hesitated before coming clean. "Yes, I inhaled," he ended up admitting. "But I must admit I feel a little uncomfortable about questions like these, which concern my personal life." The episode produced no political fall-out, but it touched off a mighty explosion on Portland Boulevard. As he was watching television, Red Charest learned that his son had smoked pot. When Jean called him that evening, Red was beside himself. "So that's what your mother and I get for killing ourselves trying to bring you up right! If you have a mistress, are you going to confess that on television, too?"

DEBATES, PLEASE

The Charest camp had only one real asset: Jean Charest. His organizers' strategy consisted of making him better known to delegates, especially the ones who had not immediately come out in favour of a candidate. Despite the Campbell juggernaut, there were still many undecided delegates in English Canada. Charest strategists felt, as one organizer put it, "if Campbell were to trip, Charest would become the alternative solution."

How was Charest to get more exposure? The party had scheduled three candidates' debates during the delegate election phase. The Charest camp managed to have two early debates tacked on to the agenda. It was a crucial strategic victory, one that few had expected the Campbell camp would allow. "I didn't feel that the Campbell people really had a strategy," says Jodi White, who negotiated the deal for Charest. It was the first hint of disarray among their adversaries.

Five candidates took part in the first debate, held on April 15 in Toronto. Besides Charest and Campbell, there were three minor candidates. Of these, the most serious was Jim Edwards, an Albertan with solid support in his home province. Garth Turner, a former populist radio talk show host, and Patrick Boyer, another MP, who had visions — poor fellow — of reforming Canada's political institutions, also participated.

Charest's entourage knew he had everything it took to do well in the debate. As the underdog, he was in a good position. Everyone expected Kim Campbell to crush the other candidates. To succeed in the debate, all Charest had to do was to impress the rank and file who had no expectations about him whatever. "Expectations were not set very high for him, but we had set pretty high expectations internally," says Bruce Anderson, Charest's top communications adviser. "If we were going to break from the back of the pack, it was going to be the consequence of some trigger event, and the most likely trigger event would be the first televised debate. We needed a win, and a clear win."

Before the Toronto debate, Anderson and Charest's little team spent two days prepping their man. Anderson showed Charest feedback from focus groups in which a few dozen people with tiny transmitters gave a blow-by-blow reaction to the candidate's speeches and interviews. The results appeared on a screen in the form of a red curve. If people liked what they heard, the line went up, and if they didn't, it went down.

The lesson gleaned from these "real-time" assessments was that Charest talked too much and filled his remarks with superfluous details, using bureaucratic jargon that Anderson called "Ottawa-speak." Worse still, the candidate sounded like Mulroney. Steadfastly loyal to the outgoing prime minister, the Environment minister felt compelled to mount a strong defence of his government's policies, even the most unpopular among them, like free trade and the GST. "People might think that the quality of the defence is fine, but it's not going to change their minds about the initiative," Anderson told his candidate. He would be well advised not to bring these issues up.

"Quite a bit of it was about how to use the information and the convictions that he had in a different organization," says Anderson, who was to remain one of Charest's closest advisers throughout his federal political career. Charest's job was to keep bringing the discussion back to key points, particularly job creation, showing that he had a structured program to attain those objectives. "Most people wanted to hear that more jobs was his priority, and that he had five ways in which he was going to achieve this goal. People will often pay attention to the fact that you have five steps in your program, but they don't necessarily want to invest the time to know what each of the five are."

The candidate was also encouraged to study excerpts from the Clinton-Bush debate in the 1992 American presidential campaign, which Clinton had won unquestionably. Clinton had the ability to show people not only that he had a firm grasp of the issues facing the country in all their complexity, but, above all, that he understood their problems, that he cared about them. "We wanted him to see the passion," Anderson went on to say, "the ability that Clinton had to show people his feelings behind an issue. People who have been in politics for a while become accustomed to not showing their feelings. We were trying to tell Jean: 'Be brave, say what you feel.'" "He was very, very good at accepting this kind of criticism," recalls Heather Conway, a Toronto economist who was part of the Charest coaching staff. "He was very open to saying: 'How can I improve my performance?'" Since the 1988 debate with Dennis Wood, when he had not taken kindly to his advisers' criticisms, Charest had matured.

The Clinton-Bush debate had also been marked by the performance of businessman and independent candidate Ross Perot, who upstaged the other candidates with a few well-placed remarks. That's where Bruce Anderson came up with the idea of "fastballs," an allusion to the scariest pitch in baseball. "This was going to be an evening that was going to drone on for a lot of people, even if they were interested," Anderson told his pupil. "And so what he really wanted to do was to try to find those two or three opportunities and the two or three messages that could break through the clutter. [He needed to] be vigilant all the time. At one or two points in the evening, he had to rear back and fire a fastball right down the middle. And that would blaze so quickly by everybody that they'd go: 'Wow! Where did that come from?'"

If two other candidates were monopolizing the television audience's attention, the "fastballs" would also make the camera focus on Charest. In the 1992 debates, Perot had succeeded in "stealing the camera" by interrupting exchanges between Bush and Clinton.

SPLITTING HAIRS

Anderson's focus groups revealed another handicap — a totally unexpected one.

"Why do you have a negative reaction to what he says?" the moderator asked one of the groups.

"His hair. He looks as if he's stuck his finger into an electric socket!"

People were really asking, "Does this person look like a prime minister?" Jodi White realized. Ill at ease, White and her colleagues screwed up their courage and broke the news to Charest: he needed a haircut.

"Listen, Jean," one of them ventured. "You may find this a bit silly. People don't like your hairstyle."

"My hair? What's wrong with my hair?"

"People say it reminds them of the 1970s, and besides, it's too bushy."

"I'm not going to change my hair. I can't control it. That's the way it's always been. This is ridiculous!"

"It may not seem important, Jean. But if people are too busy looking at your hair to listen to what you have to say, then it is important."

What people won't do to become prime minister! Michou, who had always liked her man with long hair, kept an eagle eye on the hairdresser. Recalling the scene, Pierre-Claude Nolin chuckles, "It was like a Church Council. We had to negotiate over every strand of hair!"

KO'ING KIM

In the annals of the 1993 PC leadership race, the Toronto debate is perceived as the beginning of Kim Campbell's demise. A closer look at the tape of the debate, however, reveals that the Vancouverite did not fare so badly after all. But, despite the glowing promise of Campbell-mania, she did not dominate the contest.

Chubby Charest's poise was what struck Tory supporters most that evening. When members of the audience asked questions, he addressed them by their first names, even mentioning their places of residence: "It just so happens I was in Hamilton recently and . . ." In contrast, the supposedly warm Campbell seemed distant. Charest's answers sounded precise, hard-edged; Campbell's seemed vague and theoretical. In response to a question about deficit reduction, the Sherbrooke MP confidently presented a five-point plan: "The first point is: no new taxes. The second point: no increase in tax rates. The third point: no real increase in government expenditures. The fourth point: new programs that we would put forward would have to be funded within existing spending envelopes. And the fifth point, the most important one, I think, is the streamlining of the government itself." One, two, three, four, five — Anderson & Co.'s advice seemed to be producing results. "I don't think that that's the best way to address the problem," Campbell replied. But her approach — "We have to do politics differently and invite the Canadian people in to make the changes with us" — was too vague to capture the imagination of the Tory faithful.

The Environment minister also earned applause with a few "fast-balls," such as, "Small business should be working for profit, not for government!" And Charest wrapped up the debate by saying, "Ladies and gentlemen, this race is just beginning. Make no mistake about it. The race isn't about talk, it's about ideas, alternatives, it's about the issues of the future for your children and my children. And that's what Progressive Conservatives all across Canada have to decide on the thirteenth of June. And as prime minister on the fourteenth of June, I assure you Canada will have a new beginning."

After each debate, organizers sent out their spin-doctors to work the press corps, fast-talkers whose job was to shape media coverage of the event. That evening, Jan Dymond was one of them. "We had our lines ready, you know: 'He did well under the circumstances, it was only the first debate.' But the thing wasn't over when journalists were coming to us: 'Your guy is terrific!'" The next day, the headline in *The Toronto Star* read, "Debate gives Charest the edge on Campbell."

In the Charest camp, it was the trigger event they had hoped for. The media declared Charest the winner. The Campbell forces were stunned. In two short hours, the party brass, who had decided to back her on the basis of a handful of polls, had come to realize how vulnerable their star candidate was. What had gone wrong? Suffering from overconfidence thick enough to slice, Campbell's team had given her only one day to prepare, in spite of her lack of debating experience. "It's like a hockey game. To win, you've got to be afraid of losing. But we weren't afraid of losing," admits lawyer Jean Riou, one of the pillars of the Campbell organization.

Not unlike Jean Charest in 1988, Kim chafed under the advice of her experts. A few days prior to the event they had set up a mock debate, duplicating the details, right down to the lecterns. "Three or four minutes into the rehearsal," recounts Luc Lavoie, one of Campbell's advisers, "she stalked out of the room complaining,

'This is so stupid!'" "She kept saying to us and to herself: 'I can't do this debate unless I am seized with the policy,'" recounts Ross Reid, Kim Campbell's campaign organizer. "But, let's not fool ourselves, television debates are more style than policy. Whatever her ideas were, and she had lots of them, she had to be able to communicate them or it didn't matter. And she wasn't prepared to recognize that she had to make some concessions to this process."

After the debate, Campbell had a long discussion with Reid. "She was pretty down. She was way down," he says. "She knew . . ." She knew that things had not gone very well and that she had better be prepared for the next debate. She would have to be: the debate was to be held in Montréal, in French, a language with which she was much less comfortable than people had been led to believe.

IDEAS, ANYONE?

With the Toronto debate, a real campaign had begun, just as Charest had predicted. Campbell took the offensive with the kind of clumsy arrogance that was to become her trademark: "I'm not in the habit of boasting," she said in Montréal, "but it must be admitted that I've accomplished more in my four years in Ottawa than Charest has in eight." It didn't take Charest long to parry her thrust: "I'm not afraid of saying that of all the candidates, I'm the one who has put the most ideas on the table, whether it concerns the deficit or other areas. Name me just one of Ms. Campbell's ideas!"

For the Montréal debate, Kim Campbell's Québec team made up its mind to leave nothing to chance. Perhaps they went too far.

The countdown to the debate was under way; reporters had already gathered in the Bell Amphitheatre. Kim Campbell and her entourage bustled onto the stage for the final adjustments. Around her buzzed ten people, with advice on camera angles and the colour of her suit. She looked uncomfortable, overwhelmed by a barrage of instructions.

A few minutes later, Jean Charest made his appearance. With a determined look on his face he stepped onto the stage alone, briefly checked the arrangement of the lecterns, and then went around shaking hands with the technicians. He looked relaxed, perfectly at ease.

For all his calm, Charest had just finished a particularly trying day of preparations. The suite in the Crown Plaza Hotel on Sherbrooke Street had been crowded. Besides the small Charest team, scores of well-wishers had come calling, including Transport minister Jean Corbeil and a representative of Montréal mayor Jean Doré. The circumstances weren't really ideal as discussions got under way over the thorniest subject of the day (and of the century): language.

The language debate had resurfaced in Québec. The Bourassa government would soon be deciding whether to maintain Bill 178, the legislation that banned commercial signs in languages other than French. How would Charest respond if he were questioned about the issue during the debate? There were two possibilities. First, he could dodge the question entirely by pointing out that language is a provincial responsibility. Second, he could take a position resolutely in support of English-Québecker minority rights, a move calculated to please militant English-Canadian Conservatives, but sure to displease Québec nationalists in the Tory ranks. Opinions around the table were divided. The discussion dragged on. Charest's confidants noticed that their man was growing increasingly restive. "He hates it when people argue in front of him without coming to any clear conclusion," Jean-Bernard Bélisle explains, "because where does it leave him? It makes him feel insecure. He just can't function." Jodi White decided to clear the room, leaving herself, Anderson, Michou and one or two others close to Charest. The little group gave the candidate the clear counsel he was looking for. "If you say one thing, some people will hate you. If you say the opposite, other people will be up in arms. It's not what you say that's important; what's important is that you've got your heart in it. It's not what we think that's important. It's your gut feeling that counts."

That evening, Charest snatched the opportunity as soon as it arose. To a vaguely worded question about national unity, he replied, "The government of Québec is currently revising Bill 178. It falls within the province's jurisdiction. But even though it may not be a popular thing to say, I believe that the Prime Minister of Canada has a duty to encourage the government of Québec to be more open." When Kim Campbell heard the hearty applause, she immediately switched into damage-control mode. But her reply, one of the few statements that she did not read from the cue cards prepared by Luc Lavoie the previous evening, went over like a lead balloon: "In Québec, the legal system is different from what we find in the rest of Canada. And that's an advantage because we can link to all the legal systems in the world, especially the systems in the new democracies in Eastern Europe." In the press room, journalists glanced at one another, shaking their heads, "What is she talking about, anyway?"

Charest had stolen the scene with his "fastball," and deflated the lovely strategy concocted by Campbell's overconfident brain trust in the process. Criticized for failing to articulate precise ideas, in the second debate she would unveil a clear, four-point plan to eliminate the deficit. When she did so, ministers Gilles Loiselle and Marcel Masse, who were in the press room, rubbed their hands with glee. "That's it, there's our headline! Watch for those press releases!" They had not noticed that journalists had greeted their "news" with studied indifference, first, because the plan lacked originality, and second, because the media already had their lead story: "Charest takes on language issue." Worse still for the Campbellites, there never were any press releases to watch for.

Three other debates were held following the Montréal face-off: in Calgary, Vancouver and Halifax. In all three, Campbell's performance improved, particularly in Calgary, where Charest had taken a hard hit earlier in the day from his friend, cabinet minister

Bernard Valcourt, who told him, "Jean, I've decided to support Kim." In Vancouver, Campbell stumbled once, when she labelled the people who opposed her economic policies "enemies of Canadians." No one remembers the debate in Halifax.

But it was too late. After Toronto and Montréal, the harm had been done. A chink in Kim Campbell's armour had been found, while the young paladin from Sherbrooke had displayed an exceptional talent. Back in Ottawa, Charest organizers could feel the wind beginning to turn. Their Bank Street offices had suddenly become cramped. "Fairly soon, we had people coming in the door and offering to volunteer," recalls Jodi White. "So we rented more space and we grew. We had people volunteering from beginning to end, and the money was growing too." To top it off, an Angus Reid poll hinted that Charest could lead the Conservatives to victory against Chrétien's Liberals. It was a near-miraculous turnaround. But of the two organizations, Campbell's was still the richer and more powerful.

Between April 22 and May 8, the members of the Progressive Conservative Party elected more than 2,700 delegates to the leadership convention. To these were added 700 ex officio delegates — MPs, senators and staffers — the party establishment.

On the evening of May 8, Mitch Patten, who tracked voting patterns for the Charest organization, made a prediction: assuming that two-thirds of the ex officio delegates voted for Campbell, she would have the support of 47 percent of the delegates, compared to 32 percent for Charest. Fifteen percent were undecided. If the latter were distributed proportionally, Campbell would receive 53 percent of the ballots. A scant month before the convention, a victory for the front runner seemed all but certain. "When you look at those numbers, [we had a chance to win] only if we got some help from Kim Campbell," Patten says. "In order to make it a horse race, either she had to lose significant numbers of her delegates or every single undecided delegate in the country would have to come to Charest."

Fortunately for Charest loyalists, Campbell could be relied upon to put her foot in her mouth. Which she did. In an interview with

Peter C. Newman initially published in *Vancouver* magazine, Campbell described people who didn't get involved in politics as "SOBs" and raised the spectre of "the evil demons of papacy" in a remark about the Catholic Church. Taken as a whole, the article drew a flattering portrait of the leading candidate. But taken out of context, a mere two weeks before the convention, the two statements seemed singularly tactless, even insulting. Kim Campbell's image had been further tarnished while Charest, with his customary charm, was winning over a growing number of delegates during his "Tortoise Tour." But it remained unclear who was the hare and who the tortoise. Campbell had gotten off to a flying start, but her organization seemed ponderous and clumsy, constantly tripping over itself. And Charest, though he liked to style himself the tortoise, crisscrossed the country at full speed rather than "like the old Senator" of the La Fontaine fable.

CHICKENS WITH THEIR HEADS CUT OFF

When Albert Painchaud turned up in Ottawa as a member of the Sherbrooke delegation two days before the June 13 vote, he did not like what he saw. "When we arrived at the Civic Centre [where the convention was being held], the first thing we saw was Campbell's huge pink tent," says the veteran Charest organizer. "Then we looked around for our tent." There was no tent. "There was just a small trailer where people were distributing bottles of water. Our first impression was that they had a super organization, while we had nothing." The Charest forces were supposed to congregate in Ottawa's new World Trade Centre, a few kilometres distant. The new centre was a lovely spot, all right, but far from the action. "When our delegates left the Civic Centre, there was no place for them to go and get together, so they'd end up meeting their friends in the Campbell tent," says Martin Desrochers, one of the Charest campaign's top Québec organizers. It was a strategic error of the first magnitude, one of many the Charest camp was to commit during the convention weekend.

What had gone wrong? Beneath the shell of the Tortoise, a fight to the finish was raging among the organizers to control the convention. The battle went unnoticed. Reporters were too busy analysing the disintegration of the Campbell juggernaut.

Organizing a leadership convention requires such extensive preparation that the task is usually handled by a parallel group operating at arm's length from the central party machine. As the convention draws closer, the two organizations merge. That was the theory. But in the Charest campaign, fusion turned out to be more like fission.

The convention week proper was to be co-ordinated by one Peter Vuicic, an Ontario businessman who had handled similar chores for John Crosbie in 1983. Vuicic had offered his services to David Small a few weeks before the convention. It did not take him long to realize that Charest's organization was not up to scratch. The computer network that was to provide updated information on the delegates was unreliable. It was impossible to target each delegate group with personalized letters written based on their preferences for each of the candidates. The software had been designed by a qualified programmer who lacked political experience. "Systems like those," Vuicic says, "should be set up and run by professionals, people you have to pay." Reduced by circumstances to penny-pinching, the Charest team was unwilling to make the necessary investment. The same reason — lack of funds — and a lack of conviction among Charest's organizers that they could win, resulted in slapdash convention planning. By the time Vuicic took over in Ottawa in early May, it was already getting late.

Vuicic's criticisms of the organization were given a chilly reception. Small and Vuicic vied for control of the convention, with Small finally ousting Vuicic from the strategic decision-making process. Lack of funds, poor planning and conflicts between his organizers added up to a devastating week for Jean Charest. Concludes

Jodi White: "Some people said Charest could have won it if he'd had another ten days. My view is we won it a week early, and we lost in the last week."

Albert Painchaud wasn't the only one to realize, on arrival in Ottawa, that something was wrong. Jodi White was overwhelmed by the massive presence of the Campbell forces: "At one point David Small and I were scrambling around delivering placards!" Martin Desrochers, Charest's number-two Québec organizer, remembers trying desperately to set up meetings between his candidate and undecided delegates. But Charest's schedule was crammed with social activities. "A hundred party faithful in the room make for great photos, but they weren't the people we had to convince!" he says. "We were running around like chickens with our heads cut off. We didn't know who we had to win over," says Jean-Martin Masse, another organizer.

In listing the difficulties encountered during convention week, White and Small point the finger at Vuicic. But Desrochers and Vuicic hold Small responsible. Whoever was to blame, the outcome was disastrous. When the convention opened on Friday at noon, the Campbell supporters outnumbered Charest's troops two to one. They were not only more numerous, they were more visible, decked out in pink giveaway caps signed "Kim." "They caught us off guard. We didn't have anything ready," one of Charest's organizers told reporters. Where were the Charest faithful? Well, they hadn't arrived yet. The candidates' organizations, as is usually the case, were footing the tab for conventioneers' registration fees, hotel bills and travel expenses. Bringing hundreds of delegates to the convention two days before the vote costs an arm and a leg. The Charest camp was on a shoestring budget, while Campbell had money to burn. Her people had even registered hundreds of party workers as observers. They were not eligible to vote, but they did swell the Defence minister's forces to massive proportions.

With more volunteers, the Campbell organization could welcome delegates at the airport, the bus terminal or at their hotels. No sooner did they spot a delegate than they handed him a cap and T-shirt and took him under their wing. Delegates who had doubts about their initial choice — and they were many — were caught up in a pink whirlpool that pulled them inexorably toward Kim.

To organizational problems were added outright blunders. The first of them was Bill McKnight's. When McKnight, one of the few cabinet ministers to support Charest, arrived at the convention, he compared an eventual victory by Kim Campbell to the collective suicide of a religious sect who, a few years earlier, had ingested poisoned Kool-Aid on orders from their leader, Jimmy Jones: "I can't believe they are about to drink the Campbell Kool-Aid."

Then Charest made his first mistake. In an interview with CBC the day before the convention opened, he refused to commit himself to running in the upcoming federal election if his opponent were to become party leader: "Nothing is automatic. It's a decision I'll be making with my family." When he heard the interview, former Ontario Conservative premier Bill Davis rang up Jodi White. "Jodi, tell him he can't say that! He has to be there for the good of the party." But Charest wouldn't budge. "He has a stubborn streak about certain things," says White. "Maybe he's too proud. He gets into this thing so much and he starts to take it personally. It was not good judgment." Insists veteran Tory Harry Near, "Even though it was an honest and right answer, it was a dumb answer."

On Saturday morning, at a candidates' forum, a Kim Campbell supporter repeated the question: "If you lose, will you be a candidate in the next election?" He would consult his family, Charest insisted, and a round of boos drowned out the rest of his reply. Luc Ouellet, an organizer from the Québec City region, was in the room that morning: "There was an old Conservative from Winnipeg sitting beside me. When he heard Jean say that, he turned to me with a sad look on his face, and said, 'Shit! Does he care about the party or doesn't he?'" Charest was chastened by the reaction. "He was quite devastated by the booing," recalls Jodi White. "He had never had anything like that happen to him in his life. This is the guy who's always been popular, and this was the convention of his own party, and they booed him!"

Fortunately for Charest, not all was gloom and doom in the final days. Campbell herself made a few slip-ups. Furthermore, the Charest organizers uncovered two encouraging bits of news in the morning papers. The arch-conservative *Globe and Mail* had given the Environment minister its cautious benediction.

> About Mr. Charest, we have [one] misgiving: that his natural ease in debate may be that of Bill Clinton, so consumed with the art of persuasion as to forget what he was trying to say. For good or ill, there is less complexity to Mr. Charest: what you see is what you get.[…] Mr. Charest's campaign has been the more substantive. Add to this a quick mind, a natural, likable demeanor and a plain way of speaking, and you have the makings of a prime minister.

Then, on Friday morning, a Gallup poll showed Charest as the only one who could lead the Conservatives to victory against Jean Chrétien's Liberals. Kim Campbell had lost her magic touch with Canadian voters.

Just a Mess!

There remained one last hurdle to clear in the seemingly interminable leadership steeplechase: the Saturday night speeches. It was a key moment, to be televised nationwide. The task of writing Charest's speech was handed to Larry Hagen, who had earned a name for himself with the remarkable speeches he'd crafted for Joe Clark the previous year. For two weeks he toiled over Charest's speech. "There was clearly a view at the time that his capacity to deliver a good speech was one of his advantages. Therefore, the speech itself was unusually important at that convention," Hagen recalls. "[His organizers] also thought that if the race was close enough, it could have a role in helping him win." A Charest adviser adds, "He wanted to contrast himself with Kim Campbell and show that he was the guy who could move people, that he was a real leader, a politician who could excite Canadians about the party and about himself."

Saturday afternoon. Charest had to return to his office in the Parliament Buildings to change his clothes. A lectern had been set up there so that he could rehearse the final version of the speech. But his bus got stuck in a traffic jam; it was impossible to reach Parliament Hill in time. "Joe's office isn't far!" someone piped up. So, the team stopped off at Joe Clark's downtown Ottawa office. Hardly the sort of thing to soothe the leadership candidate's frazzled nerves and hoarse voice. Added to his torments was a cold sore on his lower lip. Charest asked for a moment of peace and quiet to concentrate on the speech. Impossible! He looked around for one of his favourite pens; there was none to be found in Clark's office. He wanted to add a few sentences from an earlier draft to the final version; nobody could find it in the welter of papers. "It was just a mess!" says Heather Conway.

When Charest read through the speech in front of his advisers, they were disconsolate. "We were really worried. He didn't deliver the speech very well," says Conway. But the strategists kept mum, thinking it was better not to discourage their man less than an hour before the showdown. When Charest left the office for the Civic Centre, the whole team had a hangdog look, like the condemned on their way to the guillotine.

The Campbell organization had won the "battle for the floor" of the convention. Pink was everywhere, creating the impression that she had twice as many supporters as Charest. But Claude Lacroix, the artist of the Charest camp, had dreamed up one of his trademark surprises. On arrival in the capital a few days earlier, Lacroix had quickly understood that the Charest forces had made no preparations: no decorations, no music and no presentation for speech night. The Everest Group VP swung rapidly into action. When Charest was introduced, he made his entrance by bus: "The Tortoise Tour" coach drove right into the arena, preceded by hundreds of volunteers carrying immense banners in the candidate's colours. The volunteers, who weren't registered at the convention for lack of funds, would help counter Campbell's domination on the visual level. The plan was a master stroke: simple, original and effective. Charest stepped from the bus and climbed onto the stage to the accompaniment of his campaign theme song, Brian Adams's "Can't Stop This Thing We Started!"

His voice hoarse, the challenger spoke slowly at first, hesitating, then stumbling. It didn't look very good. Then came hurdle number one: to overcome the damage already done. "Let me be clear," Charest said solemnly. "I will be proud to serve with each and all of [my opponents] in tomorrow's Progressive Conservative government." This statement earned him an ovation. From that moment on, as if relieved of a burden, he launched into the kind of stem-winder designed to prove that no one in the party, and perhaps no one in the country, was a better campaigner.

The text penned by Hagen was loaded with "fastballs," and Charest took obvious delight in firing them with an energy that knocked the socks off the conventioneers. He ripped into the opposition parties, starting with the Liberals: "The Sixties are over, and I am telling you, Jean Chrétien, it's 1993, it's no ideas, no votes!" The house was rocking. In a plaintive tone, Charest begged, "And please, please . . . [then switching abruptly into aggressive mode] . . . turn me loose on the Bloc Québécois!" The crowd howled for more.

Next Charest waded head on into the weaknesses his opponents had identified. It wasn't the first time Charest had done so, but Hagen's sentences were remarkably suited to the task. First, the age question: "Some say I may be too young," he remarked, pausing to allow his supporters to register their indignation. "Yes, I am young, and vigorous . . . and so is Canada!" Then, his Québec roots: "Yes,

I am a Canadian from Québec, from the city of Sherbrooke, and you'd better believe it, I am very proud of that!"

Sweat pouring down his forehead, Charest concluded with a none-too-subtle reminder of his opponent's weaknesses. "We know what will bring us victory, and where victory needs to be won," he pointed out. "Our party must win in British Columbia, and I can win in British Columbia. Our party needs to win in Québec, and you know that I can do that! Our party needs to win everywhere in Canada, and I can!" Then, into the home stretch: "Some of you made judgments and declarations weeks ago, even months ago. Those were based on your best judgment then, but your role tomorrow is to exercise your best judgment now. Not the campaign when it started, but the campaign as it ended up. Not what was predicted, but what happened."

Even at several years' remove, it is an impressive performance. Vintage Charest.

When Kim Campbell's turn came, people had to wait. The delegates looked at one another, wondering. The big pink machine had put together a laser show for the star's entrance. What money won't buy! But all the money in the world can't stop a power failure. The unthinkable happened: a short circuit. Forget the lasers. Kim had to make her entrance technically unassisted. Then, flashing her most radiant smile, she began, "Tonight I want to talk to you about winning." It was a fine start, but the twenty minutes that followed seemed like an address to a chamber of commerce, with statements like "Power should not mean anything else but service." Even the hard-core Campbellites were sitting on their hands. "There was no magic in it," she was later to confess.

Still, Kim Campbell had made no major blunders. That was the only thing that counted. The history of leadership races has demonstrated that a good speech cannot prevent defeat, but a bad one can cost the victory. For all the tumult and the shouting, that Saturday night did not alter the standings one iota. There would be a final night of partying and arm-twisting and, the next day, the vote.

A Ballot to Remember

Sunday, June 13. A torrid sun blazed down from a cloudless sky. Five thousand people had crammed into the Ottawa Civic Centre to elect the next leader of the Progressive Conservative Party — and prime minister of Canada. David Small and Mitch Patten met Jean Charest a few minutes before the voting began: "What about it, guys?"

"We don't have any illusions, Jean. We haven't caught her. On the first ballot, she'll get between one hundred and two hundred votes more than us."

"And the second ballot?"

"Impossible to predict."

In fact, Patten's vote projections showed a Charest victory was possible, but not probable. The strategist had drawn up two scenarios: in the first, each camp would get the delegates who had clearly indicated they would vote for it, in addition to the votes of those who said they were leaning toward the candidate without being absolutely committed — the "soft" support. The vote of absolutely undecided delegates would then be distributed proportionally. In this scenario the first ballot would give Campbell 46 percent of the votes, Charest 45 percent, and 8 percent would go to the others. After the "other" candidates had withdrawn, the second-ballot forecast was based on the delegates' second declared choice. That would give Charest 52 percent, Campbell 48 percent. "Those numbers told us," says Mitch Patten, "that if we had the momentum, if the undecided delegates voted overwhelmingly for Charest, we had a shot."

And if everything went against Charest? That was the second scenario. It was based on the hypothesis that Charest would lose some of his "soft" support and Campbell would keep all of hers. On the first ballot, Campbell would win 49.6 percent of the votes, compared with 41.3 percent for Charest and 9.1 percent for the others. In that event, the Defence minister would be assured of victory on the second ballot, 52 percent to 48 percent, according to Patten's calculations.

Voting got under way early in the afternoon in a circus atmosphere of blaring music and waving banners. Under the constant
scrutiny of the television cameras, the candidates and their close
advisers struggled to look as serene as possible, despite the stress and
the fatigue. Robert Charest warned the fiery Red: "Be careful what
you say — the mikes pick up everything." Down on the convention
floor, Martin Desrochers, Charest's Québec strategist, was fit to be
tied. He had been cut off from the "godfathers," the volunteers
whose job it was to make sure that the Charest delegates cast their
votes. Nor could he contact the Charest entourage. "I couldn't
reach them, they couldn't reach me," says Desrochers, still fuming
years later. "We had to watch Radio-Canada to find out what was
happening!" Nerves frazzled, Desrochers ended up throwing his
walkie-talkie into the nearest wastebasket.

The results of the first ballot were announced: Patrick Boyer,
53 votes; Kim Campbell, 1,664; Jean Charest, 1,369; Jim Edwards,
307; and Garth Turner, 76. Reporters pulled out their calculators,
jotted down a few figures. But Small and Patten had already gotten
the message. The second — and worst-case — scenario had come to
pass. Campbell had gotten 48 percent of the votes, Charest 39 percent. Kim was only seventy votes short of an absolute majority.
Pierre-Claude Nolin, Harry Near and Joe Clark rushed over to
Edwards, the candidate from Alberta, in an attempt to convince
him to go over to Charest on the second ballot. But it was too late.
Edwards had already done his arithmetic and headed straight for
Kim Campbell. Charest's fate was sealed.

Shocked, Jean and Michèle left the crowd and took refuge in the
room reserved for them under the stands. It was there that Denis
Beaudoin explained to Michou that the battle was lost. She burst
into tears.

It took two long hours to complete the second ballot. Just before
the results were to be announced, Jean and Michèle took their places
with their supporters in front of the cameras. Michèle screwed up
her courage: "I thought, 'My God, how am I going to do it? I have

to look as enthusiastic as when I left. I can't let it show . . . I'll never be able to do it.'" But she managed. "I think I kept my hopes up in spite of everything, right until the end." Vain hopes. The delegates had spoken: Campbell, 1,817 votes; Charest, 1,630. Kim had won 52.7 percent of the votes. Patten's second scenario had predicted 52.4 percent!

Years later, Charest's strategists were still carrying a grudge toward Jim Edwards. Pierre-Claude Nolin and Harry Near swear they had an unequivocal deal with seasoned veteran John Laschinger, chief strategist of the Edwards campaign. Edwards, they claim, had agreed to support Charest on the second ballot, no matter what. The deal would have guaranteed him a place in a Charest cabinet and a helping hand from the party to look after his campaign debts. But unbeknownst to Nolin and Near, Laschinger had made a similar pact with the Campbell camp. Given the results of the first ballot, Edwards had no choice, as Jodi White, Charest's campaign manager, sees it. "Once I saw the numbers, I knew he couldn't. It didn't make any sense to come to us if he wanted to be in cabinet, because it couldn't make Charest win." Couldn't it? What if the Albertan had joined the Charest camp? A fair number of his delegates, like those of the other marginal candidates, would have voted for Campbell in any case. That would have been enough to give the Defence minister the majority . . . and Edwards would have lost all hope of an important cabinet portfolio.

Now that the outcome was clear, Charest had to go back on stage to concede defeat. For all his disappointment — his eyes were brimming with tears — for all the bitterness, he carried it off with class. "This great party of ours has been served by great leaders, and three of them are here tonight. The Right Honourable Robert Stanfield, the Right Honourable Joe Clark and the Right Honourable Brian Mulroney. And on this day, as a delegate to this convention, may I put to you that we should make it unanimous that this party support the next great leader of this country, the Right Honourable Kim Campbell!"

Then came the future prime minister of Canada's turn to speak. It was an important moment, a time for the healing process to begin. "If I might be permitted a special word to my friend and colleague Jean Charest," Campbell began. The crowd gave Charest a lengthy ovation. Besides exhaustion, there was a look of anticipation on the losing candidate's face. An expectation of special recognition. But instead, the winner offered him this: "John, you're one hell of a tortoise!" That was all — for the man who had started out with nothing at thirty-four years of age and had come within one hundred votes of becoming prime minister, the man who had given the party the passionate race that it had despaired of. That evening, Campbell displayed an extraordinary lack of political savvy.

Bill Neville, Joe Clark's former chief of staff, had drafted the acceptance speech. More accurately, he had jotted down the one-and-a-half-page outline of a speech at the last moment. "I assumed she would go on after that and ad lib," says Neville. "In the end, she didn't say much more than what was on the page and a half, which had only this sort of joke about Charest. In retrospect, I should have written more." The harm had been done. Jean Charest left the room dejected, bitter and furious. And Jean Charest's anger is not easily appeased.

The Loner

—⊶—

"All the kids will tease me," said Amélie, in no mood for school the day after the convention. Losing hurts even when you're only ten years old. But father Jean put his foot down. "I'm going to the office; you're going to go to school. Life goes on." The same words Red had spoken to the children when their mother died.

While Amélie was getting back to her schoolbooks, her dad was on his way to a luncheon date he would have preferred to avoid. Bill Neville, Kim Campbell's transition team manager, had prevailed upon the new Prime Minister to meet her former adversary as soon as the convention had wound up. "It was quite clearly not to have a serious discussion or negotiation about his role in the new government," says Neville. "It was rather to give her a chance to say: 'Gee! I should have said more about you.' To clear the air of any ill will after the convention and hopefully create sort of a good atmosphere for that discussion when it would happen." Such meetings had become an Ottawa tradition. Ten years before, Brian Mulroney had spent an hour consoling his perennial rival, Joe Clark.

But Jean Charest was not as gracious in defeat as Clark. Worse, he was in a particularly testy mood that morning. Campbell's slight of the day before had stuck in his craw. He thought back to Mulroney's victory speech in 1983. Charest had been a young Clark delegate then. Newly elected Tory leader Brian Mulroney had delivered a ringing tribute to his predecessor. Then he had turned to the party's interim leader, Erik Nielsen, an MP from the Yukon and a veteran of parliamentary wars. A few minutes earlier, Nielsen had reminded party workers that Mulroney had not been his "first choice." "Erik," said the victor, "I want you to know that you're my first choice as House Leader of this party." "It was an extraordinary moment," recalls Charest. "He broke the ice. People understood that their leader was capable of rising above the divisions of the leadership race." The Charest people had expected to hear a similar signal on that evening of defeat. But it never came. Campbell's victory speech left Jean Charest discouraged. "She hasn't changed," he thought. "She just doesn't have the knack."

Says Charest: "Kim wasn't good at reading a situation. A leader has to be able to express the feeling in the room. That evening, it was obvious there was a great deal of sympathy for the runner-up. But Kim couldn't express it."

That incident aside, Charest simply could not accept defeat. His people informed the Campbell camp that he was in no mood for lunch. But in the minds of Campbell's advisers, the meeting could not be put off. So, a grumpy Jean Charest made his way to Campbell's suite in the Westin Hotel. Horror of horrors, joyful delegates proudly wearing pink caps greeted him. "We love you, Jean!" "You put up a great fight!" they said, thumping him heartily on the back. Though Charest replied courteously, he could not help wondering, "If I'm so great, how come you didn't vote for me?" In the elevator, he muttered to Philippe Morel, "Philippe, I don't want to go out the way we came in! Find me the service stairs, land a helicopter on the roof, anything but this!"

Campbell greeted him at the door of her suite. Polite pecks on the cheek did little to relieve the tension. Charest barely touched the poached salmon that had been served for the occasion. The new leader described the immense joy women across the country felt over her victory, which only deepened Charest's funk. She turned to the electoral potential of a Campbell-Charest team. Stony silence. Then she asked, "What role would you like to play in the government?" and started eating her salmon so he would have to talk.

"No matter what," he replied (aggressively, claims Campbell), "I'm not interested in the deputy prime minister's job. I want to play an important role, a concrete role, in charge of an economic portfolio. It would be natural for me to be minister responsible for Québec. And the ministers who supported me should have a place in cabinet."

"Well, I have not yet made any firm decision about cabinet, and I would like to reflect on your comments."

The discussion went no further. Charest stalked out, fuming. He didn't trust the woman. "I remember him saying, 'I was lectured about how the people in the market were pleased that the next prime minister would be a woman!'" recalls Jodi White. Imagine, lecturing a Charest? Meanwhile, Campbell sought out Neville: "Bill, this lunch was a disaster!"

Brian Mulroney's last caucus meeting took place two days later. When he entered the room, the outgoing Prime Minister noticed Jean Charest's absence. Mulroney had him summoned. "Tell him that the Prime Minister desires his presence in caucus." Charest came, but remained at the back of the room, with his head bowed.

For another ten days Charest brooded, floating the threat of resignation if his demands weren't met, well aware that the party could not do without him on the eve of a general election. The trickiest item on the shopping list he presented to the new Prime Minister was the request that he be named minister responsible for Québec. How was Campbell to appoint her opponent to the post instead of handing it to a Québec minister like Pierre Blais, who had supported her? "I would have had a revolt on my hands,"

Campbell explains in her autobiography.* And there was more at stake than just the title. "There was also the question of the position she was prepared to give me," says Charest. At the time, he was convinced that she was not prepared to let him wield real influence in her government.

Charest's attitude had begun to exasperate Brian Mulroney, who was dragged into playing the mediator. Finally, the PM invited Charest and his family for a day at his summer residence on Harrington Lake, in Gatineau Park. It was a perfect opportunity for a man-to-man talk, with the elder statesman adopting the paternal tone he liked so much.

Brian Mulroney could understand Charest's frustration; after all, he himself had finished a depressing third at the 1976 leadership convention. His message could not have been more compelling: "Think about your future, Jean. People are going to make up their minds about you depending on how you conduct yourself in the days ahead. They made up their minds about me in 1976. It was like it or lump it, but I didn't say a word. Seven years later I became the leader."

The two sides finally called a truce. On June 25, Prime Minister Kim Campbell announced her cabinet. Charest got his economic portfolio — the new "super-ministry" of Industry and Science. He also became deputy prime minister. He was not named minister responsible for Québec, but Pierre Blais did not get the job, either. Monique Landry, less a political heavyweight, proved a good compromise solution. As a consolation prize, Charest became minister responsible for the Federal Office of Regional Development (Québec), and promptly appointed his organizer Martin Desrochers to head up the agency.

Campbell and Charest made peace — but the hatchet was only half buried. Loath to work in a Campbell cabinet, the new deputy prime minister had secretly made up his mind to leave politics —

---

* Kim Campbell, *Time and Chance: The Political Memoirs of Canada's First Woman Prime Minister* (Toronto: Doubleday Canada, 1996).

temporarily — in the months following the election campaign.

A few years later, Jean Charest would look back with a critical eye on his conduct during that period. "I was wallowing in self-pity, I was sulking, and I was wrong to sulk. In politics, you aren't entitled to be unhappy. It wasn't one of the high points of my political career." Truer words were never spoken.

WHO'S IN CHARGE HERE?

The summer of 1993 saw a rebirth of Campbell-mania. Canada Day, a first ministers' conference and the summit meeting of the Group of Seven (G-7) most industrialized countries combined to sweep away memories of Campbell's botched leadership campaign. By the end of August, polls showed that Kim Campbell had regained her popularity, although a larger percentage of decided voters was still leaning toward Jean Chrétien's Liberals. On September 8, Campbell called an election for October 25. Thus began one of the most disastrous election campaigns in Canadian political history.

Conservative strategists had staked everything on Kim Campbell's personality. At a meeting with party organizers in early August, the Prime Minister had told them that political promises were a thing of the past, that the party would campaign without a platform. "I remember us saying 'why not?'" says Pierre-Claude Nolin. But considering the new leader's quicksilver temperament, it was a risky wager — one that was lost as soon as Jean Chrétien published his Red Book, a detailed and well-thought-out program overflowing with facts and figures, spelling out his party's election promises. The pressure soon became too strong for the Conservatives to bear: they had to make public their own commitments. They ended up publishing a Little Blue Book, which consisted almost entirely of hot air. Meanwhile, the PM blundered from gaffe to slip-up — at least to hear the media tell it. The Conservatives' ratings were sinking rapidly to dangerous levels.

Relations between Campbell's organizers and Charest's people grew increasingly tense. Campbell had named Jodi White her chief of staff, and in Québec, Pierre-Claude Nolin became the Tory campaign manager. But nevertheless the backbiting intensified. Convinced that they had been shoved aside, Martin Desrochers, François Pilote and the other Charest organizers brooded. Charest placed himself at the disposal of the national organization but was told his services weren't required. Rather than remain idle, the MP from Sherbrooke launched a parallel campaign of his own, responding to the invitations that poured in from candidates from coast to coast. When the Campbell people called on him for special missions, he complied docilely. But Charest could not get over his former rival's lack of flair. When the Prime Minister addressed the party workers of a particular riding, she barely mentioned the name of the local candidate. It got so bad that Charest would speak up: "We're here to give our support to an excellent candidate, John Smith, who will soon be your MP in Ottawa!" "It wasn't that she ignored Jean Charest, it was that she ignored everybody!" says Huw Williams, a Charest political aide who accompanied him on the campaign trail.

Some of the organizers who had worked for Campbell's leadership campaign complained that Jean Charest was in no hurry to visit their ridings, which was creating problems, particularly for people in Eastern Québec. Says Luc Ouellet, "Things were more complicated when it came to ridings that hadn't supported Jean at the convention, that much was obvious." So envenomed had the situation become that Pierre-Claude Nolin felt it necessary to scold Charest's people in public, insisting that they get back in line.

The backstabbing climaxed in the second-to-last weekend of the campaign. In an interview with *La Presse*, Kim Campbell allowed herself the luxury of criticizing Brian Mulroney and her very own deputy prime minister, Jean Charest. Mulroney, Prime Minister Campbell suggested, could not claim full credit for the Conservative victories of 1984 and 1988. Turning to Charest, she ridiculed the economic program he had put forward during the leadership campaign.

Jean Corbeil, Transport minister and former mayor of Ville d'Anjou, an east-end Montréal suburb, had supported Charest during the leadership contest. Now he was beside himself. In a vitriolic letter he ripped into his new leader. "Out of loyalty to my party, I find it intolerable that you denigrate some of its members in an attempt to justify the derailment of a campaign whose strategists you have chosen and whose orientation you have determined." Campbell was forced to backtrack, apologizing to those who felt offended by her remarks. The episode spoiled what had begun as a particularly successful day of campaigning in Québec City. Corbeil's attack riled pro-Campbell organizers. "We put on the best show in the campaign, and what came out that evening was that she had to eat her words," says one of them. "We were mad as hell. Particularly since Corbeil was buddy-buddy with Charest."

Jean Charest had attempted to persuade his colleague not to send the incendiary letter. As a last resort, he had even asked Brian Mulroney to intervene. The former prime minister did get in touch with Corbeil, but it was too late: the letter had already been sent. "So, it was a disaster," sighs Mulroney. "Everything went to the dogs." On the night of October 25, 1993, Jean Chrétien's Liberals were swept into power with 177 seats. The Bloc Québécois, in its first general election, was runner-up with 54 seats, transforming an avowedly sovereigntist party into the Official Opposition in the House of Commons. The Reform Party won 52 seats, and the NDP 9. The once-powerful Progressive Conservative Party of Canada would have to make do with 2 seats out of 295.

Jean Charest's seat was one of the two. Was it a blessing or a curse? Throughout the campaign he had kept a wary eye on his Sherbrooke constituency. Should he continue his cross-country campaigning or should he return to his riding? His majority was solid, the organizers had assured him. In fact, Charest defeated his Bloc opponent by 8,200 votes. At a small party that night at organizer Alain Paquin's house, the MP did not appear the least bit depressed. The party had lost. But it was not *his* defeat. It was, in fact, his opportunity.

"PICK UP THE PIECES!"

The day after the vote, Jean Charest was back at work in his Sherbrooke office. His quick-thinking organizers pasted stickers that read "Thanks for your support" on the hundreds of signs that dotted the riding. With disconcerting serenity — after all, he had just gone from being deputy prime minister of Canada to simply an MP for a party that had been crushed — Charest gave interview after interview. No, the Conservative Party was not dead. No, he was not thinking of quitting politics. Yes, if Kim Campbell decided to stay on as party leader he would support her. In other words, Charest said what was expected of him. He also did what was expected of him: he got in touch with organizers and defeated candidates to boost their morale. It was as if he were preparing to become leader.

Party insiders had no doubt that Campbell would step down. And many believed Charest should succeed her. He was already anticipating the rebuilding phase. "We must reinvent conservatism," he said. However, some people in his entourage wondered whether he should be the one to pick up the broken pieces of the once-mighty Blue Machine. Martin Desrochers was skeptical. "I didn't think it was a good idea for him to get involved in the day-to-day problems of running the party. It was better for him to find a job in Montréal or Toronto and make a little money, keeping close tabs on the party all the while. Then he could return when the timing was right, either just before or right after the next elections."

Brian Mulroney urged his political scion to seize the day. "Jean," Mulroney told him, "it's a unique opportunity. You can take over the party, you can rebuild it, and it will belong to you. Of course, it's your decision. It's up to you to decide if you want to be prime minister of Canada one day." Another former leader held the same view: Joe Clark.

When Charest returned from vacation in November, he had lunch with Kim Campbell. It was hardly more palatable than their post-convention encounter. Campbell wanted to know whether her colleague would be prepared to replace her were she to resign. Charest, as usual, was evasive.

In a speech to Toronto party workers several days later, Kim Campbell announced that a commission was being set up to make recommendations for rebuilding the party. The members were to hand her their report no later than June 1994. The attendees looked at each other, incredulous. The commission would have to give *her* its report? She wanted to stay on? In the hours that followed, president Gerry St. Germain and other party leaders told Campbell in no uncertain terms that she was expected to resign as soon as possible. "I had gotten in touch with a lot of people in the business community, and everyone told me that it would be impossible to raise funds if she stayed on as party leader," says St. Germain, now a senator. Six million dollars in debt, the Conservative Party could ill afford to displease its donors.

Charest might have feigned hesitation, but he was ready. As Martin Desrochers puts it, "He wanted to be leader and now he had the chance, so he became leader." The MP's hesitation waltz put him in a strong bargaining position with the party hierarchy. Charest wanted to be in full command, particularly when it came to key appointments. He would not be merely filling in; he fully intended to lead the Conservative Party in the next election.

On December 15, 1993, Jean Charest was named interim leader of the Progressive Conservative Party of Canada. It is not certain that he was fully aware of the magnitude of the task that awaited him.

IS ANYBODY HOME?

The successor to John A. Macdonald, John Diefenbaker and Brian Mulroney inherited a party in tatters. With only two MPs, the Conservatives did not enjoy official party status in the House of Commons. That meant Charest and his colleague Elsie Wayne would have no budget, no researchers, nothing. It also meant that Charest was rarely entitled to speak during Question Period. As a result, reporters on Parliament Hill ignored him. For Charest, it was sheer torment.

The party's debts made it imperative to cut spending on a crash basis. In the aftermath of the election, most party employees were dismissed. Permanent staff in the Montréal office shrank from ten employees to one. The identical scenario was repeated in the federal capital.

But lack of funds was not the most serious problem. The Tories faced a shortage of party workers. Stunned and indebted, the defeated Conservative candidates wanted nothing more to do with politics. In riding after riding, party workers stayed home, completely demoralized. "It was like a desert," says former MP Gabriel Desjardins, who continued to be active during the dark years. "Funds had dried up, former MPs were lying low, the organization was in a shambles!" It fell to François Pilote to rebuild the organization in Québec. "The only calls I got," he admits, "came from debt-ridden MPs who wanted me to find them a job. But where?" In the first few months, Pilote spent days on end defending the party in court against its creditors. Even in an old Tory riding like Toronto's Don Valley West, it was extremely difficult to keep the local association alive. "When you don't have an MP, not many caucus members and no cabinet ministers, who do you invite as guest speaker?" asks longtime party stalwart Dennis McKeever. "You can't invite poor Jean Charest, he's running around the country doing more important things. When we sent out our Christmas begging letter, the money would fall from $4,000 to $2,000. Memberships wouldn't be renewed as much."

Confidently, perhaps a little naively, Charest drew up a three-phase plan, the Three Rs: rebuilding the party, rewriting the program, and returning to power. "We have to do our homework," he kept saying in early 1994. "There's no shortcut to power." Unable to use the Commons as a forum, the new Conservative leader turned his back on it, and set out to visit Conservatives all over the country. His travels would quickly become a trial. He was far from his family; Michèle and the children found the experience extremely trying. "He was always away," Michou recalls. "It's just as well we didn't know what was in store for us when we got involved in the first place!" Meanwhile, his MP's salary (about $64,400, in addition to a non-taxable allowance of $21,300) gave the family the feeling that it was in a financial strait-jacket, particularly because the party often took its time reimbursing the leader's expenses. And his credit card balance was cause for alarm.

Worst of all, Charest felt terribly alone. He had become accustomed to speaking in front of large crowds; now he spoke at coffee klatsches. One evening, only ten people turned up in a large rented hall. "It doesn't make any damned sense," he complained to Pilote on the way out. "We can't go on like this." The organizer reminded him of the harsh realities of political life. "He'd been on the hit parade for eight years, he'd gotten used to it," says Pilote. Charest had also become accustomed to travelling with a ministerial entourage. Now, he had to be content with the fleeting company of volunteers waiting for him at airports. Nobody was there to sort out the travel headaches, from badly booked hotels to missed flights. Added to Charest's heavy work schedule, the travel was becoming a grind. "Maybe it doesn't look all that serious," concedes Denis Pageau, who became Charest's first chief of staff after the 1993 election. "But when you're used to a pretty comfy life, a guy is bound to react. When you're a minister, you arrive at the hotel, the door of your room is open, the check-in has been taken care of, and your suitcase is on the bed! All that's left is your work."

Rick Borotsik, mayor of Brandon at the time and now an MP,

The adversaries. Kim Campbell and Jean Charest field questions from delegates at the 1993 Conservative convention. *Photo: Bill McCarthy. Jean Charest/Michèle Dionne collection.*

The orator. On the eve of the first ballot, Charest delivers a stem-winder: "And please, please . . . turn me loose on the Bloc Québécois!" *Photo: Bill McCarthy. Jean Charest/Michèle Dionne collection.*

Defeat. Jean Charest and Michèle Dionne minutes after learning of Kim Campbell's victory. Charest had expected a goodwill gesture; Campbell called him "quite a tortoise." *Photo: Perry Beaton.*

Cut! After a rousing referendum campaign, Charest delivers his victory address on October 30, 1995. But on television, Canadians were to see Prime Minister Chrétien instead. *Photo: Pierre McCann — La Presse.*

The three tenors. Jean Chrétien, Daniel Johnson and Jean Charest, minutes before the massive No demonstration held in Montréal's Place du Canada three days prior to the 1995 referendum. *Jean Charest/Michèle Dionne collection.*

The hotel room. Jean Charest, Michèle Dionne and adviser David McLaughlin in a Toronto hotel room, March 1997. *Photo: Bill McCarthy. Jean Charest/Michèle Dionne collection.*

Disappointment. Election night with the Charests. Sherbrooke, June 2, 1997.
Front: Lise Dionne and Suzanne Poulin. Rear: Jean Charest with friend and
adviser Jean-Bernard Bélisle. *Photo: Perry Beaton.*

"At the present time . . ." Toronto, March 2, 1998. Québec Liberal leader Daniel Johnson announces his resignation. Jean Charest says he is not interested in succeeding Johnson "at the present time." *Photo: Canadian Press.*

"I choose Québec." Sherbrooke, March 26, 1998. Dozens of journalists from across Canada listen as Jean Charest announces his candidacy for the Québec Liberal Party leadership. Michèle Dionne is at his side, as usual. *Photos:* La Tribune.

"Never, never!" She and her husband would never abandon the Conservative Party for provincial politics, swore Michèle Dionne. As Jean Charest bids farewell to the Commons on April 2, 1998, Michèle weeps. *Photo: Canadian Press.*

remembers when the Tory leader visited his neck of the woods in Manitoba. "Jean Charest drove up by himself, in a little rented Dodge Colt, came into the room with one hundred and somewhat people there, spoke passionately and got back in his Dodge Colt and went back to Winnipeg. There was no entourage, there was no media, and there was no attention. Here was a man who was doing this for the good of the party!" Former PC leader Joe Clark was struck by how meagre Charest's resources were: "Your responsibilities as the leader of a national party involve maintaining an overview of what the party is supposed to be doing, planning, all the major decisions come back to you. In Jean's case, all the minor decisions came back to him too. I was able to delegate out a large number of issues and I did it almost without thinking."

Not surprisingly, Charest was down in the dumps. "There were many days [when he wondered]: 'Why am I here? Why me?' Nobody ever understood how alone he was," says Jodi White. At his request, the party agreed to pay him $46,000, which brought his total salary up to ministerial level. But by-elections held in three ridings on February 13, 1995, did nothing to boost his morale. The Conservatives had their best showing in Ottawa-Vanier, with 8.9 percent of the vote. In Saint-Henri–Westmount, the Tory candidate picked up only 3.8 percent of the ballots. But the worst results were recorded in Brome-Missisquoi, a longtime Conservative stronghold not far from Sherbrooke, in which the Tory candidate registered a dismal 3 percent. "We told you so," chorused a number of Tory organizers who had advised Charest not to run candidates. One of his advisers was former MP Gabriel Desjardins, who had become president of the PCs' Québec wing. "Jean, what's the point of getting involved in by-elections when we're in the middle of rebuilding?" Desjardins had asked the leader. "They're going to bury us!"

"Gabi, we're a national party!"

"Just two years before the general election," says Desjardins, "it was a traumatizing experience. Just think of the message it sent our troops!"

In his darkest hours, Charest called Brian Mulroney. The former prime minister knew how to stir up the new leader's ambitions with his little history lessons. "Jean, from 1935 to 1957, the Conservative Party was in the opposition. It never won more than fifty seats. There were all kinds of parties, Créditiste, Reformers! For twenty-two years, we weren't in power. You, you've been in the opposition for barely eighteen months. Wait for the next election! You're bound to improve your position. And the next time after that, you'll become prime minister of Canada."

In another moment of despair, he talked with his father. "I see," Red grumbled. "But that's not the way I brought you up!" Rita would have put it more gently, but the message would have been the same: "Get back on your horse!" A Charest never gives up.

THE OASIS

A few days before the election debacle of 1993, Jean Charest addressed the Greater Montréal Chamber of Commerce. One of his organizers, when asked if he believed Charest should take the party leadership after the predictable defeat, replied, "For sure. It'll be hard slogging at first, but the PQ will win the provincial election, there'll be a referendum, and then Charest can mount one hell of a campaign." At the time, the scenario seemed based on shaky premises indeed. Events, however, were to prove the anonymous organizer right.

The federalist forces began to set up their organization in the weeks following the victory of Jacques Parizeau's Parti Québécois in September 1994. A meeting took place in November, attended by organizers from the provincial Liberal Party, the federal Liberal Party and the Conservative Party. Charest's team, represented by Pierre-Claude Nolin, François Pilote and Jean Bazin, a close friend of Brian Mulroney's, would take part in all subsequent meetings until the day of the referendum, October 30, 1995.

The Conservatives had three objectives: first, to contribute as much as possible to a No victory; second, to give their leader greater visibility; and third (an objective no one mentioned at the time), to use the campaign to recruit members and lay the groundwork for the next election. Wherever Charest spoke, an organizer would beat the bushes for sympathizers who would eventually work for the Conservative Party. Why pursue partisan politics when the country's future was at stake? Because the party simply did not have the funds to move Charest and his entourage around on its own. "In the referendum campaign," François Pilote admits candidly, "the No committee covered our expenses."

In truth, the Tories had little impact on federalist strategy. "We had one asset: Jean Charest," says Pierre-Claude Nolin. The provincial Liberals ran the show, closely monitored by their federal cousins. And the provincial Liberal Party had no intention of making room for the leader of a party on the verge of extinction. Not to mention that his presence might overshadow Québec Liberal leader Daniel Johnson.

Jean Masson, the Liberal lawyer in charge of the No road show, drew up three itineraries. There was the A tour featuring No committee leader Daniel Johnson, followed by the media bus. The B tour targeted regional centres like Chicoutimi, Sherbrooke, Hull and Trois-Rivières, and spotlighted new federal minister Lucienne Robillard and the Conservative leader. Finally, the C tour brought together the businesspeople and other federalist players. Throughout the campaign, Conservatives complained about the lack of national media coverage for their leader. They wanted what insiders called "the bus" — meaning they wanted Charest on the lead vehicle doing the cross-Québec tour. He only made it once, on October 14, when Daniel Johnson took the day off. To the Conservatives' great disappointment, many reporters did the same thing. The next morning Senator Nolin complained to Liberal Pierre Anctil, Daniel Johnson's chief of staff, who was handling relations between the No committee and the press.

"There was almost nothing about Charest in yesterday's news," Nolin grumbled.

"I know, I spoke to [the media] about it."

"You may have a loud bark, but they know you don't bite!"

To this day, Jean Masson points the finger at the media for Jean Charest's relative obscurity at the time. "During a referendum campaign, even if the Pope campaigned alongside Lucien Bouchard, you won't see the Pope on the news," offers Masson.

In strategy meetings during that unseasonably warm autumn, provincial Grits and federal Tories formed a common front to pressure the Chrétien government to hold out the prospect of constitutional change to Québeckers. In one caucus meeting, Charest voiced his concern: "I'm going into battle without the weapons I need to fight." Since the polls were predicting an easy No victory, the federal Liberals ignored the pleas of provincial Liberals and the Tories. "It was like pulling teeth to get two or three 'distinct societies' into the No manifesto," recalls Senator Nolin.

Charest displayed his oratorical gifts at large pro-federalist rallies, eclipsing the weepy Lucienne Robillard. "Charest electrified the room, then Lucienne would speak. By the time it was Johnson's turn, everyone was dozing," says Masson. Newspapers and television networks quoted from Charest's speeches more than from Johnson's. After spending two years crying in the wilderness, the Tory leader had returned to the fold.

Jean Charest focused on the desire for change that was surfacing across the country. "To say that a No vote will condemn us to the status quo is to make an extraordinary effort to conceal the truth," he said. "To pretend that nothing will change in the way Canadian federalism operates is to ignore what is going on in Alberta, in Saskatchewan and elsewhere in Canada. There is a common denominator in all these changes. That common denominator is fiscal. The catalyst for change, which is affecting every governmental jurisdiction, is both universal and inevitable."

But it was not his words that captured the federalists' imagina-

tion; it was his tone. Charest's No was inspired by passion, not statistics and fearmongering. "To reduce the history of our country, the
meaning of our decision, to mere episodes in constitutional negotiation is to misunderstand what is going on," he insisted at a press
conference. "It would be deceitful, because the choice we make
next October 30 will be about Canada. It's not about Ottawa, it's
not about Johnson, it's not about Charest, and it's not about
Chrétien. It's about Canada and everything we have been able to
accomplish together!"

Charest even conjured up a few oratorical tricks. Before the
campaign officially began, on the way to a meeting in Saint-Joseph-
de-Beauce one Sunday in September, he came up with an idea to
illustrate dramatically what separation would mean. "I could take
out my passport and tell people, 'The separatists are going to ask you
to turn in your passport!' What do you think about that?" he asked
adviser Claude Lacroix. There was a danger that the move would be
perceived as a little too theatrical, but Charest decided to try it anyway. There was one hitch: his passport, like that of all MPs, was
green. It would spoil the effect. "Claude, give me your passport!"
The passport stunt would become a favourite among federalist audi-
ences during the campaign. Who would have suspected for a
moment that the document Jean Charest held so dear belonged to
Claude Lacroix?

Charest used another gambit to illustrate the consequences of a
sovereigntist victory: he spoke of the fall-out from a Yes vote as a
"black hole." It was a striking image, and he used it to avoid taking
a stand on sensitive matters such as the consequences of a narrow
sovereigntist victory or the concept of a partition of federalist
regions from an independent Québec.

They were good moves, but Québec premier Jacques Parizeau
made a better one. On October 7, three weeks before the vote, he
announced that if the Yes side were to win, Lucien Bouchard would
be Québec's chief negotiator during talks with the rest of Canada.
The manoeuvre shifted the focus to the charismatic Bloc Québécois

leader and the notion of partnership. Suddenly, the campaign had a new edge. As he listened to focus groups set up by No pollsters, federal Liberal strategist John Rae noted that Bouchard could do no wrong. In the eyes of Québeckers, he could walk on water. On October 19, Rae got the bad news: internal polls showed the Yes forces had overtaken the No side.

At that precise moment, the federalist pressure-cooker blew a gasket. Quarrels between provincial and federal Grits that had been simmering for months finally boiled over on Saturday, October 21. Daniel Johnson told reporters that before voting day he hoped the federal government would make a commitment to defend some of the constitutional changes desired by Québec. When Prime Minister Chrétien, on an official trip to New York, was informed of these remarks, he replied tersely, "We're not talking about constitutional problems; we're talking about the separation of Québec from the rest of Canada." A crisis broke out in the federalist war room. Only with the utmost difficulty did Chrétien and Johnson issue a joint communiqué in an attempt to paper over the cracks. That weekend, federalist pollster Grégoire Gollin identified a seven-point lead for the Yes.

The federalists had no choice: they had to go on the offensive. At a rally in the Verdun Arena, Prime Minister Chrétien left the door open, however grudgingly, to constitutional change. His speech on October 24 attracted a great deal of attention, though the tone was solemn and cautious. "A No vote does not mean abandoning any position whatever related to the Canadian constitution," insisted the Prime Minister. "We are keeping open all other avenues to change, whether they be administrative or constitutional."

That same evening, Jean Charest gave what many considered the best federalist speech of the entire campaign. Seen on film several years after the fact, it is disappointing. The speech was not such an extraordinary piece of oratory after all. Charest sometimes appears hesitant, his sentences are awkward. But the speech did have passion, and that was exactly what federalist supporters wanted. It was built around two high points. First, the Conservative leader relates that on his way into the arena he encountered Chrétien. Looking the Prime Minister of Canada in the eye, Charest solemnly declares, "It is symbolic, Mr. Prime Minister. I say to you this evening in sincere friendship that as far as Canada is concerned, we will always be able to walk the same path." This statement brought the twelve thousand present to their feet, waving the flags of Québec and Canada.

After speaking at length of the desire for change he had found in the other provinces and about the opportunities this offered Québeckers, Charest declared, "The Canada camp stands for change!" From his jacket pocket he pulled not his passport, but the No manifesto. "I have a lot of things in my jacket pocket!" he quipped, to the delight of the crowd. "This manifesto, endorsed by the Prime Minister of Canada and the leader of the No camp, clearly states that change will take place!" It was a rather generous interpretation of a vague commitment hammered out under extreme duress. But Charest staked his credibility on it: "Our opponents will try to cast doubt on the sincerity of those who speak to you, particularly the Prime Minister. This evening, I am here to tell you that I have no doubt about his sincerity and his desire for change."

The second highlight of Jean Charest's Verdun speech came at the end. In crucial moments, he has always referred to his family. So frequently, in fact, that some have wondered whether it is sincere emotion or merely a ploy. "When I got into politics, I made a commitment to my family to make Québec and Canada grow," he said. "On the morning of October 31, I will turn to my three children and say, 'Now it's your turn to make Québec and Canada grow.'"

In that pivotal week, the Conservatives insisted that Charest become a focal point of the campaign, that he join the main tour. "Finally, we were promised the bus for three days," says organizer François Pilote. "But something would always come up at the last minute, and Johnson would keep the bus." Despite his frustration, the PC leader delivered another excellent performance a few days

later at an outdoor rally in Montréal's Place du Canada, before tens
of thousands of Canadians from across the country.

CHRÉTIEN AND CHAREST, THE TWO MUSKETEERS

In the final days of the campaign, Jean Charest and Jean Chrétien
seemed to have become identical twins. For Conservative supporters,
it was their worst nightmare come true. Well before the campaign,
they had warned their leader of the danger of sharing a platform
with the Prime Minister, who was very unpopular in Québec. "We
didn't want to tarnish Jean Charest's image," Pierre-Claude Nolin
explains. "As far as we were concerned, Jean Charest lost credibility when he was on the same podium as Jean Chrétien." The Tory
leader, however, had come under conflicting pressures. At a party
strategy meeting in Ottawa a few months earlier, Charest adviser
Bruce Anderson had made a long presentation, complete with over-
head transparencies, on the advantages to Charest of being seen as
a steadfast ally of the Prime Minister of Canada. The suggestion
sent shivers down the spines of some of his Québec organizers.

Shortly after the PQ election victory in 1994, Charest, at the
urging of the nationalists in his camp, had sought to set himself
apart from other federalists by using a different vocabulary. "It's time
we recognize concretely that true sovereignty-association in Canada
means the sharing of powers and responsibilities between the federal
government and the provinces," he declared before the Laval Chamber of Commerce. "Federalism is shared sovereignty." There was
nothing the least bit revolutionary about his pragmatic approach, but
his attempt to co-opt sovereigntist terminology was not appreciated
in federalist circles. *La Presse* columnist Lysiane Gagnon, for example,
wrote that the tactic was "reminiscent of the tried-and-true Bourassa
strategy which consists of confusing people by playing on words and
twisting the meaning of expressions that are popular in the polls to
his own advantage." Charest beat a hasty retreat.

So it was that the Conservative leader stood beside the Prime Minister of Canada as Chrétien delivered his three speeches of the referendum campaign. "Wherever Chrétien was, Charest had no choice but to be there," says Nolin. Dyed-in-the-wool nationalists in the party were less charitable. "In 1980, Joe Clark did not appear on the stage with Trudeau & Co. during the campaign," points out one-time Charest political aide Marie-Josée Bissonnette. "There's always a choice."

But the Sherbrooke MP had made up his mind to go for broke. He pledged to be a "guardian for change," as promised by the No camp. "I have put my personal credibility on the line for next October 30. The full autonomy that is Québec's right must be restored to Québec in the coming years." Like Trudeau in 1980, he put his head on the block. But in contrast to the former prime minister, Charest had no control over the machine. His head would be chopped off as soon as the results were announced on the evening of October 30.

It was a long evening. At last, the final outcome was announced: the No had squeaked through to victory with 50.6 percent of the vote. After Daniel Johnson had spoken, it was Jean Charest's turn, and he would address a crowd gathered at the Métropolis discotheque in Montréal. Québec — and all of Canada — was watching. It was to be the ultimate reward for his two years of self-denial. From his pocket Charest pulled two small flags, the fleur-de-lys and the maple leaf. Then, he began his speech by thanking "the man who has borne the heaviest burden that can be imposed on a political leader, the one who has defended the integrity and the future of Québec, and the future of Canada . . . our leader, the one who has led the No side to victory, Daniel Johnson!" At that very instant, Radio-Canada television viewers heard anchorman Bernard Derome announce, "We must break away from Mr. Charest — and none too elegantly — to let Mr. Chrétien speak. Over to you, Prime Minister." The Conservative leader's glory had lasted less than a minute. The screen showed Chrétien in his Ottawa office: "*Chers compatriotes,* dear fellow Canadians . . ." Charest was totally unaware of what was happening. When he finished his address, he joined Michèle on the right of the stage. She had been watching the TV monitors.

"Great speech, Jean."

"It was?"

"Too bad nobody saw it . . ."

"What do you mean?"

"They were showing Chrétien on TV."

The Tory brain trust was furious. "The election campaign has just begun," one of them remarked. To this day, the Tories remain convinced that the Prime Minister did it on purpose — an allegation Eddie Goldenberg, Chrétien's chief adviser, categorically denies. "Not long after Johnson had finished his speech, a CBC technician told the Prime Minister, 'You're on the air in ninety seconds.' So, Chrétien combed his hair, adjusted his tie . . . It was only the next day that we found out what had occurred. I guess the network wanted to put the Prime Minister on the air before everyone went to bed."

"So that's it. Blame the CBC producer. Big deal!" replies Pierre-Claude Nolin. "I've worked with a prime minister of Canada, Brian Mulroney. When he decided to speak, he spoke. When he decided not to speak, he didn't speak. It's very, very clear, the whole thing was intentional!"

As in most emotionally charged debates, the truth is neither blue nor red; it lies somewhere in between. The facts at hand are these. The feds had decided that, whatever the result of the vote, the Prime Minister of Canada would address the country after the leaders of the Yes and No committees had spoken. It had been a long, hard evening for Jean Chrétien, who had almost seen the country slip through his fingers. He had left the official residence to go to his office in the Centre Block on Parliament Hill, where a CBC producer, cameraman and sound engineer were waiting for him. Members of his team surrounded Chrétien. Everyone was exhausted and in a bleak mood. "We were in a hurry to get it over with," says press attaché Patrick Parizot.

In Chrétien's office, the TV was tuned to CBC — a crucial detail. Jean Chrétien's team fidgeted as Daniel Johnson delivered his address. Then producer Dave Mathews gave the signal to someone in the group that Jean Charest would follow. Mathews was simply following the line-up that party representatives in Montréal had hammered out earlier that evening. First Johnson would speak, then Charest, and then Chrétien. According to Mathews, there was a brief discussion, then the Prime Minister decided he would wait for his young ally to speak. But Johnson's speech seemed to go on forever. When he finally concluded, the feds alerted Mathews that the Prime Minister would speak, apparently forgetting the Conservative leader. "Mr. Chrétien was fed up — he was in a hurry to leave," the producer recalls. "When they noticed Johnson had finished, they saw their opportunity and decided to go ahead."

Neither Chrétien nor his advisers saw Charest begin his speech. CBC, unlike its French-language sister network, had not returned to the Métropolis to resume its coverage of the speech by the federalists' star orator. Mathews is categorical: neither he, nor anyone at the CBC gave the Prime Minister the signal to begin his speech. "It's certain that no one at CBC told them to go ahead, especially not the producer, because I would have suggested we wait for Charest." Once the Prime Minister had made the decision, the producer had to alert the country's six television networks and, ninety seconds later, give Chrétien his cue. Once the countdown had begun it could not be stopped. From the control booth at the Métropolis, Isabelle Perras, a communications officer for the No side, was surprised to see Chrétien's face appear on the screen.

"That's not what we agreed upon," she told the Radio-Canada people.

"What can you do — it's the Prime Minister of Canada."

The facts don't support the set-up theory. More likely, it was a foul-up caused by a witches' brew of fatigue, impatience and arrogance. Besides, if the federal Liberals had wanted to push Jean

Charest aside, they could have done so earlier that evening by supporting their provincial Liberal cousins, who didn't want to see Charest on the podium at all!

When Pierre Anctil, Daniel Johnson's chief of staff, told this to Conservative organizer Jean Bazin, Bazin exclaimed, "What did you say?"

"It's normal for Johnson to speak as the leader of the No camp; it's normal for Chrétien to speak as the Prime Minister of Canada. As for the others," Anctil explained, "many of them think they should talk, but after all, this is a formal event."

"I've got news for you! All hell is going to break loose, because you won't stop Charest from stepping up to the microphone!"

Then Bazin rushed over to see John Rae, a Chrétien insider who represented the federal Liberals: "John, if that's the way it's going to be, you'd better get ready, because the shit's going to hit the fan tonight!" Rae, however, agreed with the Conservatives that Charest should be given a chance to speak. Michel Bélanger, the chairman of the No organizing committee, agreed. Faced with a united front, Anctil backed down.

If anyone wanted to keep Jean Charest off the podium, it would have been the provincial Liberals, not Chrétien's team, whose crime was to overlook Charest in their impatience. Charest himself laughs when he recounts the episode today. "The people around me were more shocked than I was," he explains. "I was tired. The referendum was over." But Charest-watchers remember a leader who was absolutely furious that evening.

EFFECT? WHAT EFFECT?

Jean Charest had been the most effective of all the federalist spokespeople. As the lead enjoyed by the No camp eroded and federalists slipped into depression, Charest's performance lifted their spirits. But Charest did not win the referendum. In fact, his speeches would seem to have had a negligible effect on the outcome. In the campaign's final days, a poll asked Québeckers which leader had most influenced their decision. Among No supporters, 21 percent named Daniel Johnson, while only 13 percent picked Jean Charest, putting him on an equal footing with Jean Chrétien. "Charest may have put on a good show to boost morale," speculates Jean Masson, one of the senior federalist organizers. "Did his performance actually translate into votes? Maybe so, but I'm not convinced it had a decisive impact."

Nobody is in a better position to answer the question than Grégoire Gollin, a pollster for the No side. During the referendum campaign, Gollin monitored shifting public opinion on a daily basis. He believes that Jean Charest's efforts had no real effect on the electorate — in spite of his passion, in spite of the passport gimmick. "There really was a 'Bouchard effect' that completely turned the situation around, but I didn't see any evidence of a Charest effect." To Gollin, the Verdun rally was the turning point in the campaign, the event that lifted the No side back into the race, allowing it to avoid defeat. Newscasts that night covered little but Prime Minister Chrétien's timid constitutional initiatives. Charest's speech went all but unnoticed. Finally, even where Charest had the greatest influence — in his Sherbrooke riding — the Yes outscored the No.

The referendum campaign, nonetheless, won widespread sympathy for the Tory leader across the country. "[Jean Charest] has emerged as an attractive national figure with an unlimited future," wrote Peter C. Newman, distinguished *Maclean's* columnist, during the campaign. In the wake of the No victory, some federal Liberal strategists wondered aloud whether Prime Minister Chrétien should invite Charest to join the cabinet.

But the referendum night incident had chilled the relatively warm relations between the two men. After the Tory collapse in 1993, the new Prime Minister had invited Charest for coffee in his office. The two leaders replayed the defeats they had suffered in leadership races. "I really liked the man, much more than I'd expected," Charest told a journalist. After the referendum, Chrétien and Charest met again over supper at 24 Sussex Drive. Charest warned the PM against cosmetic gestures that would do nothing to solve the Québec problem. The atmosphere that night was less relaxed than it had been two years earlier. The younger man's advice went unheeded. It would not be long before Charest found the Liberal leader intolerable. In private conversation, Charest would swear when he mentioned Jean Chrétien's name: "If it wasn't for that bastard, the national unity problem would have been settled a long time ago!"

"Jean felt he'd been stabbed by Chrétien more than once, and he didn't have any confidence in him," says Conservative MP David Price, a longtime friend. Price recalls a telephone conversation between Charest and the Prime Minister very early in 1998. At the time, the Conservative leader was demanding a Commons debate about Canada's participation in the pending American offensive against Iraq. "The conversation was very civilized at first," recounts the MP, who was in Jean Charest's office. "But it didn't take long for things to heat up." It became so heated, in fact, that Charest asked his friend, "David, would you mind leaving?"

Whatever feelings of resentment Jean Charest might harbour toward Lucien Bouchard are tempered by a degree of respect for his former colleague. Charest does not have the same respect for Chrétien. "With Bouchard he sees himself in a contest, a tennis match," explains Price. "But he doesn't see Chrétien as a competitor, because he doesn't consider him his equal."

"WHO DO YOU THINK YOU ARE ANYWAY?"

With the dust of the referendum campaign settling, it was time for Jean Charest to get back to the business of leading the Progressive Conservative Party of Canada. The party had two MPs and precious little else. By then, his sense of frustration at not being able to speak in the House of Commons had reached the boiling point. When, in December 1995, the Liberal government tabled a motion recognizing Québec as a distinct society, the Bloc Québécois and the Reform Party denied Charest the privilege of speaking after the other party leaders. In a heated exchange in the Commons lobby, Bloc leader Michel Gauthier told the Sherbrooke MP to take a hike: "Who do you think you are, anyway? Is your party recognized in the Commons?" While the Mulroney government had been in power, the Tories had done nothing to make things easy for the Bloc, which had not yet achieved official party status. But Charest still couldn't get over it: "Never have I seen a parliamentarian treated like that! Talking to me like that in the Commons lobby! It was like a slap in the face." So strong was the slap that he did not even show up for the vote. Instead, he attended a Christmas party a stone's throw from the Commons. Skeptics suggest that by not voting for a distinct society Charest hoped to avoid alienating western voters. But his absence irked Québec Tories. He now admits the mistake: "Acting out of spite may not be the most rational approach."

Only a short time elapsed before the same spite led him to contemplate an alliance with the Reform Party. With the support of both Conservative MPs, Preston Manning's Reform Party could have wrested Official Opposition status from the Bloc Québécois. In exchange, Reform would have given Charest and his colleague Elsie Wayne more time to speak. Charest had always categorically rejected the idea of a merger with Reform. That he would even consider it speaks to the extent of his frustration. When Pierre-Claude Nolin heard of the deal, he got on the phone immediately. "What the hell's going on?" he asked Charest. "It'll never fly in Québec!" The reaction was unequivocal. "Charest is consorting with the devil," thundered Raymond Giroux in Le Soleil. "Pitiful," Pierre Gravel exclaimed in La Presse. "Incapable of accepting the marginal status to which voters have relegated him, Charest has shown he will resort to any compromise to keep his head above water." Realizing he'd made another blunder, the Tory leader ran for cover. "Politically, it was a mistake," he says.

That storm having passed, Charest then turned to the second R of his program: rewriting the platform. The idea was to formulate new ideas the party could present to the voters. Drawing up the platform would also keep idle party workers busy and interested. Montréal lawyer Jacques Léger and party staffer Roxanna Benoit handled the consultation process, spending six months meeting Conservatives all across the country. "We picked up a sense of excitement among the party workers," says Léger. "People wanted to speak their minds. They felt they'd been duped by the party leadership, that at the end of Brian Mulroney's term the party had lost touch with the rank and file." The sense of excitement was translated into a detailed, 150-page report submitted to the party's policy convention, held in Winnipeg in late August 1996.

The event, attended by fifteen hundred members, brought the Conservative Party precious media coverage — more than welcome after three years in the political wilderness. But it was also the scene of heated debate about party policy for the future. The youth wing proposed a series of changes that would move the party farther to the right on the political spectrum. They insisted the Conservative Party substantially cut taxes when it took power, emulating Premier Mike Harris's Ontario Conservatives, who had been elected the previous year. The young Tories also called for restoration of the death penalty and for young offenders more than ten years old to be tried in adult courts. Several resolutions sought to limit the scope of the chapter dealing with the distinct society, a chapter partially drafted by Charest himself. In the end, most of the proposed changes were rejected, with the leader making only a few concessions. One of them was to cut taxes between 10 and 20 percent upon taking office. The Winnipeg convention boosted Jean Charest's morale, and that of his party. But in the polls their support still hovered around 12 percent. And the debates that had raged between party members foreshadowed even more divisive confrontations.

From the convention emerged a sixty-page brochure containing the Conservative Party program, "Designing a Blueprint for Canadians." Only the final stage of the process remained: transforming a boring document into a list of clear, hard-hitting and attractive commitments — in other words, an election platform. Charest handed the job to Leslie Noble, an organizer he had gotten to know quite well during the 1993 leadership race. Noble had also been the principal writer of "The Common Sense Revolution," the program that helped carry Mike Harris to victory in Ontario. Charest's choice was cause for concern. It showed that winning Ontario was the leader's priority. And Noble carried a reputation for stubbornness as well as intelligence.

The first draft of the document presented by Noble to the platform committee provoked a strong reaction. French-speakers sought in vain for a few paragraphs on Québec. "There was not a word!" recalls lawyer Jacques Léger. "Ideally, Noble would have preferred not to mention it at all. We set up a hue and cry, demanding to meet Charest so that he would intervene." Charest knew he could not publish a program that did not mention, even in cautious terms, the recognition of Québec as a "distinct society." Finally, in an attempt to reassure English Canadians, Charest and the other Québeckers on the committee produced a text that offered no specific commitment: "It is not and it will not constitute special powers, privilege, preferential treatment or superiority. It is the simple recognition of a historic fact of more than two centuries."

The bulk of the text written by Noble and her colleague, Allister Campbell, focused on the economy. Based on the Ontario Tories' program, these chapters came under heavy fire from some Conservative strategists. Many thought that the proposed spending cuts were too drastic. "Employment insurance was going to be decimated!" says Andy Walker, a committee member from Prince Edward Island. Noble was sent back to her desk for a rewrite. When she returned with a second version, "Almost nothing had changed," Léger exclaims. "It was extremely difficult to make them [change their minds]. They had the leader's ear."

The platform was scheduled for publication in mid-March 1997, but the committee wasn't making any headway. The constant manoeuvring led to infighting exacerbated by personality conflicts. Two weeks before the deadline, some committee members requested a meeting with Jean Charest, where they insisted that the election platform be given to someone else who could smooth out the edges. The task was handed to Jeff Norquay, Brian Mulroney's former speech-writer, with Charest, Norquay and Noble handling the final negotiations.

Released on March 18, 1997, the platform pledged that a Conservative government's first budget would reduce income taxes by 10 percent. The Conservatives also promised to slash unemployment insurance premiums by $5 billion. At the same time, the federal government would eliminate the deficit by 2000 through massive cuts to government spending: the Agriculture department budget would be sliced by $600 million, Natural Resources by $400 million, and Public Works by $1.4 billion. "There was some appetite for a tax cut, but I don't think the party members had been promised a $12-billion set of cuts. That was not my impression coming out of Winnipeg," says Heather Conway. A loyal economic adviser for Charest since 1993, Conway had kept far away from the process in 1997 because she believed Noble and Campbell "had their own agenda." Norquay had attempted to soften the platform, but according to Jacques Léger, "It was their document, their philosophy that they'd managed to sell Jean Charest."

Another plank in the platform displeased moderate Conservatives: the promise to repeal the Liberal government's new Firearms Act. So succinct was the paragraph that it was impossible to tell whether it called only for the elimination of compulsory firearm registration, as party spokespeople contended later, or further liberalization of the rules. Leslie Noble claims that the article was written into the platform at the request of Conservative senators:

"When we met with the caucus and candidates, they insisted that it be in and the leader instructed us to put it in." Jacques Léger maintains that the leader was annoyed with the radical terms employed. "The words that were used displeased him. The ideas weren't his; he would have happily dispensed with them altogether." Which didn't stop Charest from losing his temper on the campaign trail when a reporter insinuated that the Tory leader did not really subscribe to his party's platform on the issue.

Leslie Noble's text did include an original element, the notion of a new Canadian Pact, inspired by the work of economist Tom Courchene and André Burelle, a former constitutional adviser to Pierre Trudeau. Under the new agreement, the federal government would surrender to the provinces tax points corresponding to their share of health care and post-secondary education funding. The provinces would no longer be at the mercy of Ottawa's budget cutbacks. In exchange, provincial governments would come to an agreement with the federal government on quality standards for services provided in these areas, national norms that would have the force of law.

Jean Charest had also instructed the authors of the report to include a chapter on his pet issues: youth and education. Education falls within the jurisdiction of each province but, asserted the Conservative platform, "the interests of Canada's young people are Canada-wide interests." A Conservative government would establish pan-Canadian education norms and programs. When it came to education, Charest found it difficult, as he had ten years earlier with the "Stay in School Program," to keep from treading on provincial jurisdiction.

Rarely had the Conservative Party of Canada presented so detailed a program to the electorate. The second R had been accomplished with flying colours. Yet the Conservatives had a long road to travel before they achieved the third R, a return to power.

Like Rungs on a Ladder

To gain power, political parties need a leader, ideas, money, workers and luck. Luck might well be the dominant factor. Next in importance is the leader, who conveys the party's ideas to voters. But the role of party workers cannot be overlooked. This group comprises businesspeople prepared to fund the party, organizers committed to the party, body and soul, and simple supporters who put up posters and stamp envelopes. Some party workers hope to land a contract or a job in return for their dedication. Others are in politics for idealistic reasons. But many, perhaps most, simply take pleasure in the work. For them, politics is a drug, and the party is a social club. Whatever their motivation, party workers need to feel appreciated. A wonderful reward is the yearly Christmas card from the leader — better still, a telephone call.

If it had not been for Jean Charest's exceptional qualities, his persistence, his political acumen, his oratorical skills, the Progressive Conservative Party of Canada might not have survived the debacle of 1993. But on becoming leader, Charest also revealed certain weaknesses, weaknesses that have alienated many workers from him and his party. An eminently sociable man, Jean Charest is also a loner. He relies on a small inner circle from which he ventures only out of strict necessity. All others, be they MPs, organizers or volunteers, sometimes have the feeling they are little more than cannon fodder.

Some party workers — maybe the most experienced — accept their leader's independence ungrudgingly. Others have lost patience. Jean Charest's road to political leadership is strewn with scores of disappointed, abandoned or bitter admirers, including veteran supporters and strategists such as Pierre Gagné and Albert Painchaud, who rarely hear from Charest. Perhaps an even greater loss is that of the young people who would have given everything for him, and who now feel forgotten or rejected. They include Marie-Josée Bissonnette and Martin Desrochers, without whom Charest's 1993 leadership campaign might never have gotten off the ground.

Jean-Martin Masse, a lawyer by profession and a Conservative organizer for a number of years, served as co-chairman of the party's 1997 Québec campaign and as a losing candidate in Saint-Laurent–Cartierville. He describes the telephone call he got from Charest a few days after the vote:

"Hello, Jean-Martin, it's Jean."

"Hi, Jean!"

"Thanks a lot for putting up the fight you did. I hope you're going to run in the next election. Thanks again, and see you next time."

"Hello?"

And that was that. Jean Charest had already gone on to the next call. "I would have understood if it were a candidate in the Yukon he'd never met," says Masse. "But when you've known the guy for twelve years!"

"These days, nobody believes he's going to become a millionaire by going into politics," Masse adds. "Your motivation as a party worker or an organizer is the thanks you get when you've put in twelve-hour days and the impression that you've got the leader's ear."

In politics, it's called networking. It's not just a question of how many people you know or how many people you can recognize, something at which Jean Charest excels. Instead, networking is the art of nurturing those resources.

Politics is about human relationships. In a wide-ranging study on leadership, American political scientist James MacGregor Burns quotes a turn-of-the-century municipal politician, George W. Plunkitt, who explained that to retain one's city council seat, it is necessary to "study human nature and act accordingly." And, added Plunkitt, "To learn real human nature you have to go among the people, see them and be seen. I know every man, woman and child in the Fifteenth District. I know what they like and what they don't like, what they are strong at and what they are weak in, and I reach them by approaching at the right side." Concludes MacGregor Burns, "Whatever the political culture, the effectiveness of the political party leader depended on an ability to offer material or psychic help, not abstract advice or sermons."*

Party leaders, unlike aldermen, cannot always "learn real human nature" in the flesh. The telephone must often act as the permanent link between leaders and party workers. By keeping in contact with hundreds of people, Brian Mulroney built up the formidable network of friends that enabled him to become prime minister of Canada, staying in constant touch with hundreds of people, giving them the impression that each one of them was important. "His network fed him everything from political intelligence to the latest gossip," wrote Mulroney's biographer, John Sawatsky. "It also functioned as an informal public opinion poll and kept him on top of everything going on behind the scenes in law, in business, and in government."** By developing these contacts into friendships, leaders do more than assure themselves of loyalty and devotion. They receive constant feedback from diversified sources independent of their intimate circle. "In Québec, politics is like a little family, and you have to make sure you keep up your contacts with people," says Jean-Martin Masse. "You have to keep your finger on the pulse."

Charest insiders have long been aware of their leader's inability to cultivate a network and to stroke party workers. They have attempted to remedy the situation by giving him a list of telephone calls to make regularly. But they've all run up against the same reaction: "Why should I call him? What would I have to say to him?" Denis Pageau, longtime director of operations for the Québec wing of the Conservative Party, notes, "We've all managed at one time or other to get him to do a blitz, but we've never managed to get him to make a habit of it." Québec Tories may have developed a particularly acute sensitivity to networking during the Mulroney years. Political leaders should not be constrained by this type of obsession with the telephone. However, Pageau is not alone in believing that personal relationships between the leader and the

---

* James MacGregor Burns, *Leadership* (New York: Harper & Row, 1978), pp. 311–12.
** John Sawatsky, *Mulroney: The Politics of Ambition* (Toronto: Macfarlane, Walter & Ross, 1991), pp. 214–16.

party faithful must be maintained. "If you've worked for a guy for two years and he's never picked up the phone and called you, after a while you start to wonder whether it's all worthwhile."

Charest's charismatic performances and affable style create the impression that he is an extremely warm person, raising party workers' expectations. "People would really like to be close to him!" says Pageau. But the leader won't have it. "Trust doesn't come easily to him." It's all a part of the enigma named Jean Charest.

Even when he is among people who work with him every day, he keeps his distance. Only the Sherbrooke clan can claim to be on intimate terms with the local deity. Albertan Albert Cooper, who was Jean Charest's chief of staff for a year and a half, says his boss often made deals or decisions without informing him. "I would say to him: 'Talk to anybody you wish, but I want to know about the calls and what the agreements and decisions are. I have to know that, because otherwise I will be working against you.' But he didn't like to do that. He'd sneak a call to someone without telling me about it! I often had to force him to talk to me and tell me what he was thinking and where he was going."

The distance Jean Charest keeps between himself and party workers might well come back to haunt him one day. Party workers are always extremely loyal when the polls are encouraging. The acid test comes when things turn sour. And, if leaders don't cultivate that loyalty, they might find themselves suddenly abandoned by people they thought they could count on. "It's a very, very important quality for a political leader," says former prime minister Mulroney, who is well aware of his protégé's shortcomings. "That's why my caucus remained solidly behind me through all the crises we went through. I knew everybody intimately. I entertained my MPs. If the leader doesn't do that, when things go bad, the members of the caucus think, 'It's going bad, we don't know the guy anyway, he never calls us, we're just there to be used.' In my case, people said, 'It's going bad, but it's not his fault.'"

When reminded that many people find him distant, Jean Charest replies, "Is that a fault?" Then he explains: "I'm at ease with people. I like them, but at the same time, there should be space. I like to be able to step back a bit."

The problem goes deeper than that. Even if he loves travelling and spending hours shaking hands and shooting the breeze with his supporters, Jean Charest is a hothouse politician. Until now, his protective shell has not prevented him from being extraordinarily effective. It might well be that this barrier has enabled him to survive, to maintain some semblance of a family life. History will decide whether it will be possible for him to pursue his climb to the top while keeping his distance, sometimes abandoning people he's used like so many rungs on his ladder.

A SEE-SAW CAMPAIGN

"What Charest needs is a campaign," was how *La Presse* reporter Vincent Marissal put it. As cabinet minister or party leader, he may be average, but the man from Sherbrooke truly comes into his own on the campaign trail.

The Big Blue Machine was making strange noises in the run-up to the June 1997 election. In Toronto, organizers were panicking: no one had thought to lease an airplane or bus for the leader's campaign tour. They wanted to see the polls; none was available. Meetings were taking place, conversations were being held, but, on the ground, nothing was happening. In Ottawa, national campaign headquarters had been rented — but there was no furniture. When the news finally reached Jean Charest's ears he checked with campaign co-chairmen Pierre-Claude Nolin and David Tkashuk, who hastened to reassure him. Then, one Saturday morning, he got a call from Freddy Watson, a Conservative Party bus driver. For Freddy to call him in North Hatley on a Saturday morning, the situation must have been grim indeed. "Listen, Boss, if the party doesn't reserve the bus before Monday, it won't be ready for the campaign." Charest could hardly believe his ears. "They weren't telling it to me like it was," he says.

Why get hot and bothered about a bus? Imagine the reaction of reporters if the Charest campaign couldn't get under way for want of a press bus! "It would have been game over. We might as well have forgotten the thirty-six days left in the campaign," Charest says.

A few days before the election briefs were issued, he had to bench the senators and entrust the campaign to Jodi White, who had managed his leadership campaign four years before. The loyal organizer would be able to resolve the practical problems quickly. But the change in command, coming as it did just before the battle, created confusion about campaign strategy. Ontarians like Leslie Noble believed the focus should be on the platform. Much to Noble's chagrin, the White team quickly decided to spotlight the leader's personality. Businessman Peter White, in charge of party fund-raising, also felt left out of the strategic decision-making process. Party scuttlebutt had it that Jodi White was making all the decisions herself. And she'd never really won anything, people muttered.

"The election strategy was defined much too late in the game," says Jan Dymond, a Conservative organizer from Toronto. Confusion and internal wrangling could partially explain why Charest failed to make a mark in the early weeks of the campaign. But that was only part of the picture. In all fairness, it must be said that after the Liberals, the Bloc, Reform and the NDP had been covered, there was not much media space left over.

Once again, the Tory leader would be well served by the weaknesses of his adversaries. Stumbling all over himself, Gilles Duceppe, the new Bloc Québécois leader, quickly stood revealed as a sovereigntist version of that blunderer par excellence Kim Campbell. Something totally unforeseen, even by Tory organizers, was happening. The polls showed the Bloc's support beginning to erode while the Tories' climbed rapidly.

The Conservative comeback was so startling that a number of experts pooh-poohed the first poll to report it, raising doubts about its methodology. "One Québecker in four would be prepared to vote Conservative? Give me a break!" chided pollster Jean-Marc Léger. But subsequent polls confirmed the breakthrough. For months, the Big Blue Machine had been gearing up to do battle in Ontario, and now it was making gains in Québec and the Maritimes. The problem was that the Québec organization was not firing on all cylinders. For two years, François Pilote had been struggling to rebuild the riding associations one by one, all but running himself into the ground in the process. But he was alone; no one else had faith in the party. It was difficult for Charest to find candidates who would not become an embarrassment, let alone candidates with nation- or province-wide reputations. When Charest's old friend, former Chicoutimi MP André Harvey, decided to run, even his family thought it was a harebrained scheme. Run as a Conservative candidate? In Québec, in 1997? "It was one hell of a situation," says former MP Gabriel Desjardins, then president of the Conservative Party's Québec wing. "We had a colossal rebuilding job ahead of us. It was up to us to deliver the goods, and so far they hadn't been delivered — for perfectly understandable reasons."

The number of ridings with well-run organizations could be counted on the fingers of one hand, adds Desjardins. André Harvey saw that for himself at a disastrous Jean Charest rally in the Québec City region. "I was surprised that an area as large as the Québec City region couldn't draw more than four hundred people," admitted Harvey a few months later. "The problem was an organizational one. There wasn't any structure to speak of. We had too much catching up to do."

The Québec polls were promising, but organizers were worried: who would get out the vote? Who would do the canvassing to identify potential Tory voters? Who would call them on election day to make sure they actually cast their ballots? Who would drive senior citizens to the polls? The youth and inexperience of many of the candidates was another problem. Dazzled by their moment of glory in the local newspapers, they neglected the grassroots slogging that drives a winning campaign.

So the riding organizations were feeble. Adding to these woes, the candidates felt the party's permanent staff gave them little support. "There was no provincial organization," says former Kamouraska–Rivière-du-Loup MP André Plourde, again a candidate in 1997. In contrast to previous elections, he recalls, advertising material was not even ready the day the campaign kicked off. When the candidates gathered in Sherbrooke for a training session that day, they waited in vain for the posters and signs that were usually provided by the party. "We had to organize everything on our own," laments Plourde. "When problems came up, there was no one there to solve them."

Not only was the Montréal headquarters short on resources, but infighting was rife among senior campaign strategists. Campaign co-chairman Jean-Martin Masse, former MP Gabriel Desjardins and other advisers felt increasingly alienated because power was concentrated in the hands of the people closest to Charest: Jean-Bernard Bélisle, Claude Lacroix, François Pilote and Suzanne Poulin. "It went from a table for twenty, to five, down to two," says one of the malcontents. Criticizing the leader was impossible. "It was a little like the Supreme Soviet. The trapdoor opened and someone disappeared."

Voters, of course, had no inkling of what lay behind Jean Charest's immaculate image — fortunately for the party.

In the spring of 1997, a new, slimmer, physically fit Jean Charest emerged. At home in the Eastern Townships he had been following a strict workout schedule under the supervision of a personal trainer; in Ottawa, he pedalled an exercise bike as he watched the news. "I'm doing it for my own good," he assured reporters, who suspected his motives might have had some connection with his political well-being. Charest chalked up victories in the two and a half leaders' debates that took place in mid-May — two and a half because the last segment of the French-language face-off had to be postponed by a few days when moderator Claire Lamarche fell unconscious. In the English debate, Charest uncorked some of his "fastballs." When Prime Minister Jean Chrétien claimed Canadians were beginning to see "the light at the end of the tunnel," the Tory shot back, "The light that he saw at the end of the tunnel was the whites of the eyes of the Canadian voter." Then Charest drew an ovation from the audience when he responded to the Bloc leader with a ringing plea for Canadian unity: "I have news for you, I intend to make this country work. Because if there is one commitment I have made to my children, it is that I'm going to pass on to them the country I received from my parents!" The children gambit never fails.

CHAREST DECONSTRUCTED

Laval University linguist Guylaine Martel, in a detailed study of Charest's performance in the debates, concludes: "His success is not due entirely to his undeniable qualities as an orator. It is also the result of an overall strategy that is sometimes apparent in his public speaking, which is much less spontaneous than it seems."* Without ever consulting Charest's debate-strategy gurus, the professor identified each of the tactics they had taught their pupil over the years. Charest, she points out, often enumerates his points ("What I would like to do is suggest four things . . ."), and he constantly relates the issues to personal experience, either his own or those of ordinary citizens ("If you're a businessperson and a new order comes in . . ."). She goes on to describe the tactics Charest employs to monopolize airtime. "During discussion periods, Charest has no difficulty taking the floor and, unlike his opponents, he is seldom interrupted. [. . .] He never speaks directly to the other candidates; he does not interrupt them to take the floor, he asks the moderator

---

* Guylaine Martel, "Le débat politique télévisé. Une stratégie argumentative en trois dimensions: textuelle, interactionnelle et émotionnelle." To appear in GRIC (ed.), *Les Émotions dans les interactions* (Lyon: Kimé).

for the right to speak." Charest does not look at his rivals, the study notes; he looks directly into the camera. "One of the consequences of this strategy is that he is extremely difficult to interrupt. On the one hand, the four party leaders cannot refuse the Conservative leader the right to speak since the moderator has given him the floor. On the other, it is embarrassing to interrupt a discussion with the audience — whom they seek to please above all — or to respond to a remark not directed at them."

When the Sherbrooke MP takes a question from the audience, he lowers his voice and attempts "to create a person-to-person relationship between one man — rather than the representative of an entire party — and the voters." Though Martel does not mention it, this is the Clinton method. Like the American president, Charest is a past master in the art of expressing emotions, real or feigned. "With his opponents," she writes, "he is dynamic, but never nervous; firm but never aggressive; with the audience, he is pleasant but emphatic, he admits his concerns while at the same time he reassures. As with his tone of voice, Charest displays considerable nuance in expressing his emotions, avoiding extremes like irritability and self-pity."

The Conservatives, Martel observes, present "an extremely romanticized image of their leader — a kind of Lone Ranger closer to the people than to power."

Jean Charest would probably be offended by Martel's analysis. He would have us believe that his debating success has nothing to do with techniques or tactics. "In my experience," he said not long after the debates, "an image works as long as it is genuine. Building an image that does not correspond with reality does not work." True enough. But though Charest may be genuine, he is also a politician who has honed the art of communication to a fine edge. Compare his earliest debates with recent ones, the 1993 debates with those of 1997, and it is easy to appreciate what he has learned from the advice of Anderson & Co. "For me," he went on, "debates require an enormous effort of concentration. You have to listen to what the other guy has to say, then assimilate it. Going into a debate thinking you'll score a knockout is the worst thing you can do. Good debating means being well prepared, getting your message across, then if there's an opening . . ." If there's an opening, come in with the fastball.

CHECKMATE

The Tories sustained their momentum in Québec and Atlantic Canada until the last week of the campaign. Charest even began to dream: on a swing through Québec City on May 24, he predicted his party would win forty of the province's seventy-five seats. But to the chagrin of the Tory brain trust, polls showed that the Tory wave was breaking on the west bank of the Ottawa River. Their only hope was that Ontario voters, seeing the tide rising in the East, would join the movement at the last minute. Two events would dash their hopes.

On May 23, a Reform Party television commercial attacked Québec politicians: "Last time, these men [the photos of Jean Chrétien and Jean Charest appear on the screen] almost lost our country [1995 referendum results: Yes: 49 percent, No: 51 percent]." The ad presented the Reform Party as "a voice for all Canadians, not just politicians from Québec" and ended with photos of Chrétien, Charest, Bouchard and Duceppe crossed out with a large red X. The ad touched off a storm of indignation, particularly in Québec. Furious, Jean Charest went so far as to call Preston Manning a bigot, a term some English-speaking Conservatives found excessive. "The bigot remark did not help us," says organizer Jan Dymond. "It was out of character. It's not his style to throw names at people. And let's face it: the soft Reformers we were trying to attract agreed with a lot of what Manning was saying."

The next day, in an interview with RDI, Radio-Canada's all-news network, Jean Chrétien indicated that he would not comply with a close referendum vote in favour of sovereignty: "Fifty percent plus one in a third referendum, I don't think that's reasonable." The sovereigntists were to milk the statement for all it was worth in the final week of the campaign. "He has clearly stated that he would not accept a Yes from Québec to a question he himself considered clear," said a scandalized Gilles Duceppe.

The two incidents polarized the vote. Québec nationalists, who might have been tempted by Charest, felt the need to vent their anger and flocked back to the Bloc en masse. Federalists, after a brief flirtation with the Conservatives, returned to the Liberal hard line. Tory strategists in Québec realized they were in trouble when they heard the Prime Minister's remarks. Jean-Bernard Bélisle admits, "When Chrétien made his move, I said to myself, 'checkmate.'" In the final week, Bélisle and the others tried desperately to find a way to extricate Charest from the no-man's-land into which the Prime Minister's statement had dropped him. What could he do? What could he say? Charest tried to get out of the jam by bringing back his referendum "black hole": "As soon as we get involved in a break-up scenario for the country, no one can predict what may happen." But the harm had been done; no one was listening anymore.

The Conservatives were convinced that the Prime Minister's declaration was a deliberate tactic to stem the Tory tide. They were certain that it was this statement that had broken their momentum. Tories offered as evidence results of daily polls taken in target ridings. The figures showed that around May 25, Conservative support had begun to drop after climbing steadily for several weeks.

The figures are striking, but they are not indisputable proof that Chrétien's remarks alone accounted for the Conservatives' loss of steam. This thesis ignores the possible impact the Reform Party's advertising campaign had on French-speaking voters. Also, if we are to credit Tory pollsters, the Prime Minister's declaration cut into Conservative support the day the comments were broadcast. Yet experts know that voter reaction to any given event usually takes a few days to crystallize.

A variety of factors likely came into play. The other parties reacted to the Conservative surge by attacking Jean Charest, whom they had previously ignored. At a well-attended Bloc Québécois rally in Jonquière on May 19, Québec premier Lucien Bouchard mocked his former colleague. "Jean Charest," he said, "is the closest thing we have to a political clone of Jean Chrétien!" Then, on May 21, the Grits denounced the Tory pledge to repeal the gun control legislation. The mother of one of the victims in Montréal's 1989 École polytechnique tragedy said, "Look me in the eye, Mr. Charest: we will not let you touch our law on gun control."

Was Chrétien's statement part of a deliberate strategy to undermine the Conservatives? The Grits denied it. Had they wanted to get the most out of their leader's remarks, they certainly would have gone about it in a different way. The Prime Minister could have addressed the "50 percent plus one" issue in the French-language debate; he did not. He could have tackled it in one of his speeches; he did not. Why choose an RDI Sunday program with low audience ratings? Chrétien was chafing at journalist Daniel Lessard's barrage of questions on the Constitution. "You're asking me hypothetical questions! For half of the program, we've been talking about a problem people don't want to hear about!" It was a curious reaction for a politician who was supposedly looking for an opening to drop a bombshell. A few minutes later, Lessard asked him a specific question about the "50 percent plus one" issue, and only then did Chrétien make the reply that shocked Québec Tories.

True believers can rarely be bothered with details. For Québec Conservatives, the disappointing results of the June 2, 1997, election can be attributed to one cause: Jean Chrétien's statement. Relations between Charest and Chrétien could only get worse.

FATHER KNOWS BEST

The fatal blow came from an unexpected source. On Tuesday, May 27, less than a week before election day, *La Presse* columnist Lysiane Gagnon penned a glowing profile of the Conservative leader. The Charest people were so delighted that they distributed copies of the column to reporters covering the campaign. But one quote troubled English-speaking journalists. In the offending passage, Charest characterized his friendship with Brian Mulroney as a "father-son relationship," admitting that he regularly consulted the former prime minister. "The image of Brian Mulroney loomed over Tory leader Jean Charest's campaign today," CBC TV news told viewers that evening. Given Mulroney's lack of popularity in English Canada, the report did little to help the Conservatives. Gagnon later admitted that she had misquoted the Tory leader, but, here too, the harm had been done.

How can the relationship between Brian Mulroney and Jean Charest best be described? "Almost fatherly," says Luc Lavoie, an acquaintance of both politicians. "A father-son relationship," confirms Paul Terrien, who has toiled as a speech-writer for both Mulroney and Charest. But Lavoie and Terrien hasten to add that the former prime minister takes a paternalistic attitude toward everyone. Mulroney fancies describing himself as Charest's "mentor." Privately, the former PM never misses a chance to mention the decisive role he has played in his protégé's career. Charest does not conceal his admiration for his predecessor, but he does everything in his power to dispel the notion that he is dependent on Mulroney.

A particular bond does exist between the two men. But is it truly a father-son relationship? Jean Charest has a father, after all, and an extraordinary one at that. Red Charest's powerful personality has profoundly influenced his son; Jean is indebted to his father for many of the qualities that have contributed to his success. Is there a place for a second father in John-John's heart of hearts?

THE SAVIOUR

In the final days of the campaign, the Conservative leader felt the ground slipping away from beneath his feet. Just when it had seemed that four years of toil were about to bear fruit, just when he had dreamed of becoming the Leader of the Opposition, internal polls revealed a rapid decline in his support. Exhausted, hoarse, Charest made one desperate appeal after another. Increasingly, he referred to himself in the third person, presenting himself as the only leader capable of keeping Canada united. In short, he portrayed himself as a saviour.

The climax came in Markham, Ontario, on May 21. Charest's sole preparation that evening consisted of a few notes scribbled on a paper napkin. "Since some politicians in this campaign seem so interested in our birth certificates, I want to take a moment tonight to tell you about myself, about where I'm from, and about my country," he began before an enthusiastic audience of seven hundred against the backdrop of an immense Canadian flag. With palpable emotion, Jean Charest told the party faithful about his parents' origins, his youth and the discussions the family had around the table: "I remember my mother saying to me many times how leadership makes a difference, and how your life meant something if at the end of it you could look back and say: 'I have made a difference in my lifetime.' And I remember the words of my parents telling me many times that in life it is not the victories and the defeats that count, it's what you do with them. And indeed the defeats in your life are only opportunities to test your character."

Charest spoke of Sherbrooke: "You won't find in Sherbrooke those great declarations about one group or another because the people they speak of are not strangers, they're not adversaries, they're not out there in some abstract part of the country; they are their neighbours."

He described his youthful trips on the Great Lakes: "I remember being mesmerized by an extraordinary country, a country that had boundless limits. [. . .] I remember discovering a country that belonged to me, and would one day belong to my children, a country that I was determined to pass on to them."

Then he moved on, to the history of Canada: "If you read the speeches of the Fathers of Confederation, whether it's Thomas D'Arcy McGee, Sir George-Étienne Cartier, Sir John A. Macdonald, whether it's Baldwin or Lafontaine in our [earlier] history, or, in our more recent history, Diefenbaker or Pearson, you will find a common thread: the words 'diversity' and 'tolerance.' They spoke these words with eloquence because they understood that this country we call Canada is a country that would be different from all other countries in the world. That we had set for ourselves a different challenge. Not only to fight the elements and to conquer geography. Our challenge was to learn to live with each other, to grow together, to build together. And to make that happen, we decided early in our history, that our values would be based on tolerance and diversity and compassion and respect."

As her husband was being carried along by emotion, Michèle looked on, enthralled and perhaps a trifle concerned. Then, in a tone that seemed to be verging on tears, the leader of the Conservative Party pleaded with the audience: "I know this country well enough to say to you today that a vast majority of people in the province of Québec, whether they speak French or English, want this country to work, and they are looking for the leaders that will make the country work. And I know, because I travelled Ontario, the Atlantic and the West, that everywhere else there are Canadians who share the same values and the same commitment to this country. I see this, I feel this. And why is it that, in this election campaign, I seem to be the only leader who sees this change, this will to make the country work? And I don't care in the end if I am the last leader of the country to say Canada will work."

Who knows? If every Canadian had watched that speech, the outcome of the June 2 election might have been different. But they saw only a brief excerpt on the news at most. And, in any event, the decisions had already been made.

On the evening of June 2, Jean, Michèle and their close friends gathered at Red's home in Sherbrooke to watch the election coverage. The early returns from the East were encouraging. The Atlantic provinces sent an undreamed of thirteen Conservative MPs to the Commons. But moving farther west, the portents of the campaign's last days were confirmed: Québeckers elected only five Tories, dashing the Blue Machine's hopes for thirty or forty MPs from Québec. And Ontario, into which the party had poured so much energy, had ignored Charest's plea from Markham. By evening's end, the Conservatives had to settle for twenty MPs for the country as a whole. It was much better than two, but it still left Jean Charest the leader of the fifth-largest party in the Commons, after the Liberal Party, which was returned to power, the Reform Party, the Bloc Québécois and the NDP.

Was it a moral victory or total defeat? "It was the worst thing that could have happened," says Gabriel Desjardins. Electing only twenty MPs was not in itself a catastrophe, but it was no triumph either. Would the leader be willing to soldier on? Would the party be content with so little? "Jean had raised expectations during the campaign," Desjardins continues. "He kept on hammering away that the Conservative Party would form the next government. Then we get to the election and what do we elect? Twenty MPs."

For the ambitious young politician, the outcome was a stunner. On election night he contrived to hide his feelings from his supporters. But Michèle was in tears as she left the room. And it took Charest several months to recover from a despondency far deeper than anything he had experienced after his defeat in the 1993 leadership race.

The Last Temptation of
Jean Charest

—ɯ—

Of the thousands of Canadians who followed the Tory leadership race in 1993, one looked on with an unerring eye for the finest detail. On the day of the vote, that connoisseur sat riveted to his television set on Maplewood Street in Outremont. He had just seen the young politician from Sherbrooke come within a hair's-breadth of becoming prime minister of Canada. It took him only an instant to realize that Charest's defeat presented the Québec Liberal Party with an opening, an undreamed-of opportunity to choose a new leader of the highest calibre.

That connoisseur's name was Robert Bourassa. After having guided Québec for fourteen years, Bourassa, by then suffering from a malignant skin cancer, was retiring. Only a few intimate friends knew. He had spent the June afternoon with one of them, his former chief of staff, Mario Bertrand. The next day, Bourassa described his reactions to Bertrand's successor, John Parisella. "Mr. Bourassa was astonished by Charest's performance," says Parisella.

The most serious contender for the Liberal succession was

Treasury Board president Daniel Johnson, who already enjoyed solid support in the party. "To the premier, Daniel Johnson's candidacy was perfectly acceptable," says Parisella, a friend of the MNA from Vaudreuil. "He considered Daniel a known quantity. But he also believed that a candidate of Jean Charest's standing would change the political landscape."

"Luck, be a lady tonight," is the politician's watchword. That night, Parisella got a dinner invitation from Robert Benoît, an MNA and former president of the provincial Liberal Party. Other guests at the Benoît residence, on the bank of Lake Memphré-magog, included Industry minister Gérald Tremblay, Johnson's potential rival; businessman Bruno Fortier, a friend of Jean Charest's; and Charest himself. As guest lists go, it seemed designed to persuade Jean Charest to get into provincial politics. "That wasn't it at all," swears Benoît. "I wanted to give Jean and Gérald an opportunity to discuss manpower training, which in my opinion was an issue that had to be settled before the federal election." Not once during the supper, which ended very late, did the question of the Liberal leadership ever arise . . . and yet manpower training was barely touched upon, either. Even so, Parisella returned to Montréal under the spell of the "Charest effect." One detail had struck him: the rising star had easily memorized the names of all the guests and had listened modestly to everyone. During the conversation, he had addressed Parisella's wife: "Micheline, you were saying . . ." "That made Micheline feel that she was very important, that her opinion was as important as any minister's," says Parisella. Despite his friendship with Daniel Johnson, whom he wanted to succeed his boss, Parisella gave the premier a glowing report on the young federal MP from Sherbrooke: "He's the most impressive politician I've ever met in an informal setting."

John Parisella took the matter no further. But Mario Bertrand, then head of Télé-Métropole, the private television network, joined the fray. Under no circumstances did he want to see Daniel Johnson become leader of the Québec Liberals. Like Robert Bourassa, he had been won over by the qualities Charest displayed in the PC leadership race. So, along with Pierre Bibeau — the former Liberal organizer whom Bourassa had appointed to run the Olympic Installations Board — and Health minister Marc-Yvan Côté, Bertrand made up his mind to persuade Jean Charest to get involved in another battle, this time for the leadership of the provincial Liberals. Bertrand and Bibeau met Charest several times. They also approached his brother, Robert, and a group of Québec Conservative senators. Bibeau quickly realized he was wasting his time and made no further efforts: "Not only was the door closed, it was locked." But Bertrand and Côté, who were conducting a veritable anti-Johnson crusade, would not give up so easily. "At the time, we controlled about forty MNAs who were ready to go with someone other than Daniel," says Côté.

A mid-July meeting between Bourassa and Charest was held in the premier's office in the Hydro-Québec building in downtown Montréal. Officially, the federal deputy prime minister and the Québec premier were to discuss outstanding issues, including manpower training. Bertrand urged the two leaders to discuss the Liberal leadership issue. "Charest didn't want to talk about it," he says. But the premier put the subject on the table. According to Charest, Bourassa broached the subject cautiously: "Have you ever thought of getting into politics at the provincial level?" The younger man apparently replied that he had not, which was his usual answer at the time, and this version coincides with Bertrand's. Témiscamingue MP Gabriel Desjardins, however, got a very different impression of the encounter: during a Conservative caucus meeting, Charest, who was all smiles, confided to him, "I saw Mr. Bourassa, and he told me I would be premier of Québec one day!"

Hoping to persuade both the federal MP and the Liberal caucus, Mario Bertrand commissioned provincial Liberal pollster Grégoire Gollin to sound out Québec voters on a Charest candidacy. Gollin's confidential report was very clear. "Jean Charest is by far the favourite candidate among respondents, when compared with Daniel

Johnson and Lise Bacon, in all age groups and regions," Gollin wrote. "In every area of comparison, Jean Charest wins significantly and by a wide margin." When asked who would make the best premier of Québec, 61 percent of respondents chose Charest, 17 percent opted for Lise Bacon, and 13 percent picked Daniel Johnson.

Bertrand, Bibeau and Côté were not the only ones to take up the Charest cause in the run-up to the Québec Liberal Party (QLP) leadership showdown. Prior even to the meeting in the premier's office, *Le Soleil* had published a poll that drew the same conclusion as Gollin's survey. Leaked to the newspaper "by a political source who insisted on anonymity," the survey had been financed by "private interests, people concerned for the future of the Liberal Party of Québec."

But everyone, from Robert Bourassa to those mysterious "private interests," ran up against a wall. In July 1993, provincial politics didn't tempt Jean Charest, even if the winner of the leadership race would automatically become premier. On the one hand, polls were showing that a Tory victory with Kim Campbell at the helm was quite possible. Were that to happen, Charest would be assured of a high-profile position in Ottawa. Shortly after the leadership convention, it should also be remembered, the Sherbrooke MP had decided to beat a strategic retreat into the private sector for a few months, "a little like John Turner." Mario Bertrand and former provincial Liberal minister Paul Gobeil, who was a friend of Jean Charest's, made one last-ditch effort in the wake of the Conservatives' election debacle. But it was too late. Daniel Johnson was already in the saddle — and probably unbeatable. Charest let it be known that, after a leadership campaign and a general election, he would take a pass.

Daniel Johnson's coronation as the leader of the provincial Liberal Party and his impressive performance in the 1994 election campaign — he lost, but did far better than anyone had predicted — ended plans to draft Jean Charest into provincial politics, at least for a year.

The spectre of "private interests" resurfaced right after the 1995 referendum campaign. The federalists found Charest's performance electrifying. This time, "a group of Liberals dissatisfied with the leadership of their party" leaked a poll to *La Presse*. The survey revealed that 44 percent of French-speaking Québeckers felt Daniel Johnson should resign. Among the political big guns, Jean Charest was clearly the voters' favourite to succeed him. Who were the poll-happy "dissatisfied Liberals"? One of the characters involved in the 1995 manoeuvring, as he had been two years earlier, was former radio reporter Paul Langlois. At the time, Langlois had solid ties with the Charest camp — he had taken part in Charest's leadership campaign — and also in the Liberals' camp, since he had been chief of staff to Liza Frulla, minister of Culture in Bourassa's government. But Langlois was only the messenger, and to this day he refuses to say for whom he worked. Among the suspects are Mario Bertrand and investment broker Michel Le Rouzès, who was close to both Bertrand and Tory strategist Pierre-Claude Nolin. But Bertrand had gone off to live in Europe in 1995. And Le Rouzès swears he had no part in the wheeling and dealing. The name of Guy Savard, a Liberal fundraiser and one of Charest's Sherbrooke buddies, also came up. Still, in late 1995, Charest was continuing to reject the Québec scenario. His friend and adviser Jean-Bernard Bélisle reached Paul Langlois to tell him, "For God's sake, will you please put a stop to this? There's no question of Jean going into provincial politics!"

There was another attempt to draft Charest, this time orchestrated from Ottawa. Just before retiring from active politics, veteran federal Liberal minister André Ouellet decided to include Jean Charest in his political will and testament. In a lengthy *La Presse* interview, which hit the headlines on December 23, 1995, Ouellet blamed Daniel Johnson for the near-defeat in the referendum and called on the Conservative Party leader to enter the provincial arena: "He is wasting his time, all alone in Ottawa. During the referendum campaign, he proved he could put his feelings across.

You've got to talk to Québeckers with your guts. [. . .] And I think Charest can do that."

"That outburst just about ruined my Christmas vacation," recounts the object of this political love letter. On Christmas Eve, Suzanne Poulin had to call an impromptu press conference in a North Hatley skating rink where Charest was playing hockey with his children. "Getting involved in provincial politics has never been an option for me," he told *Le Soleil* three weeks later. "I began my career at the federal level, and my interests have always been in federal politics. There's never been any question of going over to the Québec Liberal Party, and there never will be." He could hardly have made it clearer. Yet over the next two years scarcely a day would go by without people suggesting he make the move to Québec City. "There were daily faxes, there were constant letters," says Albert Cooper, then Charest's chief of staff. "It was an ongoing, non-stop thing. It was there all the time, coming sometimes from people who were prominent in the province of Québec." Suzanne Poulin did what she could to stem the flow. Senior Charest adviser Albert Painchaud, who was closely associated with the provincial Liberals, was told that there was no longer any question of meeting with the Tory leader to discuss the subject. "Suzanne Poulin closed the door on those discussions," Painchaud explains. "A wall was systematically erected around him so no one could speak to him about it."

Marcel Danis, a former cabinet minister and organizer for Joe Clark, approached Charest a few months before the 1997 federal election. Ostensibly representing a group of Conservative business-people from Québec, Danis counselled his former colleague not to try to overthrow Johnson, but to team up with the Liberal leader for the next provincial election, expected in the spring of 1998. "If Johnson wins the election, you'll be certain to be in the cabinet," Danis explained. "If he loses, you'll replace him." Danis was convinced that the coming years would be lean ones for the federal Conservatives. Charest did not share Danis's view and categorically rejected the proposal. Why would an ambitious young man like him be willing to play second fiddle in the provincial Liberal Party when he was already conducting his own orchestra?

OH! ITALY!

"It's Jean Charest on the line." It was July 16, 1997, a month after the federal election. Research on my book had begun and I was waiting to hear from its lead character, who I hoped would co-operate. "If you undertake this project, I want to be honest with you," Charest said. "I cannot rule out leaving my position at some point. I have not made my mind up yet. It's about 80 percent sure that I'll be staying on, but Michèle and I are going on holiday, and when we come back, it could be that . . . If you go ahead with the project, and the person you're writing about leaves the scene, your book won't be very saleable!" Rarely are politicians disinterested when they share secrets. In this case, however, Jean Charest was acting out of simple decency, out of pure kindness. He of course asked that his career ruminations remain "strictly confidential," but he was certainly taking a risk that the wavering might end up in the newspapers.

And he really was wavering. Jean and Michèle went on vacation in Italy. They enjoyed themselves, got a good rest — and spent not a moment discussing their future. (I continued to work as if nothing had happened, convinced that, no matter what, Jean Charest would be a leading public figure for a long time to come.) But when they returned, the couple had no choice but to face reality. The future did not look rosy. With twenty MPs in the Commons, the Conservative Party now had official status, speaking privileges in the House and a number of perks. But it was still just one of five parties, wedged in between Reform, the Bloc and the Liberals. Grumbling began to be heard in the party. Mike Harris's Ontario faction, in particular, held Charest responsible for the Tories' poor election performance. They found a prestigious spokesperson in businessman Peter White, a crony of press magnate

Conrad Black's and president of the PC Fund, the party bank. In December 1997, White signed a letter of resignation, arguing that the Conservatives could not win the next election with Charest as the leader. "In a party, there are winners and losers," says White. "In the Conservative Party, the losers were those who were around Joe Clark, and Jodi White was Clark's chief of staff. They weren't able to win. The winners were the people around Mulroney. Unfortunately, Charest has chosen the losers as his senior advisers."

That was not all. According to the authors of the Harris election program, "The Common Sense Revolution," Charest had committed an error when he strayed from the platform during the campaign and talked about national unity. What's more, Charest's message was confused. Says Peter White: "One day, Tom Long [a Harris adviser] called me to let me know that five ads were broadcast on television on the same day, each dealing with a different theme. It was a nightmare!"

Charest's popularity within his party was such that he could fend off any attempted insurrection. White's criticisms could not force him to resign. But his future prospects were far from clear. Most of Charest's advisers felt that even by 2001 the Conservatives would not become the Official Opposition. "You're going to increase the number of caucus members to forty. So what?" he was told. Charest was more optimistic: "I can deliver fifty seats in Québec. Ontario is open . . ." But he was not kidding himself. His chances of becoming prime minister of Canada were dwindling rapidly.

Throughout the autumn of 1997, Charest dithered. Would he stay? Would he go? His new MPs were concerned. At a caucus meeting in Halifax before the parliamentary session began, they asked him about his intentions. Charest told them he would stay — but his voice lacked the ring of conviction. The Sherbrooke MP was no longer his old self. "He was quieter, more distant," says Dennis McKeever, a Toronto activist. "He didn't have the same fire in the belly."

People kept trying to persuade him to jump to Québec. In August, a Léger & Léger/*Journal de Montréal* opinion poll revealed that Jean Charest inspired greater trust among Québeckers than any other politician. The Conservative leader even outdistanced Lucien Bouchard. But Sherbrooke's favourite son refused to budge. And a Charest putsch against Johnson was out of the question: he and the QLP leader enjoyed cordial relations. "Charest and Johnson are two true-blue Conservatives," points out former Johnson chief of staff Pierre Anctil. "Johnson comes from a family of Blues. There is a genuine sympathy between the two. They have the same instincts."

In November, PC fundraiser and Montréal businessman Brian Gallery met Charest in his office and repeated Marcel Danis's suggestion of a few months earlier: "You should work with Daniel Johnson. You could travel the province together, one going one way and the other going the other way. It would be the best thing for Canada, Québec and yourself."

"Thank you, Brian, for your comments. You've always been a good friend."

During those four months of hemming and hawing, Charest never seriously considered the possibility of making the leap to Québec. Instead, the choice was between staying in politics or taking up a new career in the private sector. In public, however, he made sure not to close the door too tightly. In early 1998, Stanley Hartt, Brian Mulroney's former chief of staff, suggested that Charest take a firmer line. Otherwise, Hartt believed, his ambiguous position might come in for criticism in English Canada, where many people could not understand how a Tory could be flirting with the Liberals. Hartt suggests that the Tory leader was concerned that a categorical denial would make it impossible for him to get into provincial politics at some time in the future. When he heard the argument, Hartt replied, "It will be very easy to make people forget this statement if, one day, you get into a Québec Liberal Party leadership race."

For Jean and Michèle, the primary consideration was family. Michèle was adamant: "If you can't spend more time with us, we're leaving. I don't want to go through what I've gone through the last three years, and that's that." During the fall, the Charests realized that, as Jean could now once again take part in the daily Question Period in the Commons, he was obligated to stay in Ottawa, and he was at home much more often than before the election. Moreover, Charest had rediscovered the pleasures of parliamentary life. He could debate the country's problems with the Prime Minister, teach his caucus the rudiments of Commons behaviour and watch his young lions embarrass the government. In contrast, a job in a downtown Montréal skyscraper seemed deadly dull, no matter the salary. "Would I be satisfied with a life that would keep me away from active politics?" Charest wondered. The answer was never in doubt.

In December 1997, Michèle and Jean finally made the decision: they would stay in Ottawa. To make life more pleasant, they planned to buy a new house. Charest announced the good news to Conservative Party workers at the Christmas party. This time, the Tories were convinced: the decision was cast in concrete.

But the subject slipped back onto the table over the Christmas vacation, at a dinner with the MacLarens in the Eastern Townships. George MacLaren and Robert Charest believed Jean should be prepared to make the move to Québec after the next provincial election, given the limited prospects federal politics seemed to hold out. But Charest was categorical: "I've made my decision. I announced to the caucus and the staff at the Christmas party that I would stay until the next federal election. I've thought it over and my mind is made up."

MacLaren didn't lose hope. In early 1998, Charest met with his senior advisers in Ottawa to lay plans for the coming two years. No sooner had the meeting begun than the leader slammed the door: "Michèle and I have just bought a house, we're going to stay on until the next election, and I have no intention of going anywhere else. I know there may be pressure after the next provincial election if Johnson is defeated, but I don't intend to bow to the pressure."

"Those of us who thought it was an intelligent option just kept our mouths shut," says MacLaren.

The Call

More than a few Québec Tories were surprised to see Daniel Johnson's chief organizer, Pietro Perrino, participating as an observer at the Conservative Party's National Council in Ottawa in late February 1998. Some people found his conduct bizarre. Why the devil was he taking pains to be seen with people close to Jean Charest? Why was he openly wooing candidates in the fifth-ranking federal party? When a journalist asked Perrino about the long-running rumour that would have Jean Charest moving to Québec, Perrino gave a peculiar reply. Instead of the predictable response for any party organizer — that Daniel Johnson was the best leader in the universe, that he was there to stay, and that he would win the next election — Perrino said, "Johnson controls the party machine. If he wants to stay, he'll stay. The decision is in his hands." Come again? The decision hadn't been made?

At the National Council, the Conservatives could admire Jean Charest at the top of his form. In an electrifying speech on Saturday evening he lambasted the Reform Party: "Canadians will have to choose: Progressive Conservatives or Reform. The Reform Party has lied its way into Opposition!" The hundreds of party activists greeted the speech with rapturous applause. Michou was radiant. The Conservative Party seemed to have risen from the ashes. The next day, the Tory leader invited his Members of Parliament and candidates to go to the House of Commons, where he sat down in the Prime Minister's chair and said, "One day, I will be sitting in this chair and you will be around me!"

All weekend long, however, Jean Charest was aware that a bomb might blow up in his face. He was one of the very few Québeckers who knew that Daniel Johnson might well resign in a matter of hours. "We knew," a Charest insider swore, making me vow not to reveal his name. Think back to the fate that awaits traitors in the Charest clan: the Supreme Soviet, the trapdoor. When *La Presse* published an article reporting what the Conservative leader had said in confidence, Suzanne Poulin immediately rang me up. "Jean didn't know! He only found out Sunday evening, when Johnson called." Obviously, Charest didn't want to look like a cynical leader who had psyched up his troops during the weekend, knowing full well he might have to abandon them a few weeks later. According to George MacLaren, Pietro Perrino informed Charest's people that he had important news for them. Charest then took pains not to run into the Liberal strategist over the weekend. Perrino maintains that he attended the Conservative Party meeting simply to establish contacts with the Tories with a view to the coming provincial election. Had he spoken to anyone about Johnson's resignation on the weekend?

"All I can say is that Daniel talked to Charest Sunday evening." The creaking sound was probably Pinocchio's nose growing.

In our final meeting before publication, Jean Charest finally admitted that he had gotten wind of what was about to happen: "I heard on the grapevine two days before that Johnson might possibly resign." But Charest, who was to become leader of the Québec Liberal Party a few weeks later, said he hadn't taken the rumours seriously: "You hear this kind of rumour every day. That's not what influenced events on the weekend. I kept right on course."

With the National Council meeting over, Jean and Michèle spent Sunday evening with the family. Legend has it that the political leader turned chef that evening and prepared a delicious roast of pork. When the children were tucked in, Michèle settled down in bed to read, while Jean was comfortably ensconced downstairs indulging in one of his favourite pastimes, reading the Sunday *New York Times*. At around 9:30 in the evening, the phone rang. "Hello Jean, it's Daniel." A man who is forewarned is not likely to fall out of his chair. "I'm calling to tell you that I'm resigning this week. I wanted you to know because it will obviously have some consequences for you." After the brief conversation, Jean went upstairs to see Michèle. "You'll never guess who called. It was Daniel Johnson."

Immediately Charest contacted Denis Pageau, Jodi White and

other close advisers. From that evening on, Pageau and White had the feeling that the door was not entirely closed. That a powerful gust of wind could blow it wide open, in fact. "As soon as [Jean Charest] learned Daniel Johnson was going to resign, he knew he wouldn't have any choice," says Pageau. Charest expected considerable pressure from Québec. "When you get right down to it," he told White, "it's just as well I'm leaving tomorrow for Toronto and the West. It'll give me a chance to stay far away from all that." He could not have guessed the pressure would be as great in English Canada as in his native province. But by noon the next day, after his speech in Toronto, even before Johnson made his public announcement, he would understand. "[Johnson's] resignation was only a rumour, and already the media were after me like I'd never seen before," Charest says. The media had already dubbed him Canada's saviour. "Run!" pleaded the *Ottawa Sun*. For the *Calgary Herald*, assuming the succession to Daniel Johnson was nothing less than the Conservative leader's "patriotic duty." Provincial Liberal MNAs joined the fray as well. "If he refuses Québec's call, he will go down in history as someone who could have saved the country and did not do it," said Saint-Laurent MNA Norman Cherry. "If Mr. Charest wants to be prime minister of Canada, he can hardly avoid doing everything he can to save the country," insisted Christos Sirros of Laurier-Dorion. Hot on the heels of Johnson's resignation, newspapers published poll after poll showing that the Liberals, with Jean Charest at the helm, would defeat the Parti Québécois hands down. Incredibly, the Canadian dollar was on the rise. Stockbrokers were betting on the coming of the Messiah.

Had he wished to do so, the Tory leader could have closed the door for good. The storm might have raged for a few days longer, but eventually it would have blown itself out. All he had to do was hold an official press conference and make a categorical statement: "Under no circumstances will I join the Liberal Party of Québec. I repeat, my answer is no; repeat, no. Never." Instead, Charest met briefly with a scrum of reporters in Toronto, telling them he did not intend to make the leap to provincial politics. Then he added, "At the present time, nothing could make me change my mind." At the present time? The Liberals had the opening they were hoping for. As Pietro Perrino said later, "The door was closed, then I heard it creak." From then on, the Liberal strategist's task was a simple one: flood Charest with messages from every direction to show him how badly the Québec Liberal Party wanted him as its leader. And in fact, due to spontaneous reaction from across the province, and in some part to Perrino's manoeuvres, Charest's offices were soon buried under a mountain of faxes and e-mails. The telephones would not stop ringing. Since Charest had not slammed the door, perhaps there had always been at least a one percent chance in his mind that he would join the QLP.

"There was a 1 percent chance," he admits. "Enough of a chance that I could reach the decision I made in the end."

Tory MPs were not fooled. When they heard "at the present time," alarm bells started to ring. On Tuesday afternoon, Charest set up a conference call with his MPs. The House of Commons was not in session that week; the leader was in Toronto, and his flock was scattered across the country and abroad. He explained to them that his tongue had slipped, that his No was still definite: "No ifs, ands or buts about it, I'm staying in Ottawa." But he turned down their suggestion that he convene a press conference and make it official. "It was hard to get him to say exactly what his answer was," says André Bachand. "Was it a No, a Maybe, or a No for the moment?" Finally Charest blurted out: "No means no." The MPs promptly cranked up the machine, reassuring party activists that the leader would stay. Many were convinced. Others were somewhat doubtful. They had good reason: Charest had discreetly instructed his entourage to gather as much information as possible about the situation. Who called? What are people saying? The door had cracked open a little more.

Continuing his swing through the West, the "saviour" made up his mind not to return telephone calls, particularly from Liberal

MNAs, a decision that created considerable consternation. "Every conversation was repeated and distorted," he says, "so I decided to keep the contacts to a minimum." He spoke by phone to Suzanne Poulin daily and to his closest advisers regularly. All of them confirm that in the early days he was overwhelmed by the magnitude of the movement.

"Suzanne, you can't imagine how big it is," he told his assistant in the middle of the week.

"Jean, you're not in Québec — you have no idea how big it is here!"

By week's end, Charest and his advisers, including those who wanted him to stay in Ottawa, agreed that he could not give the appearance of being insensitive to the wishes expressed by Québeckers and Canadians without paying a political price. "I hear what the people are saying," he declared. Perrino heard the door creak again.

The only provincial Liberal MNA to speak to Charest during those tension-filled days was his friend Monique Gagnon-Tremblay, whose Saint-François riding overlapped a section of the federal constituency of Sherbrooke. The two chatted on Monday evening, a few hours after Johnson's resignation. "I didn't get the impression the door was wide open, but I felt that the man had to give it serious consideration," she reports. Charest told her about some of his concerns, particularly the present state of the QLP. He had already rebuilt one party — that was enough. "The Liberal Party is alive and kicking," Gagnon-Tremblay reassured him. "We have forty-six MNAs in the Assembly and we've almost finished drafting our program. I've spoken to a lot of people today and I know that a majority of the MNAs are ready to support you."

The Hand of Brian

Some observers, including Conservative Party insiders, think they know how the Johnson-Charest transition was concocted in the spring of 1998. According to information unearthed by Denis Lessard of *La Presse*, Act I took place at the Charest home in North Hatley during the Christmas holidays. One of the dinner guests, Bombardier CEO Laurent Beaudoin, a personal acquaintance of Charest's, is said to have asked him, "If Daniel Johnson quit of his own accord, would you go to Québec?" Charest's reply is supposed to have been closer to a Yes than a No.

In Act II, as Lessard tells it, a group representing some of the most powerful businesspeople in Québec met with Premier Lucien Bouchard to prevail upon him to abandon his goal of another referendum on sovereignty. Given Bouchard's categorical refusal, the "Québec Inc." delegation then concluded that the only way to prevent a referendum was to replace Daniel Johnson with Jean Charest.

All that remained was for Beaudoin & Co. to persuade Johnson that it was time to leave. Some analysts believe that Power Corporation founder Paul Desmarais, a friend of the Johnson family's, might have kept a close watch over the proceedings. The business community, they say, even offered Charest a "golden bridge" to cover his children's education. Finally, former Prime Minister Brian Mulroney, who is close to Desmarais, Daniel Johnson and Charest, might well have been involved in the manoeuvres.

Only when historians are able to subject the month of March 1998 to intense scrutiny will it be learned what pressure, aside from the obvious public pressure, was brought to bear on Jean Charest. He has admitted speaking to Laurent Beaudoin on Wednesday, March 4, at which time Beaudoin told Charest he would like to see him as QLP leader. Charest, however, denies meeting the Bombardier CEO during the holidays. "It's not true. That dinner never took place." While the new Liberal leader also denies accepting any kind of "golden bridge," he does not rule out the possibility that such offers might have been made. "People who went around making statements like that, I avoided them like the plague. In any case, this is 1998 . . ."

What of Mulroney? Jean Charest admits he spoke to his former boss only once or twice during that period. When Radio-Canada reporter Michel Cormier revealed that he'd learned from a reliable source that the former prime minister had advised his protégé to go into provincial politics, Brian Mulroney denied it. In an interview with him in my capacity as a *La Presse* reporter, Mulroney insisted that the story was "a total fabrication." But in a conversation with the former prime minister a month later, in conjunction with research for this book, he told a totally different tale, claiming to have played a key role in the events that followed Johnson's resignation.

As is his wont, the elder statesman requested that the content of our conversation not be published. This is the notorious off-the-record rule with which journalists are too often expected to comply if they wish to learn about backstage wheeling and dealing, and behind which wily politicians hide. There can be no more skilful politician than Brian Mulroney. After considerable reflection, given that his remarks were essential to the understanding of events of public concern, particularly since he was telling me in private the exact opposite of what he had said publicly, and finally, convinced that their publication would in no way harm Mr. Mulroney, I decided not to respect the commitment I had made about the confidentiality of our discussion.*

---

* Since this decision was vehemently criticized after publication of the French-language edition of this book, I feel compelled to add a few comments. Originally, the practice of off-the-record conversations was intended to allow journalists to obtain vital information without compromising their sources. But in the political realm, off-the-record remarks have become more the politician's tool than the reporter's. Politicians and organizers abuse the reporter's confidence to manipulate the media, to spread information that suits their purposes without their having to assume responsibility for what is said. This is a practice I have already denounced in an earlier book (*Le Syndrome de Pinocchio*, [Montréal: Boréal, 1997]). When I began work on the Charest biography, I had hoped to be able to avoid off-the-record interviews altogether. This soon proved impossible. So in instances where I could not do otherwise, I decided to follow the rules of the game. Yet in the back of my mind, I kept the door open to a violation of those twisted rules if an exceptional situation came up where such a violation would serve the truth.

To explain the former PM's role in the events of March 1998, I had three choices. 1) I could stick with the public version he had urged me to write in *La Presse*; in other words, write something that I knew to be false. 2) I could break the off-the-record commitment

During the interview, Brian Mulroney revealed that Daniel Johnson had called him, even before he contacted Jean Charest, to let him know that he intended to resign. "We arranged it together," the former prime minister added. It is clear that Johnson wanted to see Charest succeed him, that this was the aim of his "sacrifice." In January, QLP pollster Grégoire Gollin had been commissioned to measure the "Charest effect" on the voters. Gollin's conclusion was clear: Charest was the only one who could beat Lucien Bouchard. Hence Johnson's statement on the day of his resignation: "I believe a new approach, a new way of speaking, a new tone and a new leader will make the difference."

During the turbulent weeks in March, Charest and Mulroney would have spoken a "great deal." And, as Johnson had hoped, Mulroney strongly advised his successor to make the leap into Québec politics: "Jean, you owe nothing to the Conservative Party. You owe everything to your family and to Canada. It's up to you to choose the way that will help you reconcile these two realities. As far as I'm concerned, the immediate problem is Québec. Even if it breaks my heart to say it, I think your future is in Québec. It goes against my personal interests because with you I was convinced that the Conservative Party could have been extremely successful. In the meantime, you're the only one who can beat Bouchard."

Political strategist that he is, Mulroney outlined two scenarios for the ensuing months. First scenario: Charest would stay in Ottawa. "There is a [QLP] leadership race between Liza Frulla and Pierre

---

and make his comments public; in that case, I would lose, but truth would win. 3) I could use what Mr. Mulroney had told me privately without revealing to readers the source of my information. Knowing Mr. Mulroney, that is probably what he wanted: to let people know the major role he played while at the same time distancing himself from this self-serving version of events.

I chose option 2. It was a very difficult choice, which involved weighing fundamental principles tugging in different directions. Many have condemned me for breaking my word. But few have taken exception to Brian Mulroney's attitude. It was he, after all, who said one thing publicly and the exact opposite privately. In the end, although I still have doubts, I am comforted in thinking I made the correct decision by one fact: no one has yet dared claim that what is written in this book is untrue.

Paradis. Paradis might do well in an election, but he would not beat Bouchard. Bouchard would win and within six months to one year there would be a referendum. And the chaos that we see in Montréal — the poverty and the lack of investment, the political uncertainty — all that would go on forever." Second scenario: Charest moves over to the QLP: "Bouchard calls an election and Charest wins. That would be the end of Bouchard; the PQ throws him out within twenty-four hours. It would not be the end of the separatist movement, but it would put an end to it for quite a long time. That gives [Charest] a chance to put together another Meech on his own terms, and then sign the Constitution."

It cannot have been easy for Mulroney to make the recommendation he did. He must have known that, with Charest's departure, his beloved Conservative Party would be in danger of becoming what it had been before a "little guy from Baie Comeau" had taken it in hand — an almost exclusively English-Canadian party. But in addition to being federalist to the bone, the former prime minister detests Lucien Bouchard.

Brian Mulroney and Paul Desmarais have been close for many years. According to Mulroney, Desmarais took a keen interest in Jean Charest's decision without getting directly involved in the affair. And the "golden bridge" Charest was reportedly offered? "Nothing of the kind," swears the retired PM. "I know what went on. I told Jean, 'Lucien is nasty enough to attack you over things like that. So, don't have anything to do with it . . . don't even discuss it.'" Charest, not unnaturally, showed some concern about the financial implications of plunging into murky political waters. "Listen, Jean," his mentor says he replied, "You don't need anything. Now you can rest assured that if it all goes well, you'll become premier and it will all be taken care of. If things go wrong and you lose and decide to go into the private sector, you'll be welcomed with open arms."

Did Mulroney have a decisive influence? Just as they did in analysing the 1993 leadership race, Mulroney claims he played a crucial role in his protégé's decision, while Charest minimizes the importance of his political father's advice.

THE FINAL STEP

Returning from his swing through the West on Friday, March 6, 1998, Charest stopped off in Montréal for a few hours before heading east to give a hand to the Nova Scotia Conservatives in the provincial election. As Jean and Michèle were wondering where they could eat without being disturbed, the MacLarens came to the rescue with an invitation to dinner. The two couples discussed recent events. MacLaren did not press the issue; his friend knew his thoughts very well already. And in any case, he felt that the wind had already changed: "It was obvious at that moment that the option was open." Michèle was still hesitant: "We've settled in. The children are happy. And we have three or four years of peace ahead of us before the next federal election."

It wasn't the first time Michèle Dionne had expressed her opposition to a move to Québec. When the rumours first started in 1993, she resisted the idea. Albert Painchaud, who was close to the Charests at the time, says that she wanted nothing to do with Québec City. In an interview — in Québec City, as it happened — in November 1997, the Tory leader's wife swore she had nothing against the provincial capital. But she could not have been more adamant about her refusal to see her husband quit the PC Party: "I have worked so hard for the party that I would never, never . . . My conscience wouldn't let me. It's not a matter of cities, of moving. It goes deeper than that. I would feel I was abandoning the people I worked with, and that I would never do — never!"

Daniel Johnson's resignation had put Michèle in a difficult position. Jean was wracked with doubt. He too felt he was abandoning a job before he'd finished it. But he felt that if he turned down a provincial career, there would be a price to pay in English Canada, even in his own party. In the days that followed Johnson's resignation, the manoeuvring had already gotten under way among the Tories. "The question was," MacLaren pointed out at the time, "would he still have a career in Ottawa if he refused?" Then, too, there was a small matter of ambition. If there was no future in Ottawa, how could he pass up the opportunity to become premier of Québec? It was one of the kid's dreams, after all, before federal politics gave him his first opportunity. Remember the law student who wanted to become leader of the Union Nationale.

From the very first week, Jean Charest had left the door ajar. Michèle resisted — but she also received telephone calls: "We love you, Michou. Sure, it's a difficult situation, but it's your duty to go to Québec, both of you. History is calling." And history shows that her husband always managed to convince her.

Charest returned to Ottawa on Monday, March 9. His first evening with his family was the decisive one. On Tuesday morning the leader met with his MPs and senators and announced to them that he wanted to take some time to reflect. Each of them expressed his opinion. Some, particularly Senator Gérald Beaudoin, wanted him to answer the call from Québec. But most of them pleaded with him to stay. Some were very emotional, especially the young MP from Asbestos, André Bachand: "Jean, you're making the biggest mistake of your life! They're not your people. Since Bourassa's gone, the federal Liberals have infested the QLP. What will you do in Québec? You're the one who convinced us that the problem was here in Ottawa!" So insistent was Bachand that a few hours later he felt compelled to apologize. In calmer fashion, Manitoban Rick Borotsik asked his leader to set a deadline: "Give me a timeline, when are you going to make your final decision? I'm on an emotional roller-coaster here, you've got to stop the ride!" The member for Compton-Stanstead, David Price, a longtime friend, was so moved that he could hardly speak: "Jean, of everyone here, I am the one who has known you the longest. I don't want you to go to Québec City. I'm afraid it's a trap by the federal Liberals — watch out."

The meeting left many MPs in a state of shock. They had the feeling that their leader was slipping away from them. "I never felt any of the arguments had reached him," says Bachand.

"This is a very difficult choice," Charest declared at a press conference called immediately after the caucus meeting. "I have a profound attachment to my party and to the people that have placed their confidence in me and have strongly supported me since 1993. I am sensitive to the sincere views expressed on this subject over the last week by those who think that my future lies elsewhere. I have consulted my wife, Michèle, and my children, and we have decided to listen and consult on the choice that has been presented to us . . ." Then he added, "I ask for one thing: a short period of time during which I invite my caucus and my party to continue to reach out and to listen to what is being said and to consult with other Canadians. It is my hope that this will help not only with the choice to be made but also with the consequences of that choice." It was as though Charest was telling his MPs: "Can't you see the pressure I'm under? Wake up, get a good look at what's happening; you'll see that I don't have any choice."

That afternoon, Charest invited Senator Jean-Claude Rivest to drop by his office. Appointed by Brian Mulroney, Rivest was a member of the Conservative caucus. But Rivest had also been an adviser to Robert Bourassa and a member of the National Assembly under Claude Ryan, so he knew the QLP like the back of his hand. At a time when he did not dare overtly contact provincial Liberals, Charest found Rivest a precious source of advice and information. As Rivest recalls the conversation, the Conservative leader was quite far along in his reflections: "For all intents and purposes, he had made up his mind." The two men spent more than two hours together. Rivest made a thumbnail sketch of the Québec Liberal Party and impressed on Charest the importance of rebuilding the great coalition that had always been the party's strength, "from Stéphane Dion right to Mario Dumont's doorstep." Charest was concerned about the issue of national unity, but the senator wanted him to focus on more down-to-earth issues: "What concerns Québeckers is health and education. You'll have to have something to say about those issues."

"I'll look after that. Just give me the files and let the people who handle them bring me up to speed. And, by the way, I'm not some kind of extraterrestrial, I know what's happening in Québec!"

Charest quickly found out what he needed to know about the practical aspects of the premier's job. How many days does the National Assembly sit? Is the work mostly in Québec City or in Montréal? Could his family live in Montréal? "He had made his mind up, but he wanted to see how he was supposed to function," says Rivest.

THE QUÉBECKER

Jean Charest had never made an important decision in his career without consulting Denis Beaudoin, the former Joe Clark organizer who had recruited Charest in 1983. Beaudoin's advice had tipped the balance prior to the 1993 leadership race. But in March 1998, Beaudoin was dying. Six months earlier, he had learned he had cancer. In a long interview conducted at the time, he had explained the reasoning behind Jean Charest's eventual move to provincial politics.

Jean Charest, his old partner confided, could not express his real feelings about the future of Canada and of Québec during the 1997 election campaign. "Jean has gone further than that." Further than a new Canadian pact? Further than a distinct society? The words were reminiscent of the fears expressed by another great friend and Charest adviser, Jean-Bernard Bélisle, about what would become of a Jean Charest transplanted into Québec's political culture. "If he has to defend Québec and he runs up against a closed-minded federal government, I can't vouch for what he will decide and the path his government would take."

I add what Charest himself told me over dinner in North Hatley when he was still the leader of the Conservative Party. I took no notes and my recollection isn't perfect, but it went something like this: "Now that I'm firmly in the saddle, I'm going to say things, and people can decide to follow me, or not."

Denis Beaudoin continues: "The decision Jean would make [with regard to his political future] would be a matter of where he could best explain his vision of Canada and the place of his province in the country. Is he dreaming of becoming prime minister of Canada or premier of Québec? I don't put the question like that, and I don't think he puts it that way, either. Nowhere is it written that a renewal of the federation cannot be initiated by one province. Turn back the clock: in 1864, four provinces created this country! The federal government didn't even exist. The provinces decided what powers they would give Ottawa! It may well be time for the provinces to sit down together, ask Ottawa to leave the room, and work out a deal." This might be one of the reasons why Jean Charest consulted the premiers of all the provinces before deciding to enter provincial politics.

In March 1998, Beaudoin might well have been ill, but he had never been more lucid. When Jean visited him at his home in Hull, the sick man turned out to be strongly in favour of Charest's joining the Québec Liberal Party. Charest left the house worried about his friend but with a new assurance about his own future.

Denis Beaudoin agreed, Brian Mulroney agreed, George MacLaren agreed, the big bosses agreed, Québec agreed; in short, everyone wanted to see Charest in Québec. Well, not exactly everyone: many Conservatives — among them some very influential people — wanted to keep him in Ottawa. The Tory leader had a long chat with one of his predecessors, Joe Clark, in whose name he had taken his first steps in politics. For over an hour, Clark explained to Charest why he should remain in federal politics. "The issue of the unity of the country has to do with more than a province and more than a referendum," Clark reminded Charest. "The very factors that are causing people to urge you to go to Québec are also factors that would allow you to play a very constructive role in Canada." Like many other Tories, Clark did not trust the federal Liberals. "I have seen what the federal Liberals did to Bourassa, Ryan and to Daniel Johnson. If anything, my view is that the current federal Liberal leadership is even more difficult to deal with than in the time of Trudeau."

It was the kind of argument that certainly struck a chord with Charest. During a conference call set up in the week of March 16 to plan the announcement of his decision, several participants sensed that Charest was still hesitating. While his advisers were deciding where the press conference should take place — in Sherbrooke, of course — the type of event — sober, solemn, triumphant? — the PC leader was still very concerned about the Conservative Party. "Leaving the Conservative Party is breaking his heart," one of the conference-call participants, Jean-Yves Laflamme, said at the time. "He's torn. He's afraid for his party. He knows that when he's no longer there, he'll have no more influence and it'll be a shambles. It's like taking your bicycle to the top of the King Street hill and letting it loose!" And, says George MacLaren, "I wasn't absolutely convinced that his decision was final until two days before the announcement."

At the same time, Charest had to take care of the practical questions. He attempted to get rid of the house he had just acquired in Ottawa for more than $400,000. The seller wouldn't hear of it: a contract is a contract, even if you are marching off to save Canada. Charest might have been offered a "golden bridge," but he still had to negotiate a mortgage with his bank manager. "You're the only one of my clients who might have an influence on interest rates," the manager laughed.

IN MOURNING

On Friday, March 13, Jean Charest was in his Sherbrooke strong-hold, where a series of public events had long been scheduled. A horde of reporters followed him around, hanging on his every word and gesture. Finally, they spotted something. In a televised interview, Charest had let drop: "I become a candidate in the race, I don't automatically become the leader of the QLP." That after-noon, he talked at length with Monique Gagnon-Tremblay, who, like Rivest, gave Charest a crash course on the Québec Liberal Party. "That day," Gagnon-Tremblay was to say later, "I felt things were very promising."

Early in the morning on Sunday, March 15, a handful of people gathered in Charest's Ottawa office. The atmosphere was one of sadness. Since 1993, Jean Charest, Jodi White, David Small and Bruce Anderson had been through thick and thin together. They had almost defeated Kim Campbell. In 1997, they had come within a heartbeat of leading the Tories to Official Opposition status.

That morning, nothing was said, but they knew it was over. Charest was headed down another road, and White, Small and Anderson, who had always exercised a great influence on him, could not follow. Soon they would be political orphans. But none of them would try to dissuade him. "By that point, we had given up," admits David Small. "We were all exasperated by the fact that we hadn't been able to control the situation."

On Wednesday morning, March 25, the Conservative Party cau-cus held its weekly meeting. Everyone tried to pretend it was just routine. Then the MPs and senators were invited to attend another meeting to be held at suppertime in a location that would not be disclosed until later that afternoon, to avoid leaks to the media. That evening, Jean Charest told his caucus he was resigning as leader of the party to enter provincial politics. Then he left the room, leaving a few dozen men and women in mourning. Some, André Bachand in particular, found that he had been a little cavalier: "In the morning he made his speech. We were wondering: is he staying or is he going? Then in the evening, it was a brutal, cold, administrative decision. He stayed ten minutes. After that, it was up to us to pick up the pieces. I was bloody mad!"

The next morning, Jean Charest set out down the road to Sherbrooke. The road to Québec.

Rolling the Dice

—⚬—

That afternoon, the Queen City of the Eastern Townships was strutting its stuff. Scores of journalists from all over the country — and even the American networks — had flocked to the town for an event some were describing as historic. On March 26, 1998, forty years after Jean Lesage had taken the leap, Jean Charest would announce his entry into provincial politics. Sherbrooke was very definitely on the map.

Few people recognized Jean-Guy Ouellette as he welcomed reporters to the Centre Culturel du Vieux-Clocher, the site of the event. Jean-Guy Ouellette? Why, he was the University of Sherbrooke track and field coach who had initiated Jean Charest, then a young minister, into the arcana of amateur sport ten years before. The same man who became such a dyed-in-the-wool Charest supporter that he bawled his eyes out the day the minister was forced to resign in 1990.

At the press conference, reporters made predictions, floated analyses and traded scuttlebutt. Cameramen got in everybody's way. Charest's people scurried about, hot and bothered. Suzanne Poulin could not sit still. Claude Lacroix scrutinized the room, on the lookout for the slightest snag that might disturb the TV coverage. Jean-Bernard Bélisle, battling a serious illness, tried to stay on the sidelines, but Charest was his friend, and he had to be there.

In the midst of the hustle and bustle, in the first row right near the stage, sat Claude "Red" Charest, imperturbable, inscrutable and no doubt very proud. His "dimwit" had not done so badly after all. Flanking him were his eldest son Robert and Lise Dionne, Michèle's elder sister.

At five-thirty on the dot, Jean Charest and Michèle Dionne made their entrance. Punctuality was of the essence: the TV networks were covering the event live. Michèle was radiant, her face showing no trace of her recent bout of tension, sadness and worry. The day when Michou would refuse to do her little song and dance had long since passed. As usual, Charest was perfectly at ease, his hands rock steady, his voice firm: "Today, I am announcing my resignation as the leader of the Progressive Conservative Party of Canada." Then he added a remark that would make the newspaper headlines, a little something someone had thought of at the last moment: "I've made my decision: I choose Québec."

That alone would have been enough to make the PQ panic. But Charest had more up his sleeve. In his first press conference as a Liberal, he launched a preemptive strike, cutting off a potential PQ line of retreat: "True to form, Lucien Bouchard is already preparing a new twist. He will look for every way possible to strip the Parti Québécois of its raison d'être by reneging on his solemn promise to hold another referendum."

Once more, Jean Charest had demonstrated remarkable political instincts. But his weaknesses emerged, too. His grasp of the issues was less than perfect. As many analysts were to point out later, his assertion that Québec's unemployment rate was higher than Ontario's because of political uncertainty had no basis in fact. Furthermore,

Charest tends to exaggerate when he talks about himself. How could he have seriously contended that sovereigntist attacks on him would constitute "an unprecedented case of character assassination"? Unprecedented? Worse than the PQ's vilification of Jean Chrétien? Worse than Duplessis's demonization of his opponents?

On the second floor of the Vieux-Clocher, Albert Painchaud waited impatiently. Though he had helped launch the young man's political career back in the days of the "Club de la Relève," he hadn't seen Jean Charest in two years. Painchaud resented being shunted off to the side, but he blamed Charest's entourage, not Jean Charest. That evening, he had chosen a strategic spot where he could intercept Charest on his way to meet party activists after the conference. This time, no one would stand in Painchaud's way. When the star made his entrance, he found himself face to face with his old friend. They embraced warmly. Painchaud was in tears. The bitterness had evaporated. It was the "Charest effect."

Painchaud was not the only one in tears. Tory MP André Bachand was inconsolable. As Charest made a rapid tour of the room, the crowd surged forward, arms outstretched, eager hands reaching toward him. Seeing their saviour up close, the Liberal supporters purred like cats that had swallowed canaries. "We're giving Québec a premier," said an old Tory Blue from Sherbrooke, with a mixture of sadness and pride. A young Conservative recruited by Charest, Dany Renauld, put it differently: "I feel like I'm meeting my ex-girlfriend with her new boyfriend."

One of Jean Charest's political fathers, Dr. Pierre Gagné, was alarmed by the frenzy that had gripped the crowd, and the province as a whole. He feared for his young friend: "I know people with the Québec provincial police — I'm going to speak to them about it."

Jean Charest's career was reflected in the faces of all the people who had devoted a part of their lives to him. But some faces were missing. The young Tory nationalists who had catapulted him into the 1993 leadership contest were no longer to be seen. Also missing was the devoted Jacques Fortier, whom Charest had hurt with an unfortunate gesture during a municipal election campaign.

Also among the missing was Denis Beaudoin, whose wisdom Charest had always been able to count on. Only cancer could prevent Beaudoin from being on hand at the Vieux-Clocher. But, loyal until his dying breath, Beaudoin had already purchased a Liberal membership card.

Then the prodigal son strode to the podium. As always, he found the right words: "This evening reminds me of the home where I grew up. When you step inside, you leave your worries at the door, you hang up your coat whether it's blue or red." The crowd burst into applause; Liberals and Conservatives made peace. The "Charest effect" had worked its magic.

But it only lasted a few minutes. No sooner had he entered than he exited stage right. His supporters stood there baffled, at a loss for words. The entire Charest enigma is captured in this scene: a man so warm that everyone would like to have him for a brother; a politician whose every step, every emotion is stage-managed and timed to the second; a rousing orator who preaches moderation but doesn't disdain demagogy; a cabinet minister who is efficient and honest, but lacking in originality; a powerful but superficial intelligence; a proud, self-assured man who is also sympathetic and generous; a charismatic, but remote leader; an extraordinary communicator who is also profoundly secretive; a hesitant leader who has an irresistible will; an ambitious politician who has finally found an ideal.

The Charest enigma includes this exuberant small town, the supporters who love him like a son, and the people who are missing, pushed aside or forgotten.

The Charest enigma is an outstretched hand that will never quite touch him.

One week later, Charest bade farewell to the House of Commons.

"Québeckers are capable of great things," he told the Members of Parliament. "They need neighbours who are not strangers, and especially not adversaries, but neighbours who are fellow citizens, allies, people who share the same values."

Michèle was in the visitors' gallery, in tears. This sacrifice would be her last.

Better slow down this time. There it is, hidden away in the shadows, the brown brick house.

Red Charest's simple, gruff welcome is the same for every visitor. At Red's house, there is no entourage, no make-up. "You want a coffee?"

"No thanks, I don't want to disturb you for long."

"You're not disturbing me. But if you don't want any, I won't force you."

Sitting at the dining-room table, Red recalls a time when you never hung up a political coat no matter whether it was red or blue. "Father was always getting defeated by the Liberals. The winners would organize a parade through the street. My father would tell my mother, 'Turn off the lights!' We'd all hide under the piano. The first time Jean won, the parades stopped."

Things have changed so much since the 1930s that Ludovic Charest's grandson has become the leader of the Liberal Party. His father is not quite comfortable with the idea. It's not a question of party allegiance. That era is long gone: "Today, it's the man, it's not the party." It's just that Red is concerned about his son: "Jean was the leader of the Conservative Party. After all his years he had a good salary, and as leader . . . it's like a guy giving up a good job. You leave it, then you get into a party where you don't know for sure whether you're going to win or not."

"Jean's off to a good start, at any rate."

"Still, an election is an election. You can start with a lead . . . It's like a horse race, and at any moment . . . Anyway . . . I'm confident, but still . . . It's a gamble."

When you hang out with Red, the fearsome father smoothed

with age like a rock by water, when you listen to him drop his weighty words of wisdom, when you go back to the house where John-John played, where the kid grew up, where the son mourned, you find the answer to the enigma. Jean Charest is neither god nor saviour. He is simply a man — with a little touch of Hamlet.

Appendix 1
The Charest Report

—𝕞—

Report of the Special Committee to Study the Proposed
Companion Resolution to the Meech Lake Accord
(May 1990, The Honourable Jean Charest, M.P., Chairman)

THE COMMITTEE'S MANDATE

Canada is in the midst of a political deadlock revolving around a package of Constitutional amendments known as the Meech Lake Accord. It was signed by the Prime Minister and Premiers of all ten provinces in 1987 but in order to become law it must be adopted in every legislature by June 23, 1990. Parliament and eight provincial legislatures subsequently adopted the Accord. In two provinces, New Brunswick and Manitoba, governments changed before ratification. The new Premiers expressed reservations about certain parts of the Accord. In Newfoundland and Labrador, the Accord had already been adopted, but following an election a new government also expressed reservations.

Discussions among First Ministers failed to produce a compromise. However, on March 21, 1990 Premier McKenna introduced in the New Brunswick Legislative Assembly two resolutions intended to break the deadlock. The first was the Meech Lake Accord (*Constitution Amendment, 1987*). The second, Premier McKenna referred to as a Companion Resolution. It proposed a number of additional Constitutional amendments to take effect after the Meech Lake Accord was proclaimed. Adoption of the

Meech Lake Accord by New Brunswick was made conditional upon some progress towards adoption of the Companion Resolution by other legislatures and the Parliament of Canada.

On March 26 Prime Minister Mulroney requested time on national television to address the nation. He suggested the New Brunswick Companion Resolution be referred to a special Committee of the House of Commons. Leaders of the federal Liberal and New Democratic Parties agreed and a motion to this effect was adopted in the House of Commons the following day with instructions to report to the House by May 18, 1990.

On April 6, the Newfoundland and Labrador House of Assembly proceeded to revoke its approval of the Accord. The same day the Quebec National Assembly adopted a resolution reaffirming its desire that the Meech Lake Accord be ratified.

Thus at the moment your Committee began its work the political situation was very difficult. From the outset your Committee faced different sets of expectations. Some dismissed it as irrelevant to the process. Others expected it to solve a dilemma that had eluded both politicians and constitutional experts.

Your Committee was convinced that the solution began by listening. From April 9 to May 4, we heard some 160 witnesses in Yellowknife, Whitehorse, Vancouver, Winnipeg, St. John's and in the National Capital Region. Eight governments including five present and two former provincial premiers appeared as did constitutional experts, and representatives of aboriginal groups, business groups, women's groups, official language minority groups, multicultural groups, labour organizations, groups representing the disabled as well as other groups and interested citizens. Opinions ranged from unconditional support of Meech Lake to absolute rejection of both the Accord and the Companion Resolution. Committee hearings were televised and attracted a good deal of media attention. We received, in addition, over 800 written submissions from a wide variety of individuals and organizations across Canada.

Our task has not been easy but despite the variety of conflicting evidence and contradictory opinion, we are convinced there are solutions.

This report is our attempt to use the information we received to assist Canadians in understanding the nature of the problem and to suggest both immediate solutions to the present impasse and a longer term process whereby future generations of Canadians can add to whatever we have been able to accomplish at this time.

We realize that for historical, political and legal reasons not everyone is going to agree with our analysis or recommendations. However, we have tried to address the problems to the best of our ability. Having done so we acknowledge that, in practical terms, the solution to the present impasse is in the hands of others and we respectfully submit the following report for consideration.

WHY A QUEBEC ROUND?

The issues under discussion in the present constitutional debate go back many years. Quebec's distinct society can be traced to the *Quebec Act* of 1774, nearly a hundred years before Confederation; discussion of Senate reform began in 1867 and has been going on ever since. The debate between supporters of greater provincial autonomy and those who believe in a more centralized federation has also been going on since 1867. And there are other issues: the quest of the aboriginal people for recognition; gender equality; the place for Canadians of multicultural heritage in the definition of the fundamental character of the country; and the impact of the *Canadian Charter of Rights and Freedoms* on our traditional approach to civil liberties.

The present round of constitutional discussion must be understood in the context of what happened in the province of Quebec on May 20, 1980. A referendum was held on the question of whether the Quebec government should be given a mandate to negotiate sovereignty association. During the referendum debate the people of Quebec were promised constitutional reform if they voted NO. The federal victory was widely celebrated across Canada and led to constitutional discussions between Ottawa and the provinces over the precise nature of the changes.

The culmination of this process was the patriation of the Canadian Constitution from Westminster in 1982 and adoption of the *Canadian Charter of Rights and Freedoms* and of a new amending formula. After extensive debate, every province except Quebec endorsed the 1982 constitutional change. Quebec did not agree with the process and maintained that substantial changes to the Canadian Constitution had been made without its consent. As a result, Quebec refused to participate in constitutional conferences except as an observer and would not vote on amendments such as those dealing with the rights of the aboriginal people.

This position has no legal effect since the Constitution was patriated legally and the *Constitution Act, 1982* applies to Quebec despite its dis-agreement. But the political consequences are very real.

Following the 1985 election a new government took office in Quebec. In contrast to the twenty-two conditions of its predecessor it agreed to support the constitutional reform of 1982 if five conditions could be accommodated in its place. These were:

    i)   explicit recognition of Quebec as a distinct society;
   ii)   guarantee of increased powers in matters of immigration;
  iii)   limitation of the federal spending power;
  iv)   recognition of a right of veto;
   v)   Quebec participation in appointing judges to the Supreme Court of Canada.

In August 1986 the 27th Annual Premiers Conference took place in Edmonton. At that time the Premiers unanimously agreed *"that their top constitutional priority is to embark immediately upon a federal-provincial process, using Quebec's five proposals as a basis for discussion, to bring about Quebec's full and active participation in the Canadian federation. There was a consensus among the Premiers that then they will pursue further constitutional discussions on matters raised by some provinces which will include, amongst other items, Senate reform, fisheries, property rights, etc."* This subsequently became known as the *Edmonton Declaration*.

It should be noted that the process of aboriginal constitutional confer-ences started in 1983 and concluded in March 1987 without an agree-ment. Thus the process of these aboriginal constitutional conferences had not been completed successfully at the time of the *Edmonton Declaration*.

Between August 1986 and April 1987 intensive discussion took place among ministers and officials on Quebec's proposals. At a meeting at Meech Lake, on April 30, 1987 the First Ministers worked out an agree-ment in principle on Quebec's five proposals. Officials were directed to draft a legal document to incorporate the agreement. On June 2 and 3, the First Ministers met at the Langevin Building in Ottawa and reached agreement on the precise wording of the Accord. On June 23, 1987, the Quebec National Assembly became the first legislature to approve the Meech Lake Accord which, as set out in Section 39(2) of the *Constitution Act, 1982*, triggered the three year period for ratification.

During the course of our hearings witness after witness, even those most critical of the Meech Lake Accord expressed support for Canadian unity and the need to make Canada's second most populous province an active participant in federal-provincial negotiations and a participating member of the Canadian constitutional family. There was general agreement that Quebec's five proposals were reasonable for that purpose.

THE NEW BRUNSWICK COMPANION RESOLUTION

A. *The Process*

The objective of the New Brunswick Companion Resolution is to encourage ratification of the Meech Lake Accord by all provinces on or before June 23 by offering assurance that other priorities will be advanced. Premier McKenna noted that in putting together his Companion Resolution he had been careful to *add to* and not to *subtract from* the Meech Lake Accord. He also noted that unlike the Accord his Resolution was not "a seamless web" that had to be adopted or rejected as a package. He pointed to the need for flexibility to accommodate other concerns around which there is a wide degree of consensus.

Questioned as to what would constitute substantive support for his Resolution he said: "We in New Brunswick will be the judge of what represents that commitment. We believe, even at some cost to our credibility if necessary, we absolutely must keep our flexibility."

Before considering the substance of the McKenna Companion Resolution your Committee had to determine if the June 23 deadline was, in fact, a real one. We heard a number of learned witnesses on this point. Your Committee acknowledges that there is a legal debate over the significance of this date.

Some argued that given political will the June 23 deadline could be extended. The First Ministers could agree to introduce resolutions in their respective legislatures to allow for more time to consider the Accord. While possible in theory, the question is whether all governments and legislatures would agree to act quickly and unanimously on such a Resolution.

Having carefully considered the various options, your Committee has drawn the following conclusions:

1. Your Committee is of the opinion that June 23, 1990 is a political reality.
2. Your Committee recognizes that if the elements of the Companion Resolution we have proposed are to provide an opportunity to break the Meech Lake impasse, the question of "certainty" will have to be addressed and unequivocally resolved.
3. It is our view that timing and process leading to additional amendments to the Constitution of Canada can only be negotiated by First Ministers. We believe our recommendations may form the basis for agreement if First Ministers move quickly to resolve the question of the timing of additional changes.

Your Committee then looked at the specific concerns of the New Brunswick, Manitoba and Newfoundland and Labrador governments keeping in mind the concerns identified by others who felt their interests were left out in the process that led to the Meech Lake Accord.

B. The Content
New Brunswick would like to see an addition in the Meech Lake Accord to the clause respecting Canada's linguistic duality and Quebec's distinct society, namely that within New Brunswick, the English linguistic community and the French linguistic community have equality of status and equal rights and privileges. This would entrench a principle presently stated in a New Brunswick statute.

4. Your Committee recommends that the clause respecting the equality of New Brunswick's two official linguistic communities is an appropriate subject for a Companion Resolution.
5. Similarly your Committee agrees with the New Brunswick proposal to affirm a role for the legislature and government of New Brunswick to preserve and promote the equality of

status and equal rights and privileges of that province's two official linguistic communities.

The Meech Lake Accord affirms the role of Parliament to preserve one of Canada's fundamental characteristics — linguistic duality. Premier McKenna has proposed in his Companion Resolution to affirm as well Parliament's role to promote our linguistic duality.

Testimony from constitutional experts is unanimous in affirming that the promotion of linguistic duality as proposed is limited to federal jurisdiction. This is also clearly understood by minority language groups who testified before the Committee.

Although the promotion role suggested by Premier McKenna is now demonstrated in law in the revised *Official Languages Act* (R.S.C. 1985, 4th Supp., 31), your Committee has been persuaded by the repeated argument made by minority language groups to the effect that even though a promotion clause may not add anything legally it would have a dynamic effect on these groups.

6. Your Committee endorses the clause in the New Brunswick Companion Resolution which calls for promotion of Canada's linguistic duality by the Parliament and Government of Canada.

On this important issue other proposals have been put forward that merit the attention of First Ministers. These include the question of "where numbers warrant" and the control and management of schools in section 23 of the Charter; and an examination of the concept of a "Code of Minority Language Rights" put forward by witnesses and the Government of Quebec.

7. In any event, your Committee suggests that minority language rights require continuing deliberation and should be included on the agenda of the Annual First Ministers Conferences on the Constitution.

The Meech Lake Accord provides for provincial involvement in the appointment of Senators and Judges of the Supreme Court. The First Ministers who signed the Accord took the position that it should be passed, unchanged, unless there was some "egregious error." The body of evidence presented to your Committee is that most Canadians perceived at least one such oversight and that was the failure to include the Yukon and the Northwest Territories in the selection process.

8.   The New Brunswick Companion Resolution would address the Meech Lake Accord's omission of the Yukon and Northwest Territories in the selection of Senators and Judges of the Supreme Court by involving the two territories in the selection process. Your Committee is convinced this oversight should be corrected.

The Meech Lake Accord would also change the amending formula required for the creation of new provinces from the 2/3 of the provinces with 50% of the population to unanimity. Prior to 1982 the process for admission of new provinces was the sole responsibility of the federal government. New Brunswick has proposed a return to the pre-1982 situation thereby ensuring that the two territories could aspire to provincehood under the same conditions as other provinces created since 1867. Your Committee has heard compelling evidence on this issue as it travelled throughout Canada and more particularly in the northern territories.

9.   Your Committee agrees with the position of New Brunswick and the territories on the creation of new provinces and recommends this be dealt with in a Companion Resolution.

New Brunswick also proposes to add an agenda item to the Annual First Ministers Conference on the Constitution. It would deal with constitutional matters that directly affect the aboriginal peoples of Canada, including the identification of the rights of those people. Representatives of aboriginal groups testified that instead of being one of the items on the agenda of annual First Ministers Constitutional Conferences, a separate process be devoted specifically to aboriginal matters. They recommended that these conferences would be held every three years.

10. Your committee agrees with the suggestion of the leadership of the aboriginal groups and recommends that a Companion Resolution should provide for a separate process of constitutional conferences every three years. The first such conference should be convened no later than one year after such a Resolution comes into force.

A concern addressed in the New Brunswick Companion Resolution in relation to section 16 of the Meech Lake Accord is to the effect that the Charter is overridden by the distinct society clause. This concern has been expressed by representatives of women's groups and other equality seekers.

There is a debate about the impact of the distinct society clause on the interpretation of the *Canadian Charter of Rights and Freedoms*. The thrust of expert legal testimony would suggest that the issue is more a matter of perception. For example a legal and constitutional expert, Roger Tassé QC, Deputy Minister of Justice under a Liberal administration when the Charter was adopted and, later, in his then capacity as legal advisor to the present government, was present at discussions at the Langevin Building. He has testified:

"This is because the distinct society clause, like the Canadian duality clause which is an integral part of it, is an interpretive clause which does not in any way change the dynamics of the Charter of Rights and the protection it guarantees. Within the framework of the Charter, the only scope of this clause is to implement section 1. You will recall that this section stipulates that the rights and freedoms guaranteed by the Charter are subject only to such reasonable limits prescribed by law as can be demonstrably justified in a free and democratic society. This extremely rigorous test was made even stricter by subsequent rulings of the Supreme Court.

No one has ever seriously claimed that the rights and freedoms guaranteed by the Charter are absolute. Section 1 stipulates the conditions under which they can be restricted. I ask you, on what principle should the special situation of francophones as a minority group in Canada, in North America, be excluded from the scope of section 1? Our courts including the Supreme Court of Canada in the notorious sign law case, had already agreed to take that situation into account even before the Meech Lake Accord was passed.

The rights and freedoms guaranteed by the Charter are in no way compromised by the distinct society clause, and, in my opinion, the adoption of this clause would only confirm that the distinct society of Quebec is a legitimate fact that should be taken into consideration in applying section 1."

Some First Ministers are themselves on the record on this point. In the interpretation of our Constitution, courts give weight to such statements of intention.

11. Therefore, your Committee recommends that First Ministers affirm in a Companion Resolution that the operation of the fundamental characteristic clause, recognizing the linguistic duality/distinct society, in no way impairs the effectiveness of the Charter of Rights. As an interpretive clause it works with the Charter and does not override the rights and freedoms contained in it. Similarly, that Companion Resolution should affirm that the clauses providing roles for Parliament and the provincial legislatures do not accord legislative powers.

Your Committee also considered the New Brunswick proposal that every five years the Senate carry out an assessment of the results achieved by governments and legislative bodies in relation to the commitments in section 36 of the *Constitution Act, 1982* on equalization and reduction of regional disparities, and that a report be presented to the first annual Conference of First Ministers on the economy following each such assessment.

12. We see merit in the idea of the Senate carrying out an assessment of the results achieved in pursuance of the commitment on equalization and the reduction of regional disparities but we would recommend it be addressed in the context of a reformed Senate.

New Brunswick has also proposed an amendment that would require the House of Commons and legislative assemblies to hold public hearings before adopting any measures related to a constitutional amendment. This would include revocation of a constitutional resolution. Your Committee agrees with this idea. Under the amending formula adopted in 1982 legislatures and not governments have ultimate responsibility for approving constitutional amendments. This may seem like a subtle distinction but the lesson of Meech Lake is that the Canadian people want a say in the development of their Constitution.

13. We believe that, in a parliamentary democracy, public participation in constitutional reform can best be accomplished by means of public hearings by Parliament and legislative assemblies and we recommend such a process for Canada's future constitutional development.

14. Your Committee recommends that a Companion Resolution process that adds, without subtracting, to the provisions of the Meech Lake Accord has the best prospect of solving the current constitutional impasse.

15. Your Committee recommends the New Brunswick Companion Resolution, with the suggested changes and additions contained in our report, as the basis from which the First Ministers and the country can address the present constitutional impasse.

Premier McKenna has asked for some assurances that there is support for his Companion Resolution.

16. Your Committee recommends the House of Commons should provide assurance of support for a Companion Resolution at an appropriate time.

However, this may be academic unless New Brunswick is satisfied and the provinces of Manitoba and Newfoundland and Labrador address their concerns by adding to the New Brunswick Companion Resolution or by proposing their own Companion Resolutions.

ADDRESSING THE CONCERNS OF MANITOBA AND
NEWFOUNDLAND AND LABRADOR

Critical to a report that would respond appropriately to the outstanding issues related specifically to this round of constitutional development was keen and sensitive understanding of the concerns expressed at the hearings in Winnipeg and St. John's. Your Committee listened carefully, searching for answers to help get through this constitutional impasse.

The provinces of Manitoba and Newfoundland and Labrador have both expressed very strong concerns about the unanimity requirement for Senate reform. While the Committee heard persuasive testimony asserting that practical political considerations underscore the desirability of unanimous consent, we are sensitive to the point of view of Manitoba and Newfoundland and Labrador.

17. Your Committee is convinced that to avoid constitutional impasse the unanimous consent rule for Senate reform should be moderated after a limited period, say three years, if it has not produced success. We should then adopt a less restrictive amending formula with some form of regional approval.

Your Committee was also interested by Manitoba's suggestion of a "Canada Clause" which would include recognition for the aboriginal people and recognize the multicultural dimension of our heritage. A similar idea was eloquently advanced by the government of Newfoundland and Labrador.

18. With respect to the recognition of aboriginal peoples and of our multicultural heritage, we encourage the First Ministers to respond to these fundamental elements of Canada by recognizing them in the body of the Constitution.

The Manitoba Task Force recommended that an invitation to participate in First Ministers' Constitutional Conferences be extended to the elected leaders of the governments of the Northwest Territories and Yukon by the Prime Minister whenever he was of the opinion that agenda items would directly affect them. Testimony reinforcing this idea was presented to your Committee during the course of our hearings across Canada but particularly in Yellowknife and Whitehorse.

Therefore as suggested by the Manitoba Task Force:

19. We recommend that the Prime Minister of Canada should invite elected representatives of the governments of the Yukon Territory and the Northwest Territories to participate in the discussions on any item on the agenda of a First Ministers' Constitutional Conference that, in the opinion of the Prime Minister, directly affects the Yukon Territory and the Northwest Territories.

This would obviously include any discussion of changes to territorial boundaries.

20. We also recommend that the Prime Minister of Canada should invite elected representatives of the governments of the Yukon Territory and the Northwest Territories to participate in the discussions on any item on the agenda of a First Ministers' Annual Economic Conference that, in the opinion of the Prime Minster, directly affects the Yukon Territory and the Northwest Territories.

Manitoba further suggested that the Meech Lake provisions dealing with immigration be reviewed every five years.

21. While your Committee agrees that a review mechanism of the immigration provisions is desirable, we believe that this is an administrative matter that may better be dealt with as required by circumstance.

Manitoba, recognizing very early that this generation of Canadians would want to participate in constitutional reform, was the first province to require public hearings prior to ratifying amendments negotiated by its Premier with the other First Ministers. This interest is held in common with other Canadians including Premier Wells of Newfoundland and Labrador who expressed concern about the need for more public partici-pation in the constitutional amendment process. Since the proclamation of the *Canadian Charter of Rights and Freedoms*, many Canadians see the Constitution as belonging to themselves to a greater extent than ever before.

We have therefore endorsed the recommendation that public hearings become an integral part of future constitutional change. (See recommen-dation no. 13)

The Premier of Newfoundland and Labrador in testifying before your Committee also expressed his government's concerns relating to the issue of the federal spending power. Your Committee is particularly sensitive to the deeply rooted feeling of Canadians in the less developed areas that federal attention to their concerns might be reduced.

22. Your Committee urges the First Ministers to provide in a Companion Resolution reassurance that the federal spending power to promote equal opportunities for the well being of Canadians and to further economic development to reduce disparity and to provide essential public services of reason-able quality to Canadians (as set out in Section 36 of the *Constitution Act, 1982*), will not be impaired by the Meech Lake Accord.

CONCLUSION

The agreement reached at Meech Lake envisaged a First Ministers conference on Senate reform to take place within months of proclamation of the Accord. Several governments are anxious to get on with the process. The province of Newfoundland and Labrador has a very detailed proposal for Senate reform, the governments of Ontario and Manitoba have already established legislative Committees to look into this subject, the Prime Minister of Canada has stated his intention to create such a Committee to conduct hearings this summer on the basis of a compre-hensive discussion paper. We continually come back to the point that unless we get over the present constitutional impasse, the prospects for Senate reform or any other constitutional change appear to be remote.

The New Brunswick Companion Resolution did not deal with Senate reform because, as Premier McKenna noted, it was an issue of more immediate interest to other provinces. We have attempted to address this priority through the idea of a sunset clause for the amending formula for Senate reform. We believe Senate reform is also of fundamental importance to the country.

23. Your Committee recommends that Senate reform should be a priority item for the next constitutional round.

There is less consensus than we expected about the shape and function of a reformed Senate and there is little chance of building a consensus as long as the present deadlock continues. We have proposed a way to get us over the initial impasse and to get talks started.

Once that happens we are convinced that Canadians will turn their attention to Senate reform and other outstanding items.

Finally, your Committee wants to thank all Canadians who testified or submitted briefs for their contribution. We have been profoundly affected by what we have heard during the course of our hearings. We have witnessed the extent to which Canada has been irrevocably changed by the entrenchment of the *Canadian Charter of Rights and Freedoms* and the patriation of our Constitution. Canadians, obviously, want to get on with their constitutional development. That responsibility starts, but does not end, with First Ministers. It extends to all legislators, to interest groups and to every Canadian.

Appendix 2
List of Interviews

—〰—

Pierre Anctil
Bruce Anderson
Robert P. Armstrong
André Bachand
Richard Baulé
Jean Bazin
Denis Beaudoin
Denis Beaudoin (journalist)
Jean-Bernard Bélisle
Paul-Marcel Bellavance
Robert Benoît
Roxanna Benoit
Denis Berger
Gabrielle Bertrand
Mario Bertrand
Pierre Bibeau
Marie-Josée Bissonnette
Jean-Pierre Blackburn

Jacques Blais
Pierre Blais
Lorenzo Boisvert
Bernard Bonneau
Rick Borotsik
Benoît Bouchard
Jacques Bouchard
Thomas Boudreau
Pierrette Bouillon
Michel Bousquet
Martin Bureau
Aldée Cabana
Daniel Caisse
Arthur Campeau
Barry Carin
Conrad Chapdelaine
Carole Charest
Christine Charest

Claude Charest
Jean Charest
Louise Charest
Brigitte Charland
Joe Clark
Heather Conway
Albert Cooper
Marc-Yvan Côté
Michel Coutu
Pierre Dagenais
Léo Daigle
Marcel Danis
Mary Dawson
Jean-Laurier Demers
Ivor Dent
Jean Desharnais
Gabriel Desjardins
Martin Desrochers
Line Desrosiers
Lise Dionne
Michèle Dionne
Philippe Dionne
Robert Dobie
Michel Dorais
Marc Dorion
Father Pierre Doyon
Jean-Louis Dubé
Laurent Dubé
Robert Dubé
Jean-Guy Dubuc
Michel Dufour
Paul Dupré
Michel Dussault
Jan Dymond
John Edwards
Gilles Émond

Lucie Émond
Marie Fabi
Bruno Fortier
Jacques Fortier
Martine Fortier
Guy Fouquet
Pierre Gagné
Monique Gagnon-Tremblay
Brian Gallery
Michel Gauthier
François Gérin
Hugh Glynn
Eddie Goldenberg
Grégoire Gollin
Len Good
Daniel Green
Camille Guilbault
Larry Hagen
Bruno Hallé
Stanley Hartt
André Harvey
Chantal Hébert
Louise Hébert
François Houle
Jean-Guy Hudon
Yvan Huneault
Roger Jackson
Pierre Marc Johnson
Robert Kaplan
Jean-Pierre Kesteman
Michel Krauss
Claude Lacroix
Jean-Yves Laflamme
Jacques Lahaie
Paul Langlois
Jean Lapierre

Marc Lapointe
Charles Larochelle
Luc Lavoie
Claude Leblond
Maurice Lefebvre
Jacques A. Léger
Frances Leonard Roy
Loretta Leonard Triganne
Michel Le Rouzès
Aline Lessard
Christian Lessard
Jovette Létourneau
Gary Levy
Benoît Long
Bernard Longpré
Rolf Lund
Lane MacAdam
David MacDonald
Yvan Macerola
Dennis McKeever
George MacLaren
Lyle Makosky
Robert Marleau
Paul Martin
Jean-Martin Masse
Jean Masson
Dave Mathews
Normand Maurice
Don Mazankowski
Claude Métras
Louise Meunier
Richard Miquelon
Philippe Morel
Pierre Morency
Michel Morin
Nick Mulder

Mark Mullins
Brian Mulroney
Lowell Murray
Daniel Nadeau
Harry Near
Bill Neville
Leslie Noble
Pierre-Claude Nolin
Geoff Norquay
Lorne Nystrom
Luc Ouellet
Rolland Ouellet
Hélène Ouellette
Jean-Guy Ouellette
Denis Pageau
Albert Painchaud
Richard Paradis
John Parisella
Patrick Parizot
Pierre Patenaude
Mitch Patten
Jean-Carol Pelletier
Adrien Péloquin
Gordon Perks
Isabelle Perras
Pietro Perrino
Pierre Perron
Yvon Picotte
François Pilote
Andrew Pipe
Louis Plamondon
Jules Pleau
André Plourde
Lisette Plourde Dionne
René Poitras
Suzanne Poulin

David Price
Toby Price
Jacques Pronovost
Mario J. Proulx
John Rae
Jean-Pierre Rancourt
Ross Reid
William Reilly
Gil Rémillard
Dany Renauld
Jean Riou
Jean-Claude Rivest
Svend Robinson
Jacques Rousseau
Nina Rowell
Maurice Ruel
Gerry St-Germain
Daniel Saint-Hilaire
Guy Saint-Julien
Christian Simard
Bob Slater
David Small
Cecil Smith

Ken Smith
Norman Spector
Alain Tardif
Roger Tassé
Paul Terrien
Claude Thiboutot
Albin Tremblay
Gérald Tremblay
Marc Triganne
André Trudeau
Pierrette Venne
Monique Vézina
Pierre H. Vincent
Peter Vuicic
Andy Walker
Wilfrid Wedmann
Jodi White
Peter White
Huw Williams
Dennis Wood
Jean-François Woods
Michel Yergeau

Index

—m—